SAINTS ALIVE!

THE FAITH PROCLAIMED

SAINTS ALIVE!

THE FAITH PROCLAIMED

By Marie Paul Curley, FSP, and Mary Lea Hill, FSP

With a foreword by Celia Sirois

Pauline
BOOKS & MEDIA
Boston

Library of Congress Cataloging-in-Publication Data

Curley, Marie Paul.
 Saints alive! the faith proclaimed / Marie Paul Curley, FSP, and Mary Lea Hill, FSP ; with a preface by Celia Sirois.
  pages cm
 ISBN-13: 978-0-8198-7286-9
 ISBN-10: 0-8198-7286-5
 1. Christian saints--Biography. I. Title.
 BX4655.3.C87 2013
 270.092'2--dc23

                    2013011122

Scripture quotations contained herein are from the *New Revised Standard Version Bible: Catholic Edition*, copyright © 1989, 1993, Division of Christian Education of the National Council of the Churches of Christ in the United States of America. Used with permission. All rights reserved.

Excerpts from the English translation of the *Catechism of the Catholic Church* for use in the United States of America, copyright © 1994, United States Catholic Conference, Inc.—Libreria Editrice Vaticana. Used with permission.

Excerpts from Daniel J. Harrington, SJ, *The Gospel of Matthew: Sacra Pagina 1*, copyright © 1991, The Liturgical Press. All rights reserved. Used with permission.

Excerpts from John R. Donahue, SJ, and Daniel J. Harrington, SJ, *The Gospel of Mark*. *Sacra Pagina 2*, copyright © 2002, The Liturgical Press. All rights reserved. Used with permission.

Excerpts from Pope Benedict XVI, *Angelus*, Saint Peter's Square, October 29, copyright © 2006, Libreria Editrice Vaticana. Used with permission. All rights reserved.

Cover design by Rosana Usselmann

"P" and PAULINE are registered trademarks of the Daughters of St. Paul.

Published by Pauline Books & Media, 50 Saint Pauls Avenue, Boston, MA 02130-3491

Printed in the U.S.A.

www.pauline.org

Pauline Books & Media is the publishing house of the Daughters of St. Paul, an international congregation of women religious serving the Church with the communications media.

2 3 4 5 6 7 8 9   21 20 19 18 17

For our loved ones who have gone before us and are part of the great company of saints, especially:

Stanley R. Curley

and

Lee J. and Alvada (Toce) Hill

Contents

Part I
THE BEATITUDES

༄༅༄

Blessed are the poor in spirit, for theirs is the kingdom of heaven.

༄༅༄

Blessed are those who mourn, for they will be comforted.

ᏳᏇᏽᎧ

Blessed are the meek, for they will inherit the earth.

ᏳᏇᏽᎧ

*Blessed are they who hunger and thirst for righteousness,
for they will be filled.*

ᏳᏇᏽᎧ

Blessed are the merciful, for they will receive mercy.

CEVD

Blessed are the pure in heart, for they will see God.

CEVD

Blessed are the peacemakers,
for they will be called children of God.

CEVD

Blessed are those who are persecuted for righteousness' sake,
for theirs is the kingdom of heaven.

Part II

THE SACRAMENTS

⟨❦⟩

The Sacrament of Baptism

⟨❦⟩

The Sacrament of Confirmation

⟨❦⟩

The Holy Eucharist

Saint Thomas Becket

༺❦༻

The Sacrament of Matrimony

Blessed Peter To Rot

Saints Zélie and Louis Martin

Foreword

The Beatitudes of Jesus, found in Matthew 5:3–12 and Luke 6:20–23, are among the best loved but most misunderstood of Gospel texts. The reason in large part is that they challenge the Christian imagination to see beyond ethical imperatives to the eschatological horizon of the kingdom of God to which Jesus, in his life, death, and resurrection, draws our attention. The Beatitudes of Jesus, in both Matthew and Luke, are neither commandments nor conditions. As W. D. Davies and D. C. Allison observe in their commentary on Matthew, the only two imperatives in the Beatitudes are "rejoice" and "be glad" (5:12; in Luke 6:23, "rejoice" and "leap for joy").[1] [*] What, then, are the Beatitudes?

Biblical beatitudes come in two varieties: the first falls under the heading of Wisdom literature. These beatitudes praise the good man who enjoys the good life in the present tense, as in Psalm 1. The second category, to which the Beatitudes of Jesus belong, is eschatological. Focused on God's future (the *eschaton*), these sayings promise good

1. W. D. Davies and D. C. Allison, *Matthew 1–7: International Critical Commentary*, vol. I (London: T&T Clark Ltd., 1988), 463.

* Unless otherwise noted, all biblical quotations are from *The New American Bible*, rev. ed. U.S. Congress of Catholic Bishops (Charlotte: Saint Benedict Press, 2010).

things to those who are presently poor and powerless and persecuted. As Daniel J. Harrington explains, "The Beatitudes' function not as 'entrance requirements' but rather as a delineation of the characteristics and actions that will receive their full and appropriate eschatological reward."[2]

A thoughtful reading of the nine Beatitudes of Matthew or the four Beatitudes of Luke reveals the key to their interpretation. The Beatitudes, first and foremost, describe the life and work of Jesus. Jesus himself was poor in fact as well as in spirit. Jesus mourned, "grieved, even to death" (Mt 26:38). Jesus was meek. Jesus hungered and thirsted "to fulfill all righteousness" (Mt 3:15). Jesus was merciful, as his healing ministry attests. Jesus was pure in heart, willing solely to do his Father's will. Jesus was a peacemaker. Jesus was insulted and persecuted and slandered. From this it follows that the Beatitudes describe the Christian life, which is life *in Christ*, as well. This is what Paul was saying when he wrote to the Galatians, "and it is no longer I who live, but it is Christ who lives in me" (2:20). The Beatitudes are not commandments that must be obeyed or counsels that might be followed. Rather, the Beatitudes describe every Christian life that is lived in intentional conformity to Christ's life.

The Beatitudes of Jesus also draw a bright line between the ways of the world and the way of Christ. This sharp contrast is made even more explicit as Jesus moves inexorably toward his passion. "You know that the rulers of the Gentiles lord it over them, and their great ones are tyrants over them," he tells his disciples. "It will not be so among you; but whoever wishes to be great among you must be your servant, and

---

2. Daniel J. Harrington, SJ, *The Gospel of Matthew: Sacra Pagina 1* (Collegeville, MN: The Liturgical Press, 1991), 83.

whoever wishes to be first among you must be your slave; just as the Son of Man came not to be served but to serve, and to give his life a ransom for many" (Mt 20:25–28; see also Lk 22:25–27). The implication of these words of Jesus is that membership in the Christian community is not just a shift in one's status quo, but a new creation—starting now.

All the saints whose stories are told in this book sought, in their own time and in their own way, to conform their lives to that of Christ. To the extent that, by God's grace, they succeeded, their lives were characterized by the paradox of Christ's own life as put forth in the Beatitudes. But that statement must be qualified. It must be noted that these saints' imitation of Christ was never simple-minded mimicry. Conformity to Christ was the prize toward which they pressed, yet they never claimed to possess it (see Phil 3:12–16).

Initiation into the life and mission of Christ is effected by the sacraments of Baptism, Confirmation, and Eucharist together. "Holy Baptism," the *Catechism of the Catholic Church* declares, "is the basis of the whole Christian life, the gateway to life in the Spirit, and the door which gives access to the other sacraments."[3] The Latin *sacramentum* originally referred to the oath by which Roman soldiers pledged their allegiance to the Roman emperor. It was Tertullian who first described Christian Baptism as "a sacrament," thus presenting Baptism as a commitment to the cause of Christ. But it is in the words of Jesus himself that the deepest meaning of this sacrament is first discerned. In answer to the ill-advised request of the sons of Zebedee, Jesus asks, "Are you able to drink the cup that I drink, or be baptized with the baptism that I am baptized with?" (Mk 10:38). John Donahue,

---

3. *Catechism of the Catholic Church*, Libreria Editrice Vaticana (Boston: Pauline Books & Media, 1994), 1213.

commenting on this verse, says that while "it is unlikely that a primary reference to baptism is intended, the image does serve to remind Mark's readers that they were baptized *into the death of Christ*"[4] (italics mine). Paul drives that point home when he writes to the church in Rome: "Do you not know that all of us who have been baptized into Christ Jesus were baptized into his death? Therefore we have been buried with him by baptism into death, so that, just as Christ was raised from the dead by the glory of the Father, so we too might walk (*peripatēsōmen*) in newness of life" (Rom 6:3–4). As Pope Benedict XVI has observed, "The rediscovery of the value of one's own Baptism is at the root of every Christian's missionary commitment, because as we see in the Gospel, those who allow themselves to be fascinated by Christ cannot fail to witness to the joy of following in his footsteps."[5] Such was the experience of the holy men and women presented in this volume.

If Baptism is "the basis of the whole Christian life," then the Eucharist is its "source and summit" (*Catechism* 1324). It is the Eucharist that nourishes and sustains the life of Christ in us. "Those who eat my flesh and drink my blood have eternal life," said Jesus, "and I will raise them up on the last day" (Jn 6:54). The sacraments of healing, Penance and Anointing of the Sick, take us back to the ministry of Jesus himself. So much of his work as described in the synoptic Gospels lay in the reconciliation of sinners and the

---

4. John R. Donahue, SJ, and Daniel J. Harrington, SJ, *The Gospel of Mark: Sacra Pagina 2* (Collegeville, MN: The Liturgical Press, 2002), 311.

5. Pope Benedict XVI, *Angelus*, Saint Peter's Square, October 29, 2006, Courtesy of Libreria Editrice Vaticana, http://www.vatican.va/holy_father/benedict_xvi/angelus/2006/documents/hf_ben-xvi_ang_20061029_en.html. Accessed on January 2013.

restoration of the sick. But it is in the fourth Gospel, in the first appearance of the risen Jesus in the midst of his disciples, that the Church has traditionally located the institution of the sacrament of Penance. Breathing on the disciples, Jesus says, "Receive the Holy Spirit. If you forgive the sins of any, they are forgiven them; if you retain the sins of any, they are retained" (Jn 20:22–23). It is important to note the passive voice of the verbs "are forgiven" and "are retained." This is sometimes referred to as the "divine passive" because it conveys the idea that the actions—forgiving and retaining—are done *by God*.

The Anointing of the Sick, too, traces its beginnings to the ministry of Jesus and his apostles. The first missionary journey of the Twelve in Mark is summed up this way: "They cast out many demons, and anointed with oil many who were sick and cured them" (6:13). That the practice of the Anointing of the Sick continued in the early church is attested in the Letter of James. "Are any among you sick?" he asks. "They should call for the elders of the church and have them pray over them, anointing them with oil in the name of the Lord. The prayer of faith will save the sick, and the Lord will raise them up; and anyone who has committed sins will be forgiven" (5:14–15).

Holy Orders and Matrimony are sacraments of ministry, described in the *Catechism of the Catholic Church* as sacraments "directed towards the salvation of others" (1534) and exemplified in the lives of many men and women described in this book. A significant portion of Paul's First Letter to the Corinthians is given to describing the many charismatic ministries that animated the faith life of the early church. In the later Pastoral Letters (1 and 2 Timothy and Titus), also ascribed to Paul, the "orders" of service in the church begin to distinguish themselves. In 1 Timothy we read that "a bishop must be above reproach" (3:2), "deacons likewise must be serious" (3:8), and that "elders who rule well be considered worthy of double honor, especially those who labor in preaching and teaching" (5:17). The *Catechism* recognizes that both the laity and the ordained participate, each in its own way, "in the one priesthood of Christ" and that "the ministerial priesthood is at the service of the common priesthood" (1547).

The Church's vision of the sacrament of Matrimony is described in the *Catechism*, as it is in canon law (can. 1055, no. 1), as a "covenant, by which a man and a woman establish between themselves a partnership of the whole of life" (1601). This partnership serves in the Letter to the Ephesians as a model for the "great mystery" that is the relationship of Christ and the church (5:32). What the Beatitudes declare, the Sacraments effect—life in Christ, our hope of glory.

CELIA SIROIS

Part I

The Beatitudes

Saint Francis of Assisi

Holy Fool

Francis saw his father, Pietro, frown at him as he walked in the front door of the textile business. Francis didn't even stop to greet his mother, but walked right past both parents into the back storage room.

He could hear his father sputtering to his mother as he continued folding and piling the material from the new shipment. "I don't understand him! He joins the duke's army . . . a splendid knight . . . he had the whole town in the palm of his hand. And in two days—*two days*, mind you—he slinks back home, a disgrace to the Bernardone name! He's a fool!"

His mother's soft voice trembled. "I don't pretend to understand him, but you know he hasn't been himself since he came back. Maybe he just needs time to find his way."

In the next room, Francis cringed. He had decided to join the duke's army to reclaim the glory he had lost languishing as a prisoner of war. But something hadn't felt right. Then he'd heard that voice, that compelling voice too demanding to ignore: "Serve the Master, rather than man." He could still hear it ringing in his ears. Coming back had made him seem a cowardly fool, but he couldn't help it.

Francis had never experienced anything like this before. He was used to being the carefree merrymaker, the life of every party. But that sort of tinsel held no more appeal for him. He yearned for something deeper, more real—but what? He slid off the pile of material he had been perched on. "Mamma, I'm going out to Saint Damian's," Francis called over his shoulder as he strode out the door. His father just shook his head, folding and piling more furiously.

As Francis walked through the winding streets toward the city walls, he was hardly aware of anything around him. Hands stuffed in his belt and head hunched forward, he worked his mind hard. *I can't just keep drifting,* Francis thought. *What am I really looking for? Had that voice belonged to God? How can I "serve the master"?*

Francis was already outside the city walls and nearly at Saint Damian's Church when a shadow fell across the path, startling him out of his reverie. Instinctively he pulled back in horror as a leper extended his trembling, rotted hand, pleading for coins. From the purse at his belt, Francis drew a few coins and threw them at the human wreck. As the leper struggled to retrieve the coins, Francis circled widely around him and tried to settle back into his interrupted thoughts. Sights like this always left him a little queasy, and he shook his head to clear it. Now, where had he been . . . oh, yes, he had been thinking of how to serve the Master. . . .

Francis stopped dead in his tracks. His stomach tightened in a knot of realization and remorse, and he spun around in time to see the leper shuffling around a bend in the road. "Wait!" he shouted hoarsely, breaking into a dead run. He caught up with the man. Panting, torn between desire and revulsion, Francis gripped those thin ragged shoulders and looked searchingly into the surprised leper's face. Before, he had seen only the ugliness of disease; now he marveled at the light that appeared in the leper's eyes. Francis embraced the leper energetically, as if he were a long-lost friend instead of a man dying of a repulsive, contagious disease. Quickly, simply, Francis emptied the entire contents of his purse into the leper's hand—not throwing the coins, but pressing them warmly into the filthy palm. Then, without a word, he turned back and walked on briskly to Saint Damian's. Francis thought to himself: *This is where I'll find my Master, not only in prayer but also in suffering, and in those who are rejected.*

Kneeling before the altar of the little, dilapidated stone church, Francis contemplated the large crucifix. His searching eyes studied the twisted, agonized face. *This* was the face he had seen reflected in the eyes of the leper. It would be in serving others—whether poor or rich, simple, or wise—that he would serve his God. But *how*? He still looked for something concrete that he could do.

As he continued praying, Francis thought he heard someone calling him. Startled, he glanced around, but no one was there, nothing stirred. Yet as soon as he had settled down again, a voice repeated his name: "Francis!" The voice came from the crucifix! "Restore my church, Francis, which is falling into ruins." Francis nodded. This was something he could do—Saint Damian's could use more than a little fixing up.

Francis returned to his father's shop, loaded some of the best brocades and silks on a packhorse, and carted them off to nearby Foligno, where he sold everything—even the horse. He went back to Saint Damian's and offered the money to the pastor. Guessing where the money had come from, the priest hesitated to accept it, so Francis left the bag of coins on a windowsill of the church. When Pietro Bernardone learned what his son had done, his long-seething temper exploded. He physically hauled his son before the bishop to demand his money back.

As his father raged on with his public accusations, Francis realized that his anger was not about the money—after all, his father had indulged Francis all his life with fine clothes, food, and luxuries. His father only wanted to stop Francis from his new way of life. It was time for Francis to choose—even though he didn't feel ready, even though he didn't know exactly what he was supposed to do. If he *really* wanted to follow the way of the servant, suffering Christ, then he must put aside everything else. He must rebel from mediocrity.

Francis squared his shoulders and turned to the bishop. "Your Excellency," he began, "I'll return not only his money, but even his clothes." So saying, he removed everything he was wearing and added, "Pietro Bernardone is no longer my father; I give everything back to him. From now on I shall say to God, 'Our Father, who art in heaven. . . .'" The bishop was deeply moved. He covered the shivering Francis with his own robe, later giving him an old gardener's tunic to wear. A furious Pietro Bernardone gathered the clothes and money and left Francis there. From then on, Francis would have to rely completely on the providence of God, having nothing to call his own.

Francis dedicated himself completely to the Lord's service. He divided his time between helping at a refuge for lepers and rebuilding the crumbling church of Saint Damian. At first he was the laughingstock of the town, but as he persevered in his determination to radically live Gospel poverty, the laughter began to lessen.

With the bishop's permission, he began preaching simple sermons to the townspeople. Before long, his Gospel lifestyle and irrepressible joy began to attract others who were dissatisfied with their lives. When Francis and his followers numbered a dozen, he decided it was time to ask the Church to recognize this order that was forming almost spontaneously around him. Together the poor men set out for Rome to seek an audience with Pope Innocent III.

When the dusty, tattered man from Assisi entered the Pope's audience hall, Innocent gasped. The Pope had seen this very man in his dream the night before: Francis had been holding up the crumbling wall of the Lateran Basilica. Surely God must have something great in store for this unknown servant!

With the Pope's full approval, the little group returned to the vicinity of Francis's hometown. They lived in a borrowed stable until they outgrew it. Then a chapel, Our Lady of the Angels, was lent to Francis by a Benedictine abbot, and the growing community built rugged shacks around it for shelter. This tiny church was called the Portiuncula, or "little portion," and was always Francis's favorite, even years later when his friars had spread all over Italy.

Francis guided his men along the simple lines of the Gospel—prayer, poverty, work, and preaching. As he gradually realized that his new order would "build the Church"—not physically but through spiritual renewal—Francis gave himself to preaching tirelessly. He alternated his preaching with times of retreat from the world, either by himself or with a few companions, dedicating himself to prayer and contemplation. Despite his many sufferings, the lighthearted cheerfulness for which he had been known as a youth blossomed into a deep, persistent joy. He would often sing his now-famous Canticle of the Sun: "Praised be my Lord for Brother Sun . . . for Sister Moon, for Mother Earth, for fruits, flowers, grass, for Sister Death. . . ."

Francis's biggest concern was that his followers—who numbered in the thousands—would remain faithful to a life of poverty, service, and obedience. Only fifteen years after the Pope's approval, Francis's health began to fail. When a doctor told him death was near, he exclaimed, "Welcome, Sister Death!" because he knew he would soon see the Lord of his canticle, face to face.

Francis asked to be taken back to the Portiuncula, and a sorrowful procession wound its way out of Assisi and began climbing a small hill. Francis motioned to the brothers to stop. Slowly, painfully he raised himself on the stretcher, breathing hard from the effort. As the stretcher was lifted once more, he begged his brothers to sing the canticle with him, for him. Their voices quivering with emotion, they began the song so loved by their spiritual father.

Francis lay for a week in a hut at Portiuncula. Toward evening on a day early in October, Francis asked to be brought into the chapel itself and laid on the floor. He joined his whispered voice to those of the friars singing his favorite song of praise to God. The last verse died away; Francis intoned Psalm 141 and then fell silent.

As darkness shrouded the chapel, the forty-four-year-old holy fool of Assisi entered the eternal light of the Master he had so faithfully served.

Prayer

Saint Francis of Assisi,
you radically lived the beatitude
"Blessed are the poor in spirit, for theirs is the kingdom
    of heaven."

In a materialistic age that pressures us to focus on
   possessions as a means of happiness,
help us to discover the true joys of following Christ:
the joy of service,
the joy of a free heart and uncluttered life,
the joy of living in reconciliation,
the joy of living in communion with all creation.
Give us the courage to live
in always greater freedom
as your instruments of Christ's joy and peace in the
   world. Amen.

About Saint Francis

Born: ca. 1182 in Assisi
Died: October 3, 1226, just outside Assisi
Feast Day: October 4
Canonized: 1228 by Pope Gregory IX
Patron: Italy and the environment

Notes on His Life

- Just after his commitment to his new way of life Francis was beaten by robbers—and rejoiced about it.
- Known as the "holy fool," Francis sought out opportunities to be ridiculed.
- Francis gave away the community's only prayer book so they could give alms to a beggar.
- Along with the Dominicans, Francis and his followers rebuilt the medieval Church by renewing it spiritually.
- In ten years, Francis's followers grew to more than five thousand.

☪ Francis inspired his contemporary Saint Clare to begin the order that was eventually known as the Poor Clares.

☪ Francis was the first known stigmatist—mystically, the wounds of Christ were reproduced physically on his body two years before his death.

Lesser-Known Facts

☪ Saint Francis didn't actually write the prayer, "Lord, make me an instrument of your peace."

☪ When he wrote (and set to music) the exultant prayer, "The Canticle of the Sun," Francis was suffering excruciating pain.

☪ He went to the Holy Land to preach to the Muslims, who greatly respected him.

☪ He wanted to be buried in a cemetery for criminals.

☪ "Friars Minor" is the name Francis gave to his new order (later known as Franciscans).

☪ One of the most beloved and popular saints, his feast day is celebrated not just by Catholics but also by the Church of England, the Episcopal Church in the United States, and others.

In His Own Words

"We adore you, O Lord Jesus Christ, here and in all your churches which are in the whole world, and we bless you, because by your holy Cross you have redeemed the world."

Saint Juan Diego

"Am I Not Your Mother?"

On a clear morning Juan Diego made his way along the dusty road to Tlatelolco (Tlat-el-ol-co), his usual route to attend Mass and to hear instruction from the priests. During the three-and-a-half hour trip, he was thinking of how life had changed in these past ten years. The conquerors had come and taken away the greatness of his people. *Our land is now their land,* he thought. *They are our rulers, we are like slaves. However, I have accepted their religion because. . . .* Suddenly he heard the strains of lovely music. *What is it that I hear? Such music must be of heaven!* And then someone called his name, "Juanito," but with such sweetness, "Juan Dieguito."

He began to look around, staring off to the east, curious about the sounds he was hearing. He was so taken by the music that, without realizing it, he began climbing Tepeyac Hill. At the top he was surprised to find a beautiful young woman, not a Spaniard, but one of his own people, a *morena*. In an instant he took in the scene: she was standing in a field of emerald hues where the ground was usually brown and dusty; the blaze of sun was behind her, whereas it should have still been rising toward midday; her clothing was regal; and she appeared to be pregnant.

She was looking at him with such a loving expression, as if she really knew who he was. "Juanito," she continued. "My smallest child, where are you going?"

"My Mother," he replied, returning her gaze, "I am on my way to your house in Tlatelolco to hear the divine things taught by our priests, our Lord's delegates."

"Know and understand, dearest of my children," the lady continued, "that I am the ever-holy Virgin Mary, Mother of the true God who gives life, Mother of the Creator of heaven and earth. I have an ardent desire that a temple be built where I can show forth all my love, compassion, assistance, and defense because I am your loving Mother: yours, and all who are with you, and of all who live in this land, and of all who love me, call to me, and trust in me. I will hear their cries and will give remedy to their sorrows and sufferings."

As he listened, Juan Diego felt great love and confidence toward this motherly figure. She urged him, "So that I can actually show my mercy as I desire, go to the bishop and explain that I have sent you to manifest what I wish, that a temple be built for me on this very site." Without losing a moment, Juan Diego said, with a slight bow, "I am on my way to do as you ask, my Lady."

As he hurried along, Juan Diego reflected on what had happened. *My heavenly Mother did not suddenly appear to me as in a dream. No, she was right there speaking to me as a mother to her son. And I could address her as I would my own mother. I must hurry and faithfully carry out her wishes.* In his heart he kept hearing her voice calling, *"Juanito, Juan Dieguito."*

Although he was fifty-seven years old, Juan Diego had no difficulty covering the miles quickly. He was received at the door of the bishop's palace and directed to a place to sit until called. He sat quietly and waited, and waited, and waited, going over and over what he must say. Bishop Juan de Zumárraga was a kindly man, who when eventually informed of his visitor, invited him in. He listened attentively to Juan Diego, but decided to give the story the test of time. "Thank you for what you have related to me, Juan Diego, but I must ask you to come again another day when there is more time. Then you can repeat what you have said and give me all the details." Juan Diego expressed his gratitude to the bishop, but outside he expressed his disappointment with a deep sigh.

Back at Tepeyac he again found his Lady waiting. "My dear Mother," he began, "I went and delivered your message, but I don't think the bishop believes me. He might think this is my invention. Please, give your commission to someone more worthy than I. I am nobody. I am like a tail or a dead leaf. You ask me to go where I do not belong. Forgive me for saying this. Do not be angry with me, my Lady."

Mary was looking attentively at Juan Diego when she replied, "My littlest one, my son, listen to me. There are many servants and messengers from whom I could choose, but I desire that you take my message so that through you my wish will be fulfilled. I beg and command you, my dearest son, go again tomorrow to the bishop. Greet him in my name and tell him that work must begin on my temple. Tell the bishop that I have personally sent you—I, the ever-holy Virgin Mary, Mother of God."

Again, this humble man accepted the Lady's mandate, but feared he would be rebuffed a second time. After all, he was only an Indian.

Early the next morning he made the trip once more to the bishop's residence, and once more he was made to wait. When kneeling before the bishop this time, Juan Diego was peppered with questions. Bishop Zumárraga wanted a description of the lady and the place where Juan Diego had seen her. Juan Diego held back nothing of what he had seen, of his impression of the lady, or of what she had requested of him. Even after all that, as he later recalled to his heavenly Mother, the bishop said he must ask for a sign, a proof of some kind that her appearance was true. In fact, however, the bishop was so intrigued that he sent men to follow Juan Diego, but they lost him somewhere near the hill.

He went home with the Virgin's assurance that tomorrow she would provide the sign the bishop requested. At home, to his dismay, Juan Diego found his beloved uncle, Juan Bernardino, very ill. He tried without success to find someone with medical expertise. So, early next day, Juan Diego set out for Tlatelolco to bring back a priest to anoint his uncle, now close to death. To avoid running into his Lady, Juan Diego went around the other side of Tepeyac Hill. In passing he glanced up at the hill just as Mary was descending toward him. "My little one, my son, what is happening? Where are you going?"

"My dear Lady," he stammered, "I hope you are well, and happy, but what I tell you may sadden you. My uncle is dying and I am rushing to call a priest to confess him and prepare him for death. As soon as I have done this, I will return to you. Please know I am being truthful. I will be back here tomorrow."

Looking at him with love, the Virgin assured him, "My son, fear not; what worries you now is nothing. Do not be frightened by that illness. Am I not your Mother? Your uncle will not die; believe me, he is healthy." Juan Diego was overjoyed by her words and immediately set off to do as she instructed. "Go, my son, to the top of the hill and collect the flowers you find. Bring them to me." At the place where he had first encountered the Lady, he found a large number of fresh, fragrant roses. When he presented all that he had cut to her, Mary took them from his arms and arranged them neatly in his cloak, or *tilma*. "Do not open your cloak for anyone but the bishop," she told him. "Tell him that I have sent you as my ambassador. You are most worthy of trust. Say that I sent you to the top of the hill to cut these flowers. Explain to him all that you saw and experienced so that he may be persuaded to build the temple I request."

This time, as Juan Diego knocked at the palace door, he felt sure of success, but again the servants tried to turn him away. As he pleaded for an audience with the bishop, one of the servants caught sight of what looked like a rose sticking out from under Juan Diego's tightly held garment. The man attempted to grab the flower, but Mary's ambassador held strong. Because of the tantalizing aroma of the roses, the servants finally decided to inform the bishop. He hurried from his study and invited his visitor to come in. Juan Diego gladly accompanied the bishop and after properly greeting him recounted his wondrous story from the beginning.

"Señor Bishop, as you ordered, I went to my Lady, Holy Mary, Queen of Heaven, and made your request. I told her that I had promised to bring a sign back for you. She agreed. And that is how, very early this morning, she sent me to the top of the hill where I first met her to cut roses. She herself arranged them in my *tilma* to be brought to you. Only cactus and dried brush grow on that hill, but this morning it was full of every variety of Castilian roses. Now I am to present them to you as her sign that I am to be trusted and that she truly wants her request to be granted."

As Juan Diego unfolded his *tilma*, not only did a glorious array of roses fall to the floor, but a stunning portrait of his Lady appeared on his *tilma*. Before the bishop and those present with him, the miraculous image of Mary, the Mother of God and of the Americas, our Lady of Guadalupe, was revealed on the poor, simple *tilma* of her faithful son.

Juan Diego was a man of his civilization, one that had been viciously subjugated, a member of a trusting people who had been sorely tried by their conquerors. Because of his personal openness to God's call, he epitomized the true disciple of Christ's kingdom, the poor in spirit. And he had personally met that kingdom's Queen. He had conversed with her. She had shown him the utmost love and respect and had commissioned him to begin the process of getting a temple built in her honor on the very place of their meeting. It was this very spot on which he now stood. "Most beloved and beautiful lady, my mother, my little one, I will be here always at your service. I will tell everyone about your tender concern for my people, for all people. I will lead them to you where they can lay down their burdens and lift up their hearts to you and to the Giver of Life."

He spent the rest of his life as caretaker of her chosen shrine and spokesman for the Mother of God. This holy and humble man, ever faithful son that he is, can still be encountered at the glorious Shrine of Our Lady of Guadalupe.

Prayer

Saint Juan Diego, Cuauthlatoatzin, "talking eagle,"
among your people the eagle is the messenger of
the Divine.

Truly you were the messenger of the Queen of Heaven,
   her most trusted son.
Our Lady of Guadalupe met with you as one meets
   a friend,
inviting you to cooperate with her
in the great work of evangelization among your own
   people.
Help us to be devoted to this Queen and to trust her
   with our needs,
and those of our world today.
Inspire us with the openness of heart needed to hear and
   act upon God's word
so that we too may be worthy of the kingdom. Amen.

About Saint Juan Diego

Born: 1474 in Tlayacac, Cuauhtitlán (north of present-day
   Mexico City)
Died: May 30, 1548
Feast Day: December 9
Canonized: July 30, 2002, by Pope John Paul II
Patron: Mexico; those devoted to Our Lady of Guadalupe

Notes on His Life

- His given name, Cuauthlatoatzin (Cuau-tla-to-át-zin), means "speaking eagle" or "one who speaks like an eagle" in his native language, Nahuatl (Aztec).

- He and his wife were early converts to the Catholic faith, though his wife died before the apparitions.

- He worked as a farmer and a weaver of straw mats.

- In studying the image on the *tilma*, scientists have found that a reflection of Juan Diego unfolding the *tilma* appears in the eye of Our Lady of Guadalupe. The bishop and several other people can also be seen.

- For seventeen years Juan Diego lived next to the shrine as caretaker and guide.

Lesser-Known Facts

- The *Nican Mopohua*, "here it is written," is the earliest extant document of the apparition.
- The dialogue, in Nahuatl, refers to Juan Diego with the suffix *tzin*, a sign of respect and tenderness ("Juantzin" or "Juan Diegotzin").
- The word "Guadalupe" is really Tequantlaxopeuh (Te-qua-tla-supe), which the Spaniards confused with the Shrine of Guadalupe in Estremadura, Spain.
- Juan Bernardino went to Bishop Zumárraga to explain his cure from smallpox.
- In Nahuatl the appearance of flower and song together designates the presence of the divine.
- Tlatelolco, a suburb of Mexico City, means "in the little hill of land."
- The *tilma* (cloak), which is still intact today, is made of maguey, or agave. Fabric made with maguey usually lasts just twenty years.

In His Own Words

"Please, give your commission to someone more worthy than me. I am nobody. I am like a tail or a dead leaf. You ask me to go where I do not belong. Forgive me for saying this. Do not be angry with me, my Lady."

Saint Germaine Cousin

God's Cinderella

In a cold, musty corner of the barn, Germaine peered through one of the cracks in the wall. The teenage girl had a clear view of the house. In the twilight, she could see the tall, familiar figure of her father trudging slowly toward the house.

Her stepmother, Madame Cousin, had been anxiously awaiting his return, and she didn't like to be kept waiting. When he got to the door he was greeted with, "Don't just stand there. Come in and close that door. You're late. What kept you?"

Back in the barn, Germaine winced as she heard that rasping voice. She watched the door shut, then she went over to the pile of straw where she slept. As she sank into the straw, one of the lambs wandered over to her.

"You're so soft and silent, little one," Germaine whispered as she caressed it. Taking care of the sheep had been her responsibility since she'd been very young. They were Germaine's constant companions and the closest thing she had to friends.

Meanwhile, inside the house, Laurent Cousin took off his hat. "Old man Larue needed me to finish up," he said.

"I've already heard that excuse four times this week." Madame Cousin shook her head and stirred the soup faster.

Happy to see their father, the children were already vying with one another, trying to be the first to greet him. After they had displayed all their exuberance in hugs and kisses, the family settled down to eat.

"Did anyone bring Germaine supper?" Laurent asked his wife.

"No. And no one will until after we have eaten. Come on now, before everything gets cold."

Laurent swallowed his soup. He didn't completely understand his wife's attitude toward Germaine. After the meal, he got up, took what leftovers he could, and went out to the barn. "Germaine! Germaine!" he called.

"Father!" Germaine ran as fast as she could. "How was your day, Father?"

"Fine! I brought your supper." Germaine and her father sat down together on a low pile of hay.

"Mother makes delicious bread," said the girl as she tore off a piece.

Laurent looked over at his daughter—her crippled arm cradled on her lap, the ugly tumors growing on her neck. No wonder his second wife kept Germaine separate from her own children. Then Laurent saw the newly formed dark bruise on Germaine's good arm.

Germaine caught his gaze, put down her bread and shifted her position so that he couldn't see the bruise anymore. She shrugged her shoulders as he looked at her. "Mother gets so impatient. Sometimes I think I am happier out here in the peace of the barn than she is." At her father's puzzled look, she explained. "In the quiet, I can sense God is with me. That makes me very happy."

Laurent studied his daughter's calm gaze, then his lips twisted in a wry smile. "Get a good night's rest."

Laurent got up and left the barn, her soft "Good night, Father," echoing in his ears. What could he do for his daughter? She was pleasant, obedient, and hard working. But with her disfigurement and crippled arm, she would always be a burden. Germaine tried to help by her spinning, but she had no future. No one knew whether her condition was contagious, so she was not marriageable. Laurent knew that his wife felt the need to discipline Germaine, but Madame Cousin often took out her anger on Germaine in cruel ways. It's her or me, he thought wearily. Germaine had been an outcast for so long, she didn't seem to mind any more. Like her comment tonight— she sounded as if she pitied his wife! Laurent shook his head. He wouldn't speak to Madame Cousin about that.

At dawn, Germaine gathered the sheep to lead them out to pasture. But her stepmother stopped her. "Germaine, today I want you to take the sheep to pasture at the edge of the Bouconne Forest."

"Bouconne Forest?" Germaine exclaimed in surprise. "But what about the wolves?"

"You heard what I said. And if you let anything happen to those sheep, girl, you'd better not come home."

"Yes, Stepmother."

Germaine puzzled over her stepmother's latest whim. What was she trying to prove? The Bouconne Forest was known for the packs of hungry wolves that roamed there. Lately some people had reported seeing them venturing out of the forest in search of food. All the farm folk were so frightened that they avoided the area as much as possible.

Germaine did as her stepmother ordered. When it was
good weather—and not too cold of a winter's day, like today—
she enjoyed taking the sheep out. Alone with God's creatures,
Germaine felt surrounded by God's love and majesty. As she
did daily, she spent much of the day in prayer. Maybe she had
no friends to talk to on earth, but talking to God was as real
to her as breathing.

Today, she entrusted her safety—and that of the sheep—to
God. The edge of the forest certainly provided plenty of good
grazing. But the starving wolves prowled the area as well.
Germaine could occasionally hear growls and the rustling of
leaves, but she stayed calm.

Madame Cousin made sure she watched for Germaine to
come home that night. Surprised to see her stepmother waiting for her, Germaine waved as she approached the barn, but
Madame Cousin did not return the greeting. As soon as
Germaine came up to her, she inspected the sheep and asked
roughly, "Did you bring back all the sheep?"

"Yes, Stepmother," Germaine said.

"Are you sure? Did you count them? You're not lying to
me, are you?" As she said this, Madame Cousin counted the
sheep herself. "I guess you know what's good for you.
Tomorrow you'll go back there again," Madame Cousin said
coldly.

The following day Germaine again pastured the sheep at
the edge of the forest. As Germaine was busily spinning wool,
she suddenly heard the rustling of leaves behind her. She turned
quickly and saw a poor beggar coming up the forest path.

"Sorry if I startled you," the man called.

"You didn't startle me," stammered Germaine. "Would
you care to join me?" She rummaged in her sack and pulled
out a few crusts of bread. "You are welcome to what I have,"
she said as she offered them to him. Germaine seldom ate all

the bread she was given. Each day she would make a little sacrifice and put some aside for anyone who needed food that day.

The man nodded his thanks as he reached for the crusts. "I was trying to get to the next village and I started to wonder if I was going to end up as food for the wolves. What are you doing, grazing your sheep here? Aren't you afraid that they will attack?"

"We are safe. God is watching over us," Germaine replied.

But the beggar was concerned for the kindly girl. "I'm telling you, they'll attack as soon as they feel sure of themselves."

"I have to go home now," Germaine said. "Maybe I'll see you tomorrow."

Germaine hurriedly gathered the sheep and headed home. When she had herded the sheep into their pen, she went to pull out the small supply of bread she had saved. She dug deep into the hay, but it was gone! All her scraps of bread, so carefully saved, had disappeared. While the girl had been at the forest that day, Madame Cousin had taken the few pieces of bread Germaine had put aside.

The girl's first thought was, "That poor man! What shall I give him if I see him tomorrow?"

Taking all her courage, Germaine headed to the forbidden house and went straight to the kitchen door. She tiptoed in and closed the door softly. Her eyes immediately fell on a basket. Picking up the cloth cover, she found the missing bread—even some straw still stuck to it. Germaine took the few stale pieces of bread, wrapped them in her apron and stepped toward the door.

"What are you doing in this house, you dirty good-for-nothing?" Madame Cousin burst into the room. "Stealing my bread, are you? You won't get away with this!"

Enraged, Madame Cousin grabbed a large wooden stick and threatened to beat Germaine. The girl pulled her apron tightly to herself and ran. Her stepmother shouted after her, "Thief! Thief!"

The neighbors flocked out to see what was going on. They had never seen Madame Cousin so upset. She was screaming and running after Germaine with a stick! "If she catches up with her, she'll kill that poor girl," yelled one of the men.

Germaine's heart pounded as she gasped for air. With her poorly nourished body, she didn't have the strength to keep running. She stopped, defenseless, arms clutching her apron. One of the neighbors tried to hold Madame Cousin back from attacking Germaine. "Stop!" the woman gasped. "Don't hit her!"

Madame Cousin raised the stick and commanded, "Open your apron and show everyone what a thief you are!"

In front of everyone, Germaine dropped the hem of her apron. Instead of hard crusts of bread, out fell a beautiful assortment of spring flowers.

The neighbors started to murmur among themselves. "Where did she get those in the middle of winter?"

"It's a miracle, I tell you!"

Shocked, bewildered, and embarrassed, Madame Cousin felt her rage fade to confusion. She quietly told Germaine to go back to the barn.

Besides the miracle of the flowers, another miracle took place that day—a conversion in the heart of Madame Cousin. Although she never actually apologized to Germaine, she was no longer as harsh and cruel as she had been. Germaine was thrilled that her prayers for her stepmother had been answered.

But Germaine didn't enjoy the newfound peace in her life for long. One morning in the summer of 1601, Germaine was found dead on her bed of straw. To some people, her life of twenty-two years might seem to consist only of sickness, beatings, loneliness, and lack of love. Yet, within the tragedies of her life, the Church recognizes the glowing heroism of a simple, disfigured farmer's daughter who discovered, clung to, and witnessed to God's love in surprising ways.

On June 29, 1867, Pope Pius IX officially proclaimed her a saint.

Prayer

Saint Germaine,
in the midst of life's tragedies—
the loss of your mother and harsh abuse—
you clung to the comfort and strength of God's love
    for you.
You didn't allow cruelty, loneliness, or suffering
    to embitter your heart,
but sought ways to alleviate the suffering of others.
Unquenchable hope allowed you to discern God's love
    and providence
in your life and in the world.
When loss, suffering, and the unfairness of life threaten
    to overwhelm me,
help me put that same trust in God, that he will comfort
    me in my suffering,
and give me the strength and compassion to stand up
    against injustice.
Give me that transforming vision of faith
to be open to how God can turn the most unlikely of events
into an encounter of grace. Amen.

About Saint Germaine Cousin

Born: 1579 in Pibrac, France (small village near
   Toulouse)
Died: 1601 in Pibrac
Feast Day: June 15
Canonized: June 29, 1867, by Pope Pius IX
Patron: those who suffer abuse and child abuse, people
   with illness and physical disabilities

Notes on Her Life

⚜ Germaine had a great devotion to the Rosary, which she
   prayed daily using a knotted string.

⚜ Germaine left her sheep in the care of her guardian angel
   when she went to daily Mass. The sheep never wandered
   off and were never harmed.

⚜ Once, a villager saw the waters of the swollen river part
   for her so she could get to Mass on time.

⚜ Visions and glorious music (witnessed by neighbors)
   sometimes accompanied Germaine's prayer.

⚜ In addition to a crippled hand, Germaine suffered from
   scrofula, a kind of tuberculosis of the neck.

⚜ In the sixteenth century, people with physical disabilities
   were often considered to be less than human. Germaine
   was considered a fool or an idiot by many in her village.
   Only gradually did the villagers recognize her holiness.

⚜ Many of the miracles attributed to Saint Germaine's intercession are connected with her own life: miraculous
   physical healings and the multiplication of food.

Lesser-Known Facts

🕮 Despite her poverty and sufferings, Germaine also fasted on bread and water.

🕮 To punish her for a mistake, her stepmother poured boiling water on Germaine's legs when she was a young child.

🕮 Germaine might have been forgotten if her body hadn't been accidentally discovered to be incorrupt in 1644, although it hadn't been embalmed.

🕮 During the French Revolution, her casket was desecrated by quicklime thrown on her body in an effort to destroy it. Afterward, her body was again found intact except where the quicklime had damaged it.

In Her Own Words

"Dear God, please don't let me be too hungry or too thirsty. Help me to please my mother. And help me to please you."

Saint Monica

The Mother Who Never Gave Up

The dignified woman opened the door and stiffly walked into the room at the seaside inn. As she looked at the drab, empty room, she thought, "Nothing special about it." It was simply supposed to be a stopover; it wasn't supposed to be the place where her heart would be broken . . . again.

She managed to hold in her tears until she closed the door behind her. Then, Monica collapsed on her knees beside the bed, burying her face in the cheap pillows and letting them absorb the sound of heartbreak.

First her husband, now her firstborn son. Monica felt so alone. How well she remembered the first time she'd wept like this—thirty years ago, on her wedding night. She had been young then, and had expected a happy wedding night. After patiently putting up with the nagging interference of her mother-in-law all day, Monica had been stunned when her new husband, Patricius, flew into a rage. He had insulted Monica in front of all their guests and then went out into the night, abandoning her.

It had been a sad prelude to what much of her married life would be like—a hostile mother-in-law who delighted in stirring up her son's discontent, a husband's fearsome temper tantrums, abandonments, and infidelities. That night, vulnerable as only a bride can be on her wedding night, she had prayed fervently that her faith would sustain her. "Dear God, please help me to be a faithful and good wife to Patricius. Help me to do your will, and to show your love to him. If our wedding night means nothing to him . . . I'm terrified of the future. . . . Help me! I mustn't think ahead. Help me now . . . just one day, one minute at a time." She had cried herself to sleep that night, and many nights thereafter, her tears alternating with her prayers, "Lord, just help me *today, now*!"

She had put up with her husband's fiery temper, dissolute habits, and infidelity for twenty years. She had found a "secret weapon"—the grace of Christian forbearance. Early on in her marriage, she had decided never to respond with anger when her husband or mother-in-law was angry. It had been impossible at first, and a constant effort—sometimes daily, sometimes minute-by-minute. But gradually, Monica had found a way to keep her peace and be unwaveringly gentle, kind, and patient.

Despite her husband's infidelity and outbursts of anger, Patricius never struck her. Finally, after twenty years, Patricius asked to be instructed in the Christian faith. When he was baptized, he became another man. He lived a fervent Christian life for only a year before falling sick and dying. Monica's grief had been tempered by the joy of their last year together and the certainty that her husband had finally found the peace and happiness he had so longed for.

How she missed him now! Maybe he would have known what to do with their wayward son. Although Patricius had not agreed to have Augustine baptized, Monica had instructed her son in the beliefs and practices of Christianity. But as a teenager away at school, Augustine fell in with bad friends and rejected Christianity in favor of Manichaeism. Monica was brokenhearted when she learned of his rejection of faith. Manichaeism claimed to synthesize all religions through intellectual enlightenment, and was particularly hostile to Christianity. Monica began to pray constantly for her son; she cried and begged God to lead Augustine to the truth. She talked and pleaded with him, but with no results. His way of life was so immoral that, for a time, she had refused him entrance to the house. But then she quickly realized that shutting him out would neither change him nor help him.

One night God comforted her with a vision. An angel appeared to her and addressed her gently, "Why are you crying? Dry your tears. Your son is with you." With that the angel pointed to Monica's right. There, in a vision, was her son—serene, calm, and resplendent in white. The next day she told Augustine, "Last night I saw a messenger from God. He told me that you were with me."

"Well, Mother," Augustine smirked, "are you coming over to our way of thinking?"

"No, son. I wasn't told that I was with *you*, but that *you* were with *me*."

Augustine couldn't hide the impression her quick answer made on him. But he didn't change. At times it seemed that the more she prayed for him, the deeper Augustine became enmeshed in immorality and error. She had begged one priest after another, one bishop after another, to speak to her son. To placate her, one bishop had told her, "It is impossible that a child of such tears and prayers will perish!" So Monica persevered in prayer. It was all she had to provide her with some sanity and hope.

And in these past few years, her son had softened toward her. While he still clung to his denial of Christianity, they spoke often. He had decided to go to Rome to teach rhetoric—although he was only twenty-nine, he had been offered a prestigious position there. Concerned about his spiritual welfare, Monica had hoped to persuade him not to go. But he wouldn't yield, so she decided to go with him. Yesterday Monica had joined him so they could travel together. Her son told her he was visiting friends and that they would leave the next day. Monica spent the day in a nearby chapel. When she went to meet him in the morning, she discovered that he had deceived her again. "Their" ship had left the day before with Augustine on board. He had deliberately left her behind.

Now, kneeling by the bed, Monica dried her tears. What could she do? It was obvious Augustine wanted her nowhere near him. He had abandoned her. Should she simply go home? Pray for him from afar? She couldn't give up on him, no matter what.

Monica thought about her son: his stubbornness, his keen intellect, his self-honesty. She knew how sensitive Augustine would be as he continued to search for the truth. Although her words seemed to have no effect on him up till now, she didn't know what a difference her presence might make at the right moment. Could she really leave his spiritual welfare to strangers?

But it wouldn't be easy traveling without him. And how would she find him? Would he even stay in Rome? Monica sighed. She barely dared to ask herself her biggest question: Suppose when she found him, he fled her presence again?

Monica turned once again to the Source of her strength. What should she do? Should she risk being rejected again by her son? Should she stay behind or go to find him? "Lord, you gave my beloved son Augustine into my care. Show me now how I can best help him to find you." In the throbbing quiet of sorrow, Monica received her answer. Just because he had abandoned her, she wouldn't abandon him. God *had* entrusted Augustine's well-being—body and soul—to her care. Perhaps, somehow, her mother's love would eventually help him to come to believe in God's love for him.

With renewed strength, Monica booked passage on the next ship to Rome. When she arrived, she found he had turned down the position and gone to Milan. So off she went to Milan.

After a long search, Monica finally found her son and learned from him that although he was not a Christian, he was no longer a Manichaean. Monica redoubled her prayers. Finally, with the wisdom and help of Saint Ambrose, the bishop of Milan, Augustine was baptized. He was thirty-two. Monica was overwhelmed with joy. With the friends who had been converted and baptized with him, Augustine went to a country villa where they could solidify their new-found faith with prayer, meditation, and discussions. Augustine wanted Monica to join them. Not only did she look after their needs, but she also contributed to their discussions.

Eventually Augustine and Monica decided to return home, and they traveled to the port city of Ostia, where they waited for a ship. One night Augustine and his mother were alone on the patio looking at the beautiful sky and God's magnificent creation. As they talked together about heaven, they fell silent. For a brief moment, God gave them both an intuition of what the joys of heaven would be like. After sharing a profound silence, Monica spoke. "Son, no longer do I find any joy in this life. I have received all I hoped for. My last desire—the one for which I lived—was to see you baptized and dedicated to God's service. Why I am still here on earth, I don't know."

A few days later Monica fell ill. She burned with fever for several days. In a lucid moment, she told Augustine, "You shall bury your mother here. It doesn't matter what happens to my mortal remains. Just promise to remember me every day at Mass, no matter where you are."

After only nine days of illness, Monica serenely passed away. Augustine was thirty-three years old. He suffered immense grief for his mother. But he did not cry at the funeral because she had died such a holy death. Later, however, when he was alone and thought about his mother's love, prayers, and constant care, he burst into tears and cried for the mother who had shed so many tears for him. He wrote, "If I am your child, O my God, it is because you gave me such a mother!"

Sixteen centuries separate us from Monica, yet she suffered the same tragedies that families face today: abuse, marital infidelity, the breakdown of the family, and family members who reject God and his commandments. She was an ordinary woman with no exceptional gifts, who was continuously disappointed by those whom she loved. Yet through these troubling, even tragic, circumstances of her life, she lived an extraordinary commitment to her vocation as wife and mother. Her perseverance in prayer, her fidelity to always being there for her husband and children, no matter how they responded to her, gradually worked the greatest miracle of all: the miracle of Love being born in their hearts.

Prayer

Saint Monica,
you were just an ordinary woman.
No miracles, no extraordinary events filled your life.
Instead, your cup was filled to overflowing with suffering
    and tears
as your loved ones broke your heart many times over.
Yet you never gave up on them, nor on God's love for
    them.
Your extraordinary love of your husband and children
wove the fraying threads of your family always more
    closely together.
You trusted in the power of your motherly prayer to
    move God's heart,
and your wayward son didn't just convert but became a
    great saint of the Church.
In times of grief and suffering, when I mourn for my
    loved ones,
give me that same confidence in God's love.
May the ordinary sufferings of my life also become
    extraordinary
through the power of God's love
working in me and through me. Amen.

About Saint Monica

Born: ca. 331 in Tagaste, Numidia (now Algeria)

Died: 387 in Ostia (in what is now Italy)

Feast Day: August 27

Patron: wives, wives who suffer abuse, mothers, widows

Notes on Her Life

- Monica was raised in a devout Catholic family.

- Monica's husband verbally abused her for almost twenty years.

- In addition to her husband's conversion, Monica's patience also won over her ill-tempered mother-in-law.

- Monica didn't pray for a miracle for her husband or son; instead she offered prayers and penances for their conversion.

- When Monica pleaded with priests and bishops to speak to her son, many of them dismissed her. Only Saint Ambrose, whom she met only a few years before she died, seemed to understand her.

- Monica had carefully prepared her own burial place next to her husband because she wanted even her physical remains to be united to his. But shortly before she died, Monica decided that it didn't matter where she was buried. She even lightheartedly joked that God would be able to find her remains wherever she was buried.

- Monica's son Augustine became not only one of the most famous converts of the Church, but also one of the greatest saints of the early Church, receiving the title Father of the Church due to his many inspiring and profound writings about the faith and the tremendous influence they have had on the Church's life.

Lesser-Known Facts

- As a youngster sent to draw the wine, Monica started to "taste" the wine and gradually started to drink cupfuls regularly. When a servant caught her and called her a "wine-bibber," Monica stopped. Shortly afterward, she was baptized.

❦ Monica had three children who survived to adulthood. Besides Augustine, they were Perpetua, who was married briefly and entered a monastery after she was widowed; and her younger son Navigius, who was also with her when she died.

❦ Monica had four grandchildren: Adeodatus, the son of Augustine and his mistress, and the three children of Navigius.

❦ Saint Ambrose became Monica's spiritual adviser, whom she promptly obeyed. When Saint Ambrose was being persecuted, Monica was one of those who stood vigil for him, risking her own safety.

❦ Saint Ambrose had a very high opinion of Monica and praised her to Augustine.

❦ Almost everything we know about Saint Monica, we know from the writings of Augustine.

❦ There is little record of devotion to Monica until the fifteenth century, when her remains were discovered in Ostia and transferred to the church of Saint Augustine in Rome.

In Her Own Words

"Remember me at the altar of the Lord."

— To her sons when she was dying

Saint Bernadette Soubirous

Unlikely Visionary

A thick fog blanketed the little town of Lourdes, France, on this cold and damp morning. In the impoverished room that served as the Soubirous family home, Mama Louise was cleaning a few vegetables for the thin soup that would be the family's noon meal. The one-room former jail cell that served as their home had only three beds and a chair for furniture. The whole family shared the small quarters—Francois Soubirous; his wife, Louise; fourteen-year-old Bernadette; twelve-year-old Toinette; and their brothers, John and Justin. Mama Louise sighed as her daughters turned to leave for school.

"Bernadette," said her mother, "go straight to school and don't wander; your cough might come back."

"Don't worry, Mama, I'll put on my cloak and cap so I won't be cold." Bernadette's eyes met her mother's and she nodded an unspoken obedience.

On her way to school, Bernadette gulped the fresh air with relief. At home, the thick, stale air could make anyone choke, and Bernadette, whose asthma already made breathing difficult, often found it unbearable. At times she would stand by the barred window and gulp great draughts of the fresh, clean air that blew down from the Pyrenees Mountains. At night she could not do this without disturbing the family, so she would lie awake next to her sister Toinette, suffering as silently as possible, but letting a cough escape her now and then.

Today, she was happy to escape not only the choking air—she was also relieved to be free of her mother's too-penetrating gaze. She had told her parents last night how unhappy she was—she had to choose between obeying her parents or the Lady. She had promised her mother she would *try* to go straight to school, but she wanted *so much* to see the beautiful Lady again!

Bernadette had first seen the Lady only a few days ago, on February 11, 1858. Bernadette, Toinette, and their friend Jeanne Abadie were gathering firewood, as they often did. A short walk from home, the girls came to the River Gave at the grotto, or cave of Massabielle. Toinette and Jeanne saw some sticks on the far side and waded across to get them, squealing as the icy water chilled their feet.

"Please throw some stones in so that I won't get my feet wet," Bernadette called. "Mama wouldn't want that!"

Jeanne, however, retorted, "You're such a nuisance! Stay where you are if you don't want to cross!" As the bells of Saint Peter's Church pealed out the Angelus and its echoes died away among the hills, Jeanne and Toinette quickly gathered the bits of wood near the river and moved farther off.

Bernadette was left alone. At first, she threw stones into the stream to make a path for her to cross, but the attempt failed, so she decided to take off her shoes and wade over as the others had done. Just then, she thought she heard a rumble of distant thunder—or was it a sudden gust of wind? Bernadette glanced about. She saw no storm clouds; nothing stirred. "I must have been mistaken," she thought, and bent down again to remove the shoe.

But then she heard that same sound! This time Bernadette stood up and looked about intently. What was happening? On the slope before her a wild rosebush was tossing violently as if caught in a gale. Everything else was still.

As Bernadette stared, the dark cave brightened and a beautiful young Lady appeared over the rose bush. Bernadette felt numb. She rubbed her eyes, closed them and reopened them, but the Lady was still there. Her warm smile told Bernadette that this was real, after all! Quickly she pulled her rosary from her pocket and began to pray. When she finished praying the rosary, the Lady disappeared from view.

When the Lady was gone, Bernadette took her shoes off to wade through the stream, eager to join the other girls. To her surprise, the water wasn't cold, but lukewarm. Bernadette caught up to the others and asked if they had seen anything. They hadn't. Then they teased Bernadette, promising to tell no one, until she confessed that she had seen "a lady in white."

That afternoon, Toinettte let the news of the Lady slip out. Bernadette's mother was unusually serious. "You must get these ideas out of your head, Bernadette," she decided. "I'm not sure you should go to Massabielle again!" The joy of Bernadette's meeting with the Lady was immediately mixed with the pain of her parents' disapproval. But the Lady had asked her to come back fifteen more times, and Bernadette had promised to return. With the reluctant permission of her parents, who were influenced by curious relatives and friends, Bernadette had already gone back to the grotto several times.

Daily, Bernadette alternately faced ridicule, scorn, threats, demands of proof, and adulation. While Lourdes buzzed with rumors and ridicule, she tried to go about her usual daily duties. Poorly educated, unable to even read and write, the humble girl hardly seemed likely to be favored by heaven.

Then one night, Police Commissioner Jacomet waylaid her, interrogated her, and threatened her father with jail. Her parents, worried about the commissioner's threats, forbade Bernadette to go back to the grotto.

Bernadette managed to make it to school and back home for lunch. But she could focus only on the Lady at the grotto. What would the Lady think if Bernadette broke her promise?

As Bernadette went back to school that afternoon, she could no longer resist the suddenly irresistible pull. She found herself heading toward the grotto!

Two policemen and a crowd of about one hundred people followed Bernadette. She arrived at the grotto and knelt in her usual place . . . but the Lady did not come that day. Shaken with shame, Bernadette was inconsolable. Her Aunt Bernarde pulled Bernadette away. All the girl could say was, "I don't know how I've failed the Lady."

That evening, Bernadette went to her confessor and explained the situation. He thought that she should be allowed to go to the grotto. When Bernadette talked it over with her parents, they realized how distressed their daughter had become, and Francois Soubirous immediately relented.

Bernadette suffered from a storm of opposition: the town officials questioned her; neighbors ridiculed her; and the clergy tested her in various ways. Despite it all, Bernadette returned to the Lady for a total of eighteen apparitions. Her faithful obedience to the Lady was tested most dramatically when, during one apparition, the Lady told her to drink from and wash in the spring. Bernadette started to go toward the river, but the Lady called her back and indicated another area. Bernadette saw no spring or water, only mud. When the Lady repeated herself, Bernadette went over to the muddy spot, dug, and finally succeeded in finding a palmful of dirty water. Obedient to the Lady, she drank it—although she had a hard time swallowing it. Then, she "washed her face" in the muddy water, streaking it with dirt. As she left the grotto, her aunt tried to wipe her face clean, but the crowd undoubtedly thought she was crazy.

But that afternoon, the trickle of water Bernadette had dug up grew into a stream of clear water. Within a month, at least two people who washed in the spring water were inexplicably cured. The miraculous spring still flows today, and healings that cannot be explained by medical science continue to occur.

At one of the last apparitions, the Lady of the grotto finally revealed her name: "I am the Immaculate Conception." Bernadette, who was still preparing to receive her First Communion, didn't know what that meant. She repeated the mysterious phrase all the way to the pastor's house, so that she wouldn't forget the Lady's name. After telling the pastor the Lady's name later in the day, she had the courage to ask the meaning of the words. She was overjoyed to learn that "the Immaculate Conception" was indeed Mary, the Mother of God.

The Virgin's message to Bernadette, and through her to the world, was simple and timeless: "Pray and do penance for sinners." For the rest of her short life, Bernadette strove to live this mandate of the Lady, and to testify to what she had seen and heard. Although the constant questions exhausted her, she would remind herself that the Lady hadn't promised happiness in this world, but "in the other."

Not long after the final apparition Bernadette went to live at the local convent of the Sisters of Charity and worked as their maid. Nothing contented her more than remaining small and hidden. Eventually she decided to ask to enter their community. The day she left Lourdes to enter the postulancy at Nevers was very difficult. She was leaving not only her family, but also the place where she had seen the beautiful Lady.

As a postulant at Nevers, Bernadette was assigned to washing pots and pans in the kitchen. Her superiors, desiring to keep her humble, would often humiliate her in front of others. Even on the joyful day of her profession of vows, when the bishop gave the newly professed sisters their assignments, Bernadette didn't immediately receive an assignment because, the superior told him publicly, "She is good for nothing." Bernadette didn't object, but the situation must have been very painful for her. The truth was that her health was frail, and she needed the protection of the motherhouse from the prying public. At the same time that the superiors humiliated her, they recognized her virtue: novices who were going through difficulties were sent to talk to Bernadette because her kindness and directness encouraged them and resolved their difficulties.

Eventually, Bernadette was assigned to help in the infirmary; two years later she was given the position of sacristan, a duty she loved because it obliged her to spend many hours in the chapel. But her health, which had always been poor, was now failing rapidly. Soon she returned to the infirmary, but as a patient. In her months of spiritual and physical suffering—both excruciating—Bernadette remained strong in character and never swerved from the course the Immaculate Virgin had shown her: to pray and to do penance for sinners. One of Bernadette's dearest hopes had been to return to

Lourdes, to visit once more the grotto so dear to her. Her superiors even hoped that she might be healed there. But poor health and other obstacles prevented her from ever returning.

As she was dying, Bernadette was accompanied by her sisters. Her last prayer was to the beautiful Lady she so longed to see again, "Holy Mary, Mother of God, pray for me, a poor sinner."

Prayer

Saint Bernadette,
God favored you with the special grace
to see his Mother many times while you were
 on earth.
Instead of allowing this to go to your head
you let the attention—both friendly and hostile—
root you more firmly in the truth that you were chosen
so that others could know of God's great love
 and mercy.
Always aware of your littleness,
you put yourself fully at the service of the message
 entrusted to you.
Help us to draw closer to the ever-beautiful Virgin Mary,
 Mother of God,
so that she can lead us to Christ,
and we can more fully experience God's mercy,
and share it with those who need it most. Amen.

About Saint Bernadette Soubirous

Born: January 7, 1844, in Lourdes, France

Died: April 16, 1879

Feast Day: April 16 in France. The universal Church fittingly celebrates the Feast of Our Lady of Lourdes on February 11, the anniversary of the first apparition

Canonized: December 8, 1933, by Pope Pius XI

Patron: France, those who are ill, those who are poor

Notes on Her Life

- Bernadette was "small" not only in her humility but also physically, being only four feet seven inches tall.

- Bernadette was the saint's nickname; Bernadette's baptismal name was Marie Bernarde, which she also received as her profession name.

- Bernadette contracted cholera when she was six years old, and after that her health was never good. She suffered from both asthma and stomach ailments.

- Francois and Louise Soubirous were particularly vulnerable to the threats of the police commissioner because the previous year, Francois had been accused of stealing food. The accusations were never proved, but Francois lost his job and almost went to jail.

- The Virgin Mary appeared to Bernadette eighteen times in all. Her message was a twofold invitation: Do penance for the conversion of sinners, and come to pray at the grotto.

- The hidden, muddy spring that Bernadette dug up at the request of the Blessed Mother produces thousands of gallons of water each week, and has been attributed as the source of many miraculous cures inexplicable to modern medicine.

⚜ Bernadette's attraction to service—especially nursing the sick—helped her to discern her call to the Sisters of Charity.

Lesser-Known Facts

⚜ The Lady used the respectful form of you—*vous*—when addressing Bernadette, and spoke to her in her dialect, not in standard French. This allowed Bernadette to understand the Lady, but made her account of the apparitions less credible to the better-educated.

⚜ Bernadette is the first canonized saint to be photographed while she was alive.

⚜ So ill that she couldn't attend school regularly, Bernadette learned to read and write after the apparitions.

⚜ Bernadette was a great mimic, and she entertained the sisters in the infirmary by imitating the doctor who came to see them.

⚜ Bernadette worked hard to tame her spontaneous reactions; occasionally she talked about her "boiling nature."

⚜ When Bernadette entered as a postulant at Nevers, she was invited to speak once to all of the sisters about the apparitions. After that, none of the sisters in the community was ever allowed to speak to her about them again.

⚜ Her superiors often called on Bernadette to talk about the apparitions to bishops and other special visitors.

In Her Own Words

"Jesus alone for my Goal; Jesus alone for my Master; Jesus alone for my Model; Jesus alone for my Guide; Jesus alone for my Joy; Jesus alone for my Riches; Jesus alone for my Friend!

"My Jesus, fill my heart with so much love that one day it will break just to be with you."

— Excerpts from her notebook

Saint Gregory the Great

Servant of the Servants of God

The year was 590. For almost two centuries, Europe had been overrun by barbarian invasions, which brought terror, killing, and devastation everywhere. Rome itself had been sacked repeatedly. In only twenty years, it had been conquered four times. Now, flooding and famine had set off a plague that was devastating the population of Rome. News arrived at Saint Andrew's monastery that the plague had just taken the life of their pope, Pelagius II.

The frail but erect abbot pondered the latest tragedy and made it the subject of his prayer. "Lord, whom will you choose to guide your people now? Whoever it is, give him the grace, light, and strength to bear this heavy burden." The people would need the consolation of their clergy, and since the abbot also served as deacon of Rome, he must go immediately. He rose from his prayer as one of the monks came running in.

"Gregory, they are calling for you—" the breathless monk gasped out.

"I am on my way," Gregory nodded.

"—to be the new pope!" the monk managed to get out.

Gregory's spare frame froze as his mind started to race. This couldn't be! God had given him a monastic vocation, in which he was deeply happy. "Don't worry, they'll change their minds," Gregory told his brother monk. "God is not calling *me* to be pope! But our people need comfort; and we need to see what else can be done to stop the plague."

Gregory immediately set about helping the city out of its current crisis. From the pulpit, he announced that the people would hold a great procession through the streets of Rome, offering public prayer and penance for the end of the plague. The procession lasted for three days, with the people chanting, "Lord, have mercy." But even as they walked through the streets, both watchers and marchers fell ill and died. Still, Gregory walked with them, and after the procession of faith was completed, the plague quickly disappeared.

The clergy, officials, and people of the city adamantly declared Gregory the new pope. Despite all their arguments, he remained unconvinced. His appointment had to be approved by the emperor (see p. 54 in Notes on His Life) and Gregory saw an easy way to resolve the situation. Along with the request for confirmation, he sent a personal letter asking the emperor not to confirm his appointment. But unknown to Gregory, the prefect of the city replaced Gregory's letter with one of his own, begging the emperor to confirm Gregory's appointment.

During the months Gregory waited for word from the emperor, he continued to serve his beloved Church and the city. But daily, he interiorly argued with himself. He cherished his monastic vocation, even more because it had been tested several times—even by the previous pope. Gregory mused, "God has truly led me throughout my life; he will make his will clear."

Gregory was born of wealthy Roman nobility with deeply Christian roots. Two of Gregory's aunts (his father's sisters) were considered saints. Gregory's own mother, Sylvia, would also be acknowledged a saint. Gregory was as well educated as he could be in a city that suffered constant chaos from invasion and oppression. His studies in law enabled him to follow his father into civil service. Energetic and wise, with a keen sense of the law, he was a popular and successful politician. At the age of thirty, he took the highest civil office in the city—prefect of Rome.

Yet, after only a short time, Gregory felt God was calling him to a different kind of service. He gave up his position and much of his estate, using some of it to establish seven Benedictine monasteries, including one at his own home, where he himself became a monk.

Those had been the happiest years of his life. He dedicated himself completely to prayer, penance, and pastoral ministry. Yet, his happy seclusion was short-lived. Despite his reluctance to leave the monastery, Gregory obediently accepted when the Pope appointed him one of the seven deacons of Rome, thrusting him into a more active role in the Church. When Rome was once again besieged—this time by the Lombards—the Pope sent a delegation to Constantinople to beg military assistance, appointing Gregory as papal ambassador.

The magnificent center of the Eastern Mediterranean world, Constantinople was a far cry from the pillaged ruins of Rome. Yet once there, Gregory did not see how he could succeed in his mission. He was at a disadvantage because he didn't speak Greek, and he refused to take part in the many court intrigues. He was troubled by signs of corruption in the government and evidence of heresy in the clergy, with whom Gregory heatedly debated. The emperor was too occupied fighting his own battles against the Persians to offer help to Rome. The failure of the mission became conclusive proof, in Gregory's mind, that God had called him to life in the monastery. After six long years, Gregory had happily returned there, serving as abbot in addition to his responsibilities as deacon.

Now, as Gregory used the time of waiting to examine the trajectory of his life, it seemed clear that God was calling him to continue as a simple monk. "Perhaps," he mused to himself, "one day I will be able to fulfill my dream to become a missionary to England."

After six months, word arrived from Emperor Maurice. Gregory's appointment had been confirmed, much to his consternation! Dismayed, Gregory immediately thought about fleeing the city. Instead, he fled to the monastery chapel.

There, Gregory wrestled with himself. How could *he* become pope? He overwhelmingly desired to offer his life for the world through prayer and suffering—the life of a simple monk. Gregory didn't feel himself worthy. He wasn't even a priest—just a deacon. He had no desire to become immersed in the affairs of Rome! In the absence of any real political authority, Gregory knew that whoever served as the next pope would also need to act as protector of the people.

Yet, despite his own desires, Gregory's path was no longer clear to him. How could he in good faith ignore the pleas of the people, the officials, even the emperor when they were all raised together? Could God be speaking to him through the needs of the people? After a great deal of prayer, it seemed after all that despite his immense reluctance, it was God's will that he *should* become pope.

On September 3, 590, after being ordained a priest, the new pope and bishop of Rome was consecrated as Pope Gregory I. In his writings, he speaks often of this sacrifice: "My poor soul is forced to endure the burden of secular business . . . and returns back far less fit to think upon those affairs that are inward, spiritual, and heavenly. . . . When I remember my former state of life, I cannot but sigh to look back upon the forsaken shore."

Yet Gregory's struggle to continue his intense prayer life amid his astounding achievements is not evident when we look at the lifetime of service he crammed into his short thirteen years as pope. Gregory brought a wealth of managerial genius and pastoral energy to the papacy. At heart a true pastor, his first concern was the welfare of the people. He gave down-to-earth sermons, aimed at nurturing the spiritual lives of his flock. These centered on Gospel themes—his favorite topics—and each sermon ended with a practical, moral conclusion. Gregory's writings are recognized more for their excellent summaries of the theological works of other Fathers of the Church than for being original. Gregory also reformed the liturgy and established guidelines for promoting the use of sacred music in the liturgy, especially encouraging and even teaching chant (which received his name in honor of his support). He also paid special attention to the formation of the clergy. His *Book of Pastoral Care* was used as a guide for bishops and priests throughout the Middle Ages.

Pope Gregory's care for the people was not confined exclusively to the pulpit and the spiritual life of his flock, although these always took precedence. Gregory urged social reforms for the poor and underprivileged, including land reforms for the more humane treatment of servants and tenant farmers. His huge charities—which took every form of relief imaginable—saved multitudes from starving, and also ransomed countless prisoners from the invaders overrunning southern Europe. He strongly urged bishops to do the same, recommending they even sell church property when needed to raise the ransom for prisoners of war. He also sought to protect the rights of the Jewish people against unjust treatment and oppression, convincing one town to restore a synagogue to its Jewish citizens.

When, in 593, a barbarian army approached the walls of the city, Pope Gregory himself went out to meet the invading army and negotiated a truce that spared Rome and the surrounding areas another ruthless round of sacking and killing.

As Pope, Gregory was able to achieve one of his greatest desires: that of spreading the Gospel to England. While still a monk, Gregory had been saddened to learn that the Gospel had not yet been preached in England. Eager to give everyone the opportunity to learn about Christ, he resolved to go to Britain himself as a missionary. However, when wind of Gregory's plan reached the ears of his superiors, he was forced to abandon it and continue what he had already begun nearer home.

Now Gregory shared this deep desire with Saint Augustine of Canterbury, whom he sent to lead a band of monks to begin evangelizing in England. The Pope followed the missionaries' efforts closely and encouraged them in the dangers they faced.

His secretary, the deacon Peter, testified that Gregory never took a rest or vacation, even though he suffered from various chronic ailments. The severity of his monastic penances compromised his health, leading to stomach problems that tormented him the rest of his life. Ill health prevented him even from rising on some days, but he continued to work from bed. In the end, Gregory's physical frame was reduced to almost a skeleton. Yet he continued to dictate letters and to look after Church affairs. After Pope Leo the Great, Gregory was only the second pope to have the title "the Great" added to his name Yet, in his humility, while he decisively defended the authority of the papacy, he never personally became attached to the authority of his office. Instead, he called himself the "servant of the servants of God"—a title still used by his successors.

Gregory's last action on earth was to send a warm winter cloak to a poor bishop who suffered from the cold. This final act of charity characterized Gregory's entire life of loving and generous service.

Prayer

Pope Saint Gregory,
how you lived the paradox of the Gospel!
While Christlike in meekness, you fearlessly shepherded
  the Church
and defended its rights.
You unified a profound life of prayer
with your availability to serve the needs of the world.
You discovered God's invitations
not just through his Word
but in the signs of the times and the needs of the
  Church.
Enlighten me to understand the call of the Gospel:
to be "in the world but not of it,"
and to be faithful to a vital life of prayer.
Help me to allow God's love for me to shape my life
and my response to others' needs.

By your example, teach me the humility of service
and the courage of true leadership.
Protect the Church today, also living in perilous times,
and ask for us the gift of your spirit of generous service.
    Amen.

About Saint Gregory the Great

Born: ca. 540 in Rome

Died: March 12, 604, in Rome

Feast Day: September 3 (anniversary of his consecration
    as Pope in 590)

Canonized: By popular acclaim immediately after his
    death

Patron: England, musicians, singers, teachers, victims of
    plague

Notes on His Life

- Gregory made several significant career changes: from politician to monk to pope.

- When Gregory was called out of the monastery to serve the Church, he brought a few brother monks with him wherever he went.

- In the sixth century, popes were elected by the clergy, the senate, and the people of Rome, and the Byzantine emperor confirmed the appointment. That's why Gregory almost refused the office of pope twice.

- Gregory was the first monk to become pope.

- After Pope Leo the Great, Gregory was only the second pope to be given the title, "the Great."

☙ In the chaotic breakdown of civil and military power, Gregory was such an effective administrator that, as pope, he was virtually the civil leader of Rome as well as leader of the universal Church.

☙ In many ways, Pope Gregory I could be considered the architect of the Church in the Middle Ages—and thus of the Church today. His influence is still felt in many areas of Church life.

Lesser-Known Facts

☙ Not just Gregory's family, but some of his friends were saints. Saint Leander of Spain was an especially close friend to whom Gregory opened his heart in his letters; Saint Peter the Deacon was his secretary to whom Gregory dictated four books.

☙ Gregory may have written some of the prayers still used at Mass today.

☙ Gregory liked to tell stories in his homilies.

☙ Gregory was criticized for emptying the Church's treasury to help the poor.

☙ By calling himself "the servant of the servants of God," Gregory was simultaneously expressing humility, reaffirming the universal authority of the papacy, and rebuking an Eastern patriarch for using a title that claimed Petrine authority (arising from Saint Peter, the first pope).

☙ Gregory suffered severely not only from constant indigestion, but also from gout.

☙ In 1904, Pope Saint Pius X wrote an encyclical celebrating the thirteenth centenary of Pope Saint Gregory the Great's death.

In His Own Words

"For one who undertakes the office of preaching ought not to do but rather to suffer wrong, and so by his meekness calm the anger of his persecutors, and heal the wounds of sinners, though weighed down himself by affliction."

— From a homily on pastoral care

Blessed Pier Giorgio Frassati

A Hunger for Holiness

The young man rushed up the stairs while calling out, "Mama, tell Papa I'm out this weekend. Off to the mountain with the crowd." As he galloped back down loaded with his climbing gear, Pier Giorgio almost ran into his father.

"Whoa, whoa, son! What is the rush here, Giorgetto," cajoled Signor Frassati. "Supper is almost on the table. Surely you will stay home with us tonight."

"No, Papa. Sorry. Must go, must go!" Blowing a kiss to his mother, out he went into the night.

"I don't understand that boy, Adelaide," Signor Frassati said to his wife. "I had hoped he would follow me into journalism. So much in our society needs straightening out, but no, he is supposedly studying engineering. Supposedly, I say, because he never seems to be in school."

"Oh, Papa," interjected Pier Giorgio's sister, Luciana. "Of course you are upset, but we all know Giorgio is the apple of your eye."

"Yes, I admit it is true. He is a wonderful son. Just exasperating sometimes. He seems determined to give away everything he owns. And everything we own, if we let him. Did you note the sack of 'gear' he had with him? His life is all friends and fun. It is time he settled down."

It was true. Pier Giorgio Frassati was often involved in adventures. Sometimes he seemed to be more interested in having a good time than in being responsible. However, Pier Giorgio was a good-natured, upright young man with a definite goal in mind. He was a man who lived the Beatitudes, intent on being a genuine disciple of Christ. In fact, his intention in choosing to pursue a degree in engineering was to be able to live and work among miners, to assist them in their social needs, but especially to help them to live fully their Christian vocation.

As a child Pier Giorgio had already understood the living connection between Christ and his followers. He was only four years old when he spontaneously gave his shoes and stockings to the child of a beggar. At seven he ran to his mother pleading that she intercede with his father who had just closed the door on a poor man. "Mama," he cried, "what if Jesus sent that man to us?" This concern grew and deepened within Pier Giorgio as he matured. As a young man he spent a good deal of time secretly visiting and serving the poor of Turin. Countless stories tell of how he would spend his last coins on food, clothing, medicine, or fuel for the poor. One classic account concerns his graduation gift. His father, Alfredo, offered his Giorgetto the choice of a car or the equivalent in money. Pier Giorgio, of course, opted for the money. His father assumed his fun-loving boy planned to spend it entertaining his many friends. Little did he know that his son used it to entertain the needs of his very special friends, the poor and needy.

Pier Giorgio did indeed intend to settle down. He had fallen in love with Laura Hidalgo, a friend from his student group and a member of his mountain climbing club. He told no one of his infatuation with Laura; in fact, he had never even broached the subject with her. He recognized in her a soul companion, someone virtuous, hard-working, and compassionate, with whom he could build a solid Christian marriage. He feared, however, that his parents would not approve. They had other expectations for him, imagining that because his father had been a senator and an ambassador to Germany he would marry into the higher social class. Hoping for a sign of their acceptance, he hatched a secret plan to introduce the girl of his dreams to his family. On the chosen day she and two other young women were his guests for tea. Mother and Luciana had an opportunity to meet his love without anyone knowing his plan. The encounter was very revealing, but not as Pier Giorgio had hoped. Neither his mother nor his sister was favorably impressed. Judicious comments were made about his lovely friends who were obviously in over their heads at the former ambassador's residence. Pier Giorgio was heartbroken, and remained silent about his hope. He confided later to a friend: "How deeply saddened I am. I was so ready to reveal my intentions to Laura, but now I must hold them inside. God must want me to concentrate more on my spiritual life." He could not be chided into going against his parents' wishes that he make "a good match." His parents lived in a state of constant tension and bickering and, as Pier Giorgio later said, he could not bring himself "to break one family in order to begin another." His own heart would have "to pay the price."

Pier Giorgio seemed to be a contradiction of qualities. He wasn't rowdy, but exuberant with the pure-hearted joy of youth, a well-known practical joker, an instigator of fun and ferment. He was always a leader, but in an unassuming way. He never shied away from confrontation in order to defend principles. Once when Pier Giorgio was defending the rights of the Christian students' group, the police roughed him up. When they realized that he was the son of Senator Frassati, Pier Giorgio refused any special treatment. He remained with the students and waved their torn and dirty banner as a badge of honor. Another time Fascist ruffians burst into his parents' house. These troublemakers began to break up furniture and smash windows until Pier Giorgio grabbed a fireplace poker and chased them all out into the street. Satisfied that they were gone for good, he calmly returned to table and resumed eating his dinner.

From his youngest years Pier Giorgio enjoyed the challenge of sports, especially hiking, mountain climbing, and skiing. Sometimes he enjoyed going out alone to contemplate the beauties of God's creation, and at other times he enjoyed the company of friends. On these excursions, he was the life of the party. He would sing at the top of his notoriously off-key voice. If his friends objected, he would say, "I don't care one bit. The important thing is the singing!" For Pier Giorgio times of fun always included some moments for prayer. On these trips he would disappear into wayside shrines for prayer. The rosary was so much a part of his daily routine that calling out the "Aves" on a trek up a mountain was as natural to him as breathing in the crisp air. His companions, motivated by his example, would enthusiastically answer. He unassumingly prayed the rosary as he walked the streets of Turin and as he visited the sick to console and to aid them.

To support his many good intentions and charitable works Pier Giorgio joined many organizations, including the Saint Vincent de Paul Society, the Catholic Student Federation, Catholic Action, Milites Mariae, Apostleship of Prayer, the

Company of the Most Blessed Sacrament, and the Cesare Balbo Club at the Royal Polytechnic University of Turin. He was everywhere and anywhere that needed a voice for justice. And he spent much time in adoration of the Blessed Sacrament.

In June 1925 his grandmother began her journey toward death. Around that time, Pier Giorgio began to feel a great deal of pain, which quickly sapped his energy and left him with an advancing paralysis. It seems that during one of his pilgrimages to the poor he had contracted the dreaded polio-myelitis virus. He was never one to oversleep, but now he found he needed more rest. In the frenzy of caring for her own dying mother, his mother lost patience with Pier Giorgio, thinking he was being inconsiderate. She scolded him, "Son, you are being so thoughtless. Grandmother is dying and you are carrying on over a little flu."

In just five or six days the health of this robust young man had deteriorated to the point that he could not get up from bed. Doctors offered little hope to the Frassati family. They made a frantic effort to obtain a useful serum from Paris, but a thunderstorm delayed the plane. Pier Giorgio knew the Lord awaited him. True to his nature, he focused his last thoughts on others: Would his parents be all right without him? Would others continue his visits to the poor? Would Luciana help him write a note about the medicine needed for one man, and a policy to be renewed for another? These things weighed on his generous heart more than the thought of his own death.

"The day of my death will be the best day of my life," he had said a year earlier. That day, July 4, certainly brought untold blessings to Pier Giorgio's family and friends. At the funeral his family became acutely aware of the depth of their loss. While they were comforted by the presence of all the influential people of Turin who had gathered within the church for the funeral, it seemed that the rest of the city was outside. Hundreds of Turin's poor and troubled citizens paid their respects to the Frassatis' son. They were brothers and sisters whom Pier Giorgio had cared for in such a Christlike manner. Now his family understood his apparent inability to hold on to money, his habitual lateness, his nocturnal wanderings, his coy replies to their questioning. Pier Giorgio had ascended the Lord's mountain not merely by his athletic climbs, but by his hidden and heroic charity.

Prayer

Blessed Pier Giorgio, you answered the psalmist's cry:
"Who can climb the mountain of the Lord?"
   (cf. Ps 24:3)

You climbed the mountain of holiness by your many
   steps to the homes of the poor;
you held fast with your tenacious love for life;
you breathed in the pure, crisp air of prayer,
and exhaled from your whole being the spirit of
   the living God.
Teach us your secret hunger and thirst to live
   Gospel holiness
within the parameters of our own lives.
Help us concentrate on what truly matters. Amen.

About Blessed Pier Giorgio Frassati

Born: April 6, 1901, in Turin, Italy

Died: July 4, 1925, in Turin, of acute poliomyelitis

Memorial: July 4

Beatified: May 20, 1990, by Pope John Paul II

Patron: World Youth Day, athletes, young people

Notes on His Life

- In 1918 he joined the Confraternity of the Rosary, the Saint Vincent de Paul Society, and the Italian Alpine Club.

- In 1918 he began studies toward mining and an engineering degree. (He was preparing for exams when he died.)

- In 1920 he joined the Peoples' Party and the Nocturnal Adoration Society.

- His father, Alfredo, was appointed ambassador to Germany in 1921. He stayed in Freiburg with the family of the Jesuit theologian Karl Rahner.

- Pier Giorgio joined the Dominican third order in 1922, taking the name Girolamo (Jerome) in honor of the Renaissance Florentine cleric Savonarola. He also joined the Legion of Mary.

- In 1923 he helped to found the Shady Character Society, calling himself "Citizen Robespierre."

- The miracle accepted for his beatification occurred when an unbeliever, Domenico Sellan, was cured of a fatal disease and requested confession.

- When exhumed in 1981, his body was found to be incorrupt.

- His tomb is now at a side altar in the Cathedral of Turin.
- Pope John Paul II called him "the man of the eight Beatitudes."

Lesser-Known Facts

- His full name is Pier Giorgio Michelangelo Frassati, and he had the nicknames Dodo (as a child) and Terror (as a young man).
- In junior high he failed the Latin examination twice.
- He liked to smoke a pipe.
- He signed his many letters with "*Saluti in G. C.*" (Greetings in Jesus Christ—in Italian, *Gesu Cristo*).

In His Own Words

"It is to Jesus that I go. He comes to me each morning in Holy Communion. I repay him in a small way by visiting the poor."

Venerable Teresita Quevedo

The Champion

Dashing across the tennis court, sixteen-year-old Teresita Quevedo bumped into a girl she knew.

"Hi, Teresita," her friend called. "I hear you're in the tennis competition today. Did you warn them you'll need an extra-large crown if you win; your head is way too big for the normal size."

Teresita laughed as she sped off to begin her set.

When she returned home that evening, Teresita greeted her mother with a big smile.

"Well, Teresita," Senora Quevedo asked, "do we have a champion in the family?"

The girl paused and her eyes filled with tears.

"No, Mama," she replied. "Not really, at least not the way you have in mind. But if you consider the winner of a spiritual victory a champion, then you have one."

Senora Quevedo was aware of her daughter's desire to win a tennis championship before graduating from high school. She knew Teresita had prepared nonstop and that she was clearly everyone's favorite. So she gently encouraged, "Tere, please tell me what happened."

"Mama," Teresita began, "I told the Blessed Mother that I was leaving it in her hands. I'm afraid I wanted the win more out of vanity than anything else. And so I stopped at church on the way home to tell her I was happy she decided that my opponent should win instead of me. I saw an old lady begging at the church door, and I gave her an offering. When she thanked me, she gave me a holy card. It wasn't a picture, but only an inscription in large blue print. Can you guess what it said, Mama?"

"No, Teresita, tell me," her mother said.

With a victor's smile Teresita replied, "*Love makes all things easy.*"

A few months later, trusting in these words, Teresita slipped into her father's room.

"Papa," she whispered, "are you asleep?"

"No, come in, Teresita," Doctor Quevedo invited. "What can I do for you?"

Teresita walked close to him and began, "Papa, I dread telling you this, because it's going to hurt you, but. . . ."

"Go on, tell me, Teresita. What is it you want?"

"I want to become a Carmelite, Papa."

"Teresita, do you realize what that means? You are so full of life—so fond of sports . . . dancing . . . and parties. . . ." His voice trailed off.

"Yes, but none of that satisfies me, Papa."

"My dear child, do you know that religious lead a life of sacrifice?

"Yes, Papa. That's why I want to enter the convent."

"And," her father continued, "when do you want to enter?"

"Well, Papa, I've been thinking about that, too. I'd like to enter next month."

At first, Teresita's vocation was a bitter blow for Doctor Calixto Quevedo and his wife. How could they get along without their youngest daughter, who was only seventeen, and so full of energy and enthusiasm?

But soon, with God's grace, Teresita's parents understood that her vocation was a blessing from God.

On February 23, 1947, Teresita Quevedo entered the Institute of the Carmelite Sisters of Charity, which was located in a little town just outside of Madrid.

Days at the novitiate turned into weeks and weeks into months. Before Teresita knew it, profession was not far away. But walking down the hall one day, she suddenly winced in pain. *Oh, well,* she thought, *maybe it's just another headache like the one I had yesterday.* However, the throbbing increased until Teresita could no longer concentrate on her work.

When she told the superior how severe her headache was, the superior sent her to the infirmary for some medication. Two days later, Doctor Quevedo was summoned to the novitiate.

He arrived within an hour and gave Teresita a thorough examination, only to discover that his daughter had tubercular meningitis.

With anguish tearing at his heart, Doctor Quevedo told the Reverend Mother, "I fear my daughter will die in a matter of months. Not even the best care will prevent it. Usually patients are paralyzed, but in her case death isn't far off."

One morning the sister in charge of the infirmary walked over to her bedside and asked, "Sister, don't you feel a bit sad when you think of leaving everything you love?"

"Why should I, Sister?" Teresita replied. "Besides I'm not really leaving everything I love. I have a Father in heaven who is waiting for me and a Mother who will come to bring me to God. I've always loved our Lady and she is my greatest comfort now."

Smiling down into Teresita's glowing eyes, the other sister felt impelled to say, "Everyone here knows that you have an extraordinary love of our Lady. How did you acquire it?"

"All I did was try to do the little things perfectly. I've had to overcome many difficulties and I have never done anything great in life, but I've found that Mary is a great means for reaching heaven. I have done everything for God through Mary. My gifts to Mary have been little ones. But, it's the little things in life that count."

As the sister-nurse resumed her infirmary duties, she thought about Teresita's words. Was it just a coincidence that especially on Saturdays and feasts of the Blessed Mother the sisters would be surprised to find their shoes "mysteriously" shined, or their stockings suddenly mended? Although the sisters knew she was the culprit, Teresita never gave herself away. She would go quietly from room to room, leaving behind shoes polished to perfection, and then slip unnoticed into the laundry to darn a few pairs of black stockings before the wash would be divided.

The infirmarian recalled another episode.

One of Teresita's fellow novices had been bedridden in the infirmary. Worn out by a long illness, she wasn't talking much. She didn't want to read; she didn't even care to have the other sisters read to her. Whoever stayed with her had to be resigned to silence. Still, the superior wanted someone to spend at least the recreation period with the patient. She hoped for volunteers, but none was forthcoming . . . none except Teresita. Right before the eagerly awaited recreation, she would ask, "Mother, could I spend recreation in the infirmary today?" The request always ended with "today," but the sister-nurse and the superior noticed that "today" became day after day, for quite a while. The permission was always granted. And Teresita, delighted with her triumph, would hurry off.

That must have been quite a sacrifice for her, mused the sister-nurse. Teresita, so naturally joyful and exuberant, had looked forward to recreation more than all the other novices combined! She loved to chat and laugh, to enjoy the warm companionship and homey fun that bubbled up spontaneously among her sisters. Yet Teresita had sought out her quiet, suffering companion instead.

Her love for Mary played no small part in that victory. In her private notebook, Teresita had written, "May all who look at me, see you, O Mary!" And whether others knew of her resolution or not, it certainly wasn't hard to see the likeness of Mary mirrored in her joyful kindness.

Death drew near Teresita gradually. On Holy Saturday morning, April 8, 1950, pain racked every bone in her body, yet the young sister remained joyful and serene. When her father, Doctor Quevedo, came to visit her that morning he realized that Teresita was on the verge of death. He thought back to when his beloved daughter had been a little girl. He could still hear her bursts of laughter and delight as she ran along the Spanish seacoast, chasing waves.

Then as he sat helplessly, watching her facial expression reflect the agony in her once vibrant body, he recalled an incident that had taken place a few summers before. At a swimming club a lifeguard approached to say, "Doctor Quevedo, your daughter is an outstanding swimmer and diver. Has she ever entered a diving contest?"

"Juan," the doctor replied, "if you have in mind what I suspect you do, I don't encourage you to ask Teresita about it. She already declined one of my friends last summer when he asked her to join in the diving contests."

Juan thanked Doctor Quevedo and then went down to the beach to see if he could find Teresita. Well, he thought, no girl has yet refused me. I just don't understand how a girl like Teresita could say no when she thinks of the trophies she would easily win.

Minutes later he ran into Teresita. "May I speak with you for a minute?" he inquired. "I won't take much of your time, Senorita Quevedo. I know you might be in a hurry. . . ."

"No, Juan," Teresita said, "I'm not in a hurry. What do you need?"

"Well, Teresita, I was speaking with your father not long ago, and I understand that you are an excellent swimmer. Why don't you take part in the diving contests that are coming up soon? None of the participants in your age bracket can match your speed or technique as a diver. Think of the honor it will give you and of the glory it will bring your parents!"

Teresita thought a moment before she answered. Then she said, "Juan, will it bring honor and glory to the Mother of God?"

For a second Juan was speechless. Teresita's decision hung upon the answer he was now searching for.

"Well, Teresita, let's leave her—I mean the Blessed Mother—out of this."

"Okay, Juan, if that's what you really want . . . but I'll stay with our Lady."

Now Doctor Quevedo felt helpless and alone as he looked at Teresita, who was dying of a disease that medicine could not cure. It took all the courage he had to just stand there and watch Teresita draw nearer and nearer to death. But thinking over her past life and her great devotion to Mary, he began to pray to the Blessed Mother for the strength he needed to accept God's will in his daughter's regard. When the phone rang the next morning, the doctor answered in a natural tone of voice. The superior asked him to come as soon as possible. Teresita had passed to eternity. When Doctor and Senora Quevedo reached the convent, the superior related the details. An aura of joy filled the air as she spoke. . . .

Teresita had been sinking rapidly. The white bed that had become an altar trembled from the pain that racked her body, and she gave no sign of consciousness. Suddenly, she opened her eyes, and her usually soft voice filled the room:

"My Mother, Mary, come for me! Bring me back to heaven with you!"

The community was summoned and filed prayerfully into the room, which seemed more like a cathedral than a sickroom. The sisters knelt around Teresita's bed. She was quiet, almost motionless except for the gentle rise and fall of the sheets as she labored to breathe.

Then it happened, like the bursting crescendo in a hymn of victory. The dying nun opened her eyes and a radiant smile lit her face for the last time:

"Oh, how beautiful! O Mary, how beautiful you are!"

Those who knew her well all agreed that "Mary was her life." And Mary had come to lead her into the dawn of life eternal.

"Death has been swallowed up in victory.

Where, O death, is your victory?

Where, O death, is your sting?" (1 Cor 15:54–55)

Teresita Quevedo had won the victory.

⋐❉⋑

Prayer

Dear Jesus,
We ask you to give us the insight you gave
    Teresita Quevedo
to realize the importance of life. At a young age
she was inspired to offer her life to you through your
    Mother Mary.
She knew the secret of pleasing you is found in living
    with your Mother,
imitating her virtues, sharing her intentions.
Make this desire for holiness a part of our vocation
    in life as well,
no matter what path we follow. Amen.

About Venerable Teresita Quevedo

Born: in Madrid on April 14, 1930
Died: April 8, 1950, in Madrid of tubercular meningitis
Declared venerable: June 9, 1983, by Pope John Paul II
Model for students, young athletes, novices, devotees of
    Mary

Notes on Her Life

❦ Her full name was Maria Teresa Josefina Justina Gonzalez-Quevedo y Cadarso. She was the third child of Dr. Calixto Gonzalez Quevedo and his wife, Maria del Carmen Cadarso.

❦ Teresita was baptized by Father Ignatius Navarro, chaplain to King Alfonso XIII, at Saint Francis Church across from the Royal Palace.

- A lover of fashion, she was once voted "best dressed" in her class.

- Her interests included dancing, swimming, tennis, basketball (team captain), and the Marian Sodality.

- Four of her aunts were Carmelites of Charity, and two uncles were Jesuits.

- She entered the novitiate of the Carmelites of Charity on February 23, 1948.

- She desired to be a missionary to China.

- She predicted that she would be in heaven for the declaration of the dogma of Mary's Assumption into Heaven, which occurred on November 1, 1950.

- She was allowed to anticipate her profession of vows due to her illness.

Lesser-Known Facts

- She was sometimes called Tere.

- She wrote a "Code or Ten Commandments of Amiability."

In Her Own Words

"May all who look at me see you, O Mary."

Saint Frances Xavier Cabrini

"What About China?"

What was Mother Cabrini thinking about that evening in December 1917 as she prepared little parcels of candy for poor children of the neighborhood? To her sisters she had announced that "this Christmas must be a special one." Perhaps she thought of all the preceding Christmases or of all the little ones she had cherished through the years.

Francesca Cabrini was born July 15, 1850, in the small farming community of Sant'Angelo Lodigiano, Lombardy, the youngest of the eleven children of Agostino and Stella (Oldini) Cabrini. Cecchina, as she was affectionately called, was born prematurely to a couple who had suffered the loss of several children already. She was beautiful and beloved. As she grew, Francesca delighted in listening to her father read from *The Annals of the Propagation of the Faith*. Her little heart absorbed the tales of the great missionaries, and she longed to follow them to far-off places. These dreams almost led to disaster one day as Cecchina placed her little paper boat full of missionaries in a stream and sent them off to China. She was leaning over the embankment to watch as they swirled away when her foot slipped and she tumbled into the fast-moving stream. Floundering about and gulping water, the little missionary was on the verge of panic when a stranger lifted her out. Relatives had come running when they lost sight of her. "Cecchina," they cried. "You're soaking wet."

"I fell in the water," she whimpered.

Eyeing the moving stream, they asked, "But how did you get out by yourself?"

"A man picked me up," she replied, shivering from the cold.

"But there is no one anywhere to be seen," they exclaimed to one other. It was concluded that this "someone" must have been her guardian angel. Meanwhile, the little girl was bundled in someone's coat and brought quickly home.

As a young woman, Francesca kept her ideal before her. "I will go to the missions. My heart is set on spreading the Gospel to the people of China," she would repeat. She enrolled in the boarding school of the Daughters of the Sacred Heart to prepare for a teaching degree, which she obtained in 1868. Consecrating herself totally to God as a religious now held sway over her heart, and she asked to enter the community. The superior replied, "No, Francesca. We think very highly of you, but your health will not support this way of life. However, we believe you are destined to honor the Sacred Heart in another way." Francesca turned away, teary-eyed. Later she applied to the Canossian Sisters, but they also told her that God must have other plans for her.

Indeed, God did have other plans, but sadly they began with the sudden deaths of both of her beloved parents. For now Francesca felt she could be a missionary in the confines of Sant'Angelo, so she helped her older sister Rosa with the school she had begun and with nursing the neighborhood's poor and shut-ins. During an outbreak of smallpox Francesca fell ill, but soon recovered through Rosa's loving care. Despite this further health setback, Francesca took her first steps toward the missions in 1871, when her pastor invited her to take a position as a substitute teacher in nearby Vidardo. For two years she diligently taught her young charges not only to read and write, but also to love and serve their God.

The pastor of Vidardo, Don Serrati, was pleased with her abilities and suggested that she assist some ladies who were running an orphanage in Codogno, where he had recently transferred. It seems the ladies who donated the home and finances for the orphanage were not very practical; things needed turning around. Don Serrati gave her two weeks to perform this "miracle" at the House of Providence. Francesca did bring about the transformation, and the pastor invited her to stay. She was happy to agree, but the ladies who were operating the house were not so pleased. Two months later the priest was inspired to invite the group of women to don a habit and form themselves into a religious community. For the next six years the group lived their new life in great hope and great tension, and in September 1877 they made their profession of vows. Francesca added the name Saveria (Xavier) to her own in honor of her favorite missionary saint. Suddenly the joy of the occasion turned to apprehension as the bishop looked at the newly professed group and announced, "I have decided to appoint Sister Francesca as your superior." Certainly, the young religious, only twenty-seven years old, never expected this. However, she saw God's will in the bishop's wishes and obeyed. What began that day came to a sudden end in 1880 when the bishop was forced to suppress the House of Providence and disband the sisters. This was not Mother Francesca's fault at all. In fact, the other sisters had witnessed the harassment she had to endure from the original "foundresses" of the House. Nothing pleased them and they went out of their way to criticize and threaten their new superior. And so, the bishop invited Mother Francesca to begin her dream of a missionary community, along with several of the sisters and some former students. They found an abandoned monastery in Codogno and thus began the Missionaries of the Sacred Heart of Jesus. The blessing of God was definitely on this new institute, which grew rapidly. Membership soon increased, for many young women were inspired both by the name of the new institute and by its spirit. Soon Mother Cabrini established five convents in Lombardy, and then set her sights on Rome. "If we can open a house in Rome, we will be in the heart of the Church," she thought.

Standing in the presence of the cardinal vicar of Rome, Lucido Parocchi, Mother Cabrini stated her desires. "Your Eminence, we would like to receive recognition of our institute and your permission to begin our missionary work here in Rome."

The cardinal's welcoming smile turned to a frown as he replied, "Mother, your congregation is very new. Others are still awaiting this permission. Return to Codogno and your work there." Stifling tears, Mother Cabrini and her companion had no choice but to leave.

She was inspired, however, to return soon after and ask permission to stay at least until the institute's constitutions were approved. Cardinal Parocchi agreed and promised to ask the Holy Father about their request. In October, the cardinal called for them and asked, "Mother, are you ready to obey?"

"Yes, certainly," she replied.

"Then," the cardinal proceeded with a slight smile, "you will open, not one house, but two." This wonderful surprise from the Lord led to another opportunity of grace. While in Rome, Mother Cabrini met Bishop Giovanni Battista Scalabrini, founder of the Missionary Institute of Saint Charles, who ministered to Italians living overseas. He told her about the needs of their countrymen who had emigrated to the United States. They faced great trials, and many were abandoning the practice of their faith. Certainly she would find a fertile field there for the Gospel. In her mind Mother Cabrini kept asking, "But what about China?" She still had to get approval to begin missionary life in earnest. When she finally was granted a meeting with Pope Leo XIII, she told him about her great desire to go to China. He asked many questions about her plans for the new institute. Then, looking at her expectant face, he said, "No, Mother! You must not go east, but west! Go to America. Evangelize among the Italians who are living there. That will be your mission." The Sacred Heart had spoken through the Pope, and Mother Cabrini believed this was indeed the will of God. So in a very short time she, along with six of her daughters, boarded a ship to New York.

Although Bishop Scalabrini had said that Bishop Michael Corrigan of New York would be expecting the Sisters, he actually was not. When the Sisters arrived, he unceremoniously suggested they should take the same ship back to Italy. "No," said Mother Cabrini firmly. "Your Excellency, we have come with letters from the Holy Father. We must stay." So Bishop Corrigan agreed, and accommodations were found with the Sisters of Charity. The great missionary life of Mother Cabrini had begun. In an unbelievably short time, the Missionaries of the Sacred Heart began schools, orphanages, catechetical programs, and other works of charity in various places. Bishop Corrigan soon came to love and to count on these courageous women. He asked Mother Cabrini to start a hospital for the poor. At first she declined, saying that nursing was not part of their mission, but then she came back, stood before his desk and said yes. The bishop asked, "Mother, what caused this change?"

Simply, she explained: "I had a dream in which I saw Mary caring for the sick. I asked her what she was doing. She replied, 'What you refused to do.' And so I understand that this too is part of God's plan."

Not knowing anything beyond her early days of assisting Rosa in nursing the sick of Sant'Angelo, Mother Cabrini began in faith. Soon doctors and other medical personnel volunteered their services, and Columbus Hospital was born. In the years that followed, Mother Cabrini traveled not only across the United States opening schools, hospitals, and orphanages, but she also made her way to Nicaragua, Panama, France, Brazil, Spain, Argentina, and England, establishing the Missionaries of the Sacred Heart to serve God's people and give him glory.

And how much glory God received through the boundless love of this missionary heart! The years passed, and now Christmas was approaching in 1917. Mother Cabrini recalled all those Christmases in the past, when she had given so many gifts to the heart of Jesus and received so many in return. Now, God had prepared a final gift for this generous soul who had given herself as a mother to so many. Mother Cabrini had been feeling tired this morning and was now praying in her room. When a sister came to call her for the midday meal, she found Mother had locked her door. Returning a little later, the sister was shocked to find the door unlocked and Mother sitting peacefully in her chair. She had been quietly called home to God.

Mother Cabrini's legacy to the Church is one of unstinting love, which translates itself into mercy. Through her efforts and those of her sisters, not only Italian immigrants but persons of every nationality and need found the love of Christ in search of them, ready to assist them in their struggles, giving them the hope to begin again.

She was canonized in 1946, just twenty-nine years after her death. One word can define this great woman of faith: *missionary*. Saint Frances Xavier Cabrini herself offers the definition of a missionary, which is a résumé of her own incredible life: "What is a missionary? To me a missionary is an uncompromising lover of the Sacred Heart. She is his candle that radiates light while she consumes her life embracing everything—labors, joys and pains—for the salvation of all people."

Prayer

Saint Frances Xavier Cabrini, mother of all who are
    uprooted from their homelands,
who seek a new and better life in unknown lands,
help us open our hearts to the immigrants of our day.
Like you may we love all people, no matter their race,
    religion, or country of origin,
with the same love that you learned from the Sacred
    Heart of Jesus.
Through your intercession we ask the strength
    and ingenuity

to show that love in works of mercy
toward those who suffer material or spiritual want.
Amen.

About Saint Frances Xavier Cabrini

Born: July 15, 1850, in Lombardy, Italy
Died: December 22, 1917, in Chicago, of malaria
Feast Day: November 13
Canonized: June 7, 1946, by Pope Pius XII
Patron: immigrants, emigrants, hospital administrators

Notes on Her Life

- In her twenty-eight years as missionary, she founded sixty-seven institutions in the United States, Argentina, Brazil, Spain, England, France, Nicaragua, and Panama.

- Many miraculous and prophetic things occurred throughout her life.

- She wrote extensively to her sisters during her travels.

- She was buried in West Park, New York, but her body was later transferred to the shrine at Mother Cabrini High School in New York City.

- She is the first American citizen proclaimed a saint.

- One miracle for her canonization was the simultaneous cure of a man from three serious illnesses; the other was the instantaneous cure of another man's foot ailment.

Lesser-Known Facts

- She was named "Italian Immigrant of the Century" in 1952.

☙ Her image is found in many places, including the bronze doors of Saint Patrick's Cathedral in New York; the National Shrine of the Immaculate Conception in Washington, DC; the museum on Liberty Island, NY (home of the Statue of Liberty); and Saint Peter's Basilica in Vatican City.

☙ Although she was deathly afraid of water, she crossed the ocean thirty times.

In Her Own Words

"That which, being women, we are not allowed to do on a large scale, such as helping to solve important social problems, is being done in our little sphere in every state and in every city where our houses have been opened."

— Letter to the students of the Teachers' College in
Rome, February 1906 (written in Chicago)*

---

* See *Travels of Mother Frances Xavier Cabrini* (The Missionary Sisters of the Sacred Heart, Chicago: 1946), 26.

Saint Martin de Porres

A Man Among Men

November 3, 1639—seemingly a day like any other. In Lima, Peru, however, it was a day of tragedy and triumph—of tragedy because Peru had lost one of her best loved sons; of triumph, because this son was Lima's glory.

In a small room of the Dominican monastery of the Holy Rosary, the commanding voice of the Archbishop of Mexico City broke through the stillness:

"Let us learn from the edifying death of Brother Martin how to die well. It is a most important and most difficult lesson."

The body of Martin de Porres was laid out before the main altar in the monastery chapel. Then the friars opened the doors of the chapel to permit Martin's closest friends—the poor, the homeless, the old, and the sick—to bid him a final farewell.

As the body grew colder and more rigid, a disappointed confrere, who had hoped for a miracle that would indicate Martin's holiness, went near and affectionately chided him, "Why is your body stiff and rigid, Brother Martin? Ask God to show his almighty power by permitting it to remain lifelike." Within a few moments, a fragrance of roses and lilies issued from the coffin, and Martin's rigid body relaxed and grew soft.

Now the crowds could not be held back. The people cut to shreds Brother Martin's habit, which had to be replaced several times. Numerous authenticated miracles took place.

Martin's story had begun quite differently just sixty years earlier.

He was the son of a Spanish nobleman and a free black woman. His father deserted the family shortly after the birth of Martin's younger sister, Juana. Unfortunately, like other children, Martin learned at a very early age just how bitter life can be.

"Half-breed," people whispered as he passed the more fashionable quarters of Lima on his way home to the poorest section of the city. But Martin's bright face never clouded, and his happy disposition never changed. He smiled and waved to passersby as he skipped through busy city streets. Martin's job as a delivery boy added a few coins to his mother's meager earnings. By the time he was eight, he had learned where he could find the best buys.

Shopkeepers and open-air merchants knew that the food Martin bought at the market was not all for himself, nor only for his mother and sister. In fact, Martin often gave away more than half—he gave away everything he had to his beggar friends. Then he would turn to old benefactors who would refill Martin's basket and send him on his way with a warning, "Remember, go straight home this time."

But one day someone asked, "Do you know who is on the ship that docked this morning?"

What a strange question, Martin thought. "Sailors, I guess," he replied.

"No, Martin, not just sailors. Your father, Don Juan de Porres, is on that boat."

"Don Juan—my father—is in Lima now?" Martin raced toward home so fast that his neighbors looked to see who was chasing him.

He dashed inside the house, dropped his basket on the table and quickly glanced around. He caught his breath, and then announced seriously, "Juana, our father is here in Lima and he is coming to see us."

"Our father?" Juana responded, wide-eyed. "Do you mean we have a father, too?"

"Yes, and we'll have to tidy up the house and put on our church clothes. . . ."

In the space of a few weeks, great changes took place in Martin's life. He and Juana went to Ecuador, where they lived with their father's uncle, Don Diego. Used to lacking even the barest necessities, the children were overwhelmed by the lifestyle of their wealthy relatives.

Martin remained in Ecuador almost three years, but he never forgot his poor mother, whom he had left behind in Lima. Although the boy was grateful for all that his father and Don Diego were doing for him, his heart ached when he thought of how lonely his mother must be.

Back home, the youth took up a heavy round of prayer, work, study, and visits to the sick. He was apprenticed to a barber-surgeon and learned his profession well. He spent whatever money he made on the poor, and he again became a regular visitor to the marketplace, now as the bene-factor.

A year or two later, the keeper of the house where Martin was staying was abruptly awakened early one morning by a loud noise in the street. As she passed Martin's room, she noticed a sliver of light under the door. "He must have fallen asleep studying," she said to herself. "I'd better wake him up and make him go to bed."

The landlady knocked on the door, but there was no answer. She tried a second time. Still no answer. Then the door swung open. She gasped in astonishment. Wrapped in a state of ecstasy, Martin was kneeling in front of a crucifix, his whole body enveloped in a bright light. She closed the door again and thanked God for having given her the privilege of lodging a person so dear to him. More and more, one could hear talk in the streets of people whom Martin had helped in strange and almost miraculous ways.

Another year passed, and Martin longed to do something more for God. After praying for light and guidance, he presented himself to the prior of the Dominican Monastery of the Holy Rosary. He told the priest that he would like to live at the monastery as a lay helper.

A few days later, sixteen-year-old Martin said goodbye to all his friends, packed his medical instruments, and left for the Dominican monastery. Shortly after he arrived, he was assigned to work in the infirmary, where he accomplished wonders for souls as well as bodies. When Martin's father heard that his son had such a lowly position, he demanded that he be accepted at least as a professed brother. "But, Señor de Porres, that was our wish as well, but your son said that he preferred simply to serve." Only later, when Martin was twenty-four, did his superiors persuade him to take vows. He made his novitiate and donned the habit of the Dominican brother. Unknown to most, he also took up wearing a heavy chain around his waist under the habit and regularly did other severe penances. Martin slept very little and often gave away his own meal, yet seemed to have unrelenting energy. He performed jobs normally assigned to several brothers. He was in charge of supplying food, caring for the clothing, nursing the sick, cleaning the monastery, and many other duties.

The amount of work he continued to do was miraculous in itself. But the countless and inexplicable cures he obtained were even more miraculous. One of these cures involved a certain Brother Francis, who was tempted to abandon his vocation. He was scheming to secretly leave the monastery to take up a government post. The young man went about his duties as if all were well. Approaching the dining room for the evening meal, Martin, who knew the brother really had a vocation, stepped in front of him and whispered, "Are you really going to leave your vocation to become a bookkeeper for the city? That will never do!"

That evening Brother Francis went to bed with a high fever. When he recovered, he tried again to leave. The fever felled him a second time, but recovering he set his mind to depart the monastery. Now, the third time, the fever put him in bed with pleurisy. He struggled to breathe. The superiors, afraid a companion might give him some remedy that would cause greater harm, locked Brother Francis in his room. But God sent in Martin. Just after midnight, as Francis lay mournfully in bed, he sensed someone near him. "Who is it?" he rasped. Then he recognized Martin's smiling face. Martin said nothing, but set down the brazier he always carried and placed sprigs of rosemary on the coals. As the sweet fragrance filled the room, Martin began attending to Francis. He washed him and changed his nightclothes. He then wrapped him in a warm blanket and put him back to bed. "The door is locked, Brother Martin. How did you come in?" the young man struggled to ask.

The answer ended any discussion. "This is not something to try to understand, my son."

"Will I die?" was his next question.

"Do you want to?" Martin asked.

"No," came the quick reply.

"Then you will not die," said his visitor vanishing as silently as he came. The next morning found Francis restored to health and convinced of his vocation.

Martin not only took care of his confreres, but he also often cared for sick people of the city. Martin sometimes even gave them his own bed. Once he found a man outside the monastery who was bleeding and terribly dirty, and Martin brought him in for care. When the man recovered and was sent back home, the brother in charge of laundry accosted Martin. "Look at these sheets. They are filthy. We'll never get them clean again!"

"Some elbow grease along with soap and water will do the trick, my brother," Martin replied. "You know that will work on our clothes, but our souls require tears and penance to be clean of our thoughtlessness."

Martin's concern was not limited to his fellow human beings; he is also known for his love of animals. He did not search out furry friendships, but animals seemed to sense he was their friend and protector. Dogs often appeared after fights or run-ins with impatient masters. He would clean and dress their wounds and have the poor beasts stay in his room, telling them to be quiet and behave well. When they were sufficiently healed he would send them off with a good word.

Martin is famous for his kindness to the mice. Once the little pests got into the monastery linen closet and feasted on the cloth. The brothers were furious and wanted to put poison around. Brother Martin interceded. "They can't go into a dining room and find meals prepared as we do, but they still have to eat." He went to the closet and caught one of the little vandals. Holding it in his hand, he put forward a plan. "My little friend, you must not eat the things set aside for the sick. Assemble your family every day at the far side of the garden. I will bring you food." The tiny mouse must have agreed, because after that the linen closet was not disturbed. The little band of mice arrived each day for the meal set out by Martin in the garden.

So much charity, so many signs and wonders. Martin had labored hard and long, with never a complaint or a moment of respite. He was a man among men, big enough to overcome prejudice and humble enough to hide the special powers he wielded. He was a man who lived solely for God, as the instrument of his mercy.

Prayer

Dear Saint Martin de Porres,
We look to you with such admiration,
not so much because you were able to work wonders,
but because you were a true man of God.
You were a man of intense yet tender prayer.
You gave yourself generously to the work at hand
and gave your own time and talent to the needs
    of others.
It did not matter to you if you were serving the rich
    or the poor,
your brothers or strangers, the kind or the impertinent.
We see this in your example,
but help us find this same merciful spirit in our own
    hearts. Amen.

About Saint Martin de Porres

Born: December 9, 1579, in Lima, Peru

Died: November 3, 1639, in Lima

Feast Day: November 3

Canonized: May 6, 1962, by Pope John XXIII

Patron: social justice, racial harmony, barbers, surgeons, nurses, innkeepers, Peru, animals, poor people, public education, television, Dominican tertiaries, public health

Notes on His Life

- He was the son of a noble Spanish gentleman, Juan de Porres, who later became governor of Panama, and a free black woman named Ana Velásquez.

- When Martin was eight years old, his father took him and his sister to Ecuador for schooling.

- At twelve Martin was apprenticed to a barber-surgeon in Lima.

- Martin learned herbal medicine from his mother.

- At sixteen he became a "donado" or lay helper, in the Third Order of Saint Dominic.

- He desired to be a missionary martyr.

- He was known as Martin the Charitable.

- He possessed exceptional gifts: bilocation, elevation, infused knowledge, miraculous healings, prophecy, and the power to raise the dead.

- He was a vegetarian.

- He established a hospital, an orphanage, and an animal shelter in Lima.
- He was a contemporary of Saint Rose of Lima, Saint John Macias, and Saint Turibius of Mogrovejo.

Lesser-Known Facts

- He was known to contemporaries as "father of charity" because he so inspired people to share in the care of other people.
- Letters permitting the opening of his cause went down in a shipwreck, but were recovered unscathed.
- The miracles for his beatification were the restoration of a removed eye, and the instant cure of a child whose skull had cracked open in a fall.
- He was beatified one week after John Macias, his friend and fellow Dominican.
- The miracles for his canonization were the instant cure from an inoperable intestinal blockage of an elderly woman, and the complete restoration of the crushed foot of a child.
- A scent of roses accompanied his exhumed body to a new tomb in 1664.

In His Own Words

(Having been berated by one of his patients) "I must take better care of him and love him more because he knows me better than anyone else."

Saint Kateri Tekakwitha

Mystic of the Wilderness

Tekakwitha watched the happy faces around the fire inside the longhouse. For some reason, even her aunt looked pleased. Her uncle, Chief Iowerano, caught her glance as he smoked on his pipe. Her stomach tightened with tension at his knowing eyes, although his face remained expressionless. Something was going on. Was she the only one not to know? She scanned the faces in the longhouse and caught a glimpse of the impassive face of their guest, a young warrior—this young man did not seem caught up in the excitement of a secret.

Behind her, her aunt motioned to the young man to sit down beside Tekakwitha, and gave Tekakwitha the bowl of sagamite (hominy stew) to pass to him. Suddenly, Tekakwitha's throat closed. Her aunt was trying to trick her into marriage—an exchange of gifts meant betrothal—and if she hadn't realized it in time, she would have had to marry him! She dropped the bowl, got to her feet, and fled the longhouse.

As she left, she glanced back at her uncle. He did not seem surprised, only disappointed. Tekakwitha was shaking so badly that she stumbled her way out of the palisade into the privacy of the forest. Tears streamed down her face. She was not afraid of her uncle's displeasure. What he thought best for her was irreconcilable with her own desires, and that had soured much of the joy in their kinship. Yet, she knew that he loved her and valued her diligence in farming and around the longhouse. And her aunt's deception did not anger her as much as frighten her. Tekakwitha had almost been tricked into a marriage that she had made clear to her family she could never accept!

The young man himself was not the objection. Tekakwitha simply did not want to get married, even though it was unheard-of for a young maiden to remain single. She had gone along with some of the customs for young women only to please her aunts and uncle. She had obeyed them in everything except their urging her to marry. Even in the face of ridicule and cruelty, she stubbornly refused.

Tekakwitha had just two desires: the first was to continue to serve her family as she always had. The second she dared not share with anyone. She desperately wanted to become a Christian, as her mother had been. Ever since she had met the blackrobes and heard them speak about God, she had been drawn to their loving God, Rawanniio. If she married, she would probably lose the chance to become a Christian and to dedicate her life to this God she longed to know. The blackrobes had been living at her village for some time, but she hadn't asked for instruction because it would displease her uncle. He didn't like the French, including the blackrobes. He remembered, as Tekakwitha did, that French soldiers had burned down their village ten years ago, and they had had to flee with nothing, barely surviving the winter.

If Tekakwitha could just speak with one of the black-robes! She was drawn to their goodness and their desire for peace. She knew that they did not approve of the cannibalism and torture of war prisoners that so disturbed Tekakwitha. But she only knew fragments of prayers. And she had so many questions!

Tekakwitha quieted her sobs and offered a prayer. "Rawanniio, if you want me to know you, help me!"

Some days later, Tekakwitha was sitting in the longhouse all alone. The other women were working in the fields, but she had injured her foot and had been left behind for the longhouse chores. She didn't mind. The bright sunlight hurt her eyes, making it impossible to see. In the dim light of the longhouse fire, she could continue her skilled beadwork.

As she leaned over her work, someone stepped into the entrance of the longhouse and spoke in the silence. "Is someone here?" an unfamiliar voice asked. Tekakwitha's breath stopped. God had answered her prayer!

"Yes, Father," she said calmly. But her heart was beating rapidly.

He walked over and looked down at her. "You know who I am?" he asked.

"Oh, yes," she breathed. "You are a blackrobe who can tell me about Rawanniio!"

The blackrobe seemed surprised, then he sat down by the fire and started telling her about his Christian God of love. As he spoke, he noticed how she paid close attention, eagerly drinking in every word.

"Why don't you come to the mission?" he asked as he got up to leave. "You can join us for prayer and instruction."

Tekakwitha explained as simply as she could. "My uncle, Chief Iowerano, would be displeased."

"Have you asked him?" the blackrobe asked.

"No," Tekakwitha said.

The blackrobe nodded, turned away, then turned back. "I will pray for you," he said. Then he left.

Tekakwitha's heart leaped for joy. The blackrobe would pray for her! As he walked away, she thought, "My uncle is displeased I do not choose to marry, but he has given up trying to force me. Maybe . . . this will displease my uncle, but he will let me do as I ask?"

Tekakwitha was right. Reluctantly, Iowerano gave Tekakwitha permission to be instructed, probably suspecting that in this, too, Tekakwitha's determination would not fail. As she got to know the blackrobes better, Tekakwitha confided her story to Father de Lamberville.

Tekakwitha was born in April 1656 in the Mohawk settlement of Ossernenon, located in what is now Auriesville, New York. She was the daughter of the Mohawk warrior chief Tsaniton-gowa and his kind and gentle wife, Kahontake—an Algonquin woman captured during a Mohawk raid on her settlement. Kahontake's goodness irresistibly attracted the attention of Tsaniton-gowa, who brought her to Ossernenon not as a slave, but as his wife.

As Tsaniton-gowa's wife, Kahontake enjoyed complete freedom, except that she could not practice Christianity openly. When God blessed their marriage with a baby girl, Kahontake secretly taught her child a knowledge of Rawanniio and the desire to practice Christian virtue.

But smallpox struck the village when Tekakwitha was only four years old. Both her parents and her younger brother died. Tekakwitha, too, contracted smallpox. Anastasia, a Christian friend of her mother's, nursed her back to health. But Tekakwitha was scarred on her face and left partially blind, so painfully sensitive to bright sunlight that she covered her head with a blanket when she was outdoors.

Her uncle, Iowerano, now a new chief, had been as devastated as she by the loss. He had picked her up and carried her off to his own longhouse, adopting her as his own and placing her in the care of her two aunts.

As Tekakwitha grew, so did her skill at beadwork and her dependability in domestic affairs. Iowerano was very pleased with his niece in many ways, though she sometimes puzzled him. She was not like other girls her age: she kept apart and silent, and she didn't like to go to dances or village gatherings. He didn't know if this was due to her inability to see clearly in sunlight, her pockmarked face, her natural shyness, or the suffering she had undergone as a child.

When she was free, Tekakwitha loved to run off into the forest to pray. She longed to know Rawanniio and begged for his help. The words and examples of her good mother had made a lasting impression on her, an impression time intensified rather than softened. Finally, when missionaries came to the village, they found this unique young Mohawk maiden, although unbaptized and uninstructed, deeply Christian in her manner of speaking and living.

After a year of instruction, Tekakwitha managed to prevail on her uncle once more: he gave her permission to be baptized! On Easter morning, April 18, 1676, she received Baptism and the Christian name Katherine, which the converts pronounced "Kateri." The next few months, Kateri spent her days working busily in her uncle's house and helping the needy of the village, including the aged and the sick. But some in the village, including her aunt and other relatives, grew suspicious of Kateri's resistance to marriage and the way she practiced her faith. Calumny, taunts, threats, and hostility soon became a daily part of Kateri's life. At last, a young warrior wearing war paint stopped her and pretended he was going to kill her, raising a tomahawk over her head. Eyes lowered, she awaited the blow, showing no signs of fear. The man ran off, impressed with her courage.

Father de Lamberville realized that it was too dangerous for Kateri to remain among her people. He suggested that she flee to Saint Francis Xavier, the Christian native village in Kahnawake near Montreal, where Kateri's mother's friend Anastasia and an adopted sister lived. Kateri resisted this plan for quite a while. She did not want to leave her people, nor break her uncle's heart. Finally, Kateri's brother-in-law made the trip to visit her village with the secret purpose of rescuing Kateri. His descriptions of the "Praying Village" where Christian converts lived peaceably together so appealed to her that she decided to take the risk. That night, several young men guided Kateri out of the village and hid her in the forest.

Terribly hurt and angry, Iowerano went searching for her. It was rumored that he threatened to kill Kateri for her betrayal. Yet, when he met one of the young men getting supplies in Fort Orange, he merely greeted him and went on. Kateri, who was hiding in the woods, would never see her uncle again.

After an arduous three-week journey, Kateri and her companions arrived at Kahnawake. The village was full of the fervor of new converts, and the Christian women happily welcomed her, including her mother's old friend Anastasia. Three months after her arrival, on Christmas Day, Kateri made her first Holy Communion. She impressed everyone with her deep prayer, unceasing kindness, and great desire to do penance and offer sacrifices for the enlightenment of her people. Kateri was greatly devoted to Jesus in the Eucharist. At every moment free of work or service, Kateri could be found at the chapel, usually arriving earlier than the priests in the morning. She also loved to pray out in the woods, where she would carve a cross in one of the trees to make her own little chapel.

Even here in Kahnawake, Kateri soon found herself being urged to find a good husband. But Kateri resisted any suggestion to marry. On a visit to Montreal she had seen the Religious Hospitallers of Saint Joseph and had finally understood her vocation. She felt called, like the sisters, to dedicate her whole life to Jesus. When her sister-in-law and her mother's old friend pressured her unfairly one day, she went to see Father Cholenec, the village blackrobe who was directing her. Resolutely she told him of her decision to renounce marriage in order to love only Christ. On March 25, 1679, the Feast of the Annunciation, Kateri confirmed her resolution with a vow of virginity. Kateri also wanted to start a community of sisters for native women, but the priest discouraged her. Perhaps he could see how her strength was failing. Or perhaps he felt it was too soon after her conversion.

Barely one year later, the young maiden lay on her deathbed. She had never been strong, her penances had weakened her, and she caught a persistent fever. On Wednesday of Holy Week, April 17, 1680, Kateri went to the embrace of Jesus, whom she had loved and for whom she had suffered so much. She was twenty-four years old. Fifteen minutes after her death, Father Cholenec was startled by the change that came over the young woman's scarred face. The pockmarks disappeared, and her face became radiant and completely unblemished. After death, this simple, pure Mohawk-Algonquin woman would be recognized for who she was—a mystic of the North American wilderness.

Prayer

Saint Kateri Tekakwitha,
lover of Jesus,
the secret of your life is that you allowed
the Good News of God's love to transform you.
Your courage, love for your people, and purity of life
were nurtured by your special devotion to Jesus in the
Eucharist and on the cross.
You have been called "mystic of the wilderness."
Pray for me,
that my love for Christ may grow,
that I may respect the sacredness of God's creation,
and that I may discover and faithfully live what God
wants. Amen.

About Saint Kateri Tekakwitha

Born: 1656 in Ossernenon, New York

Died: April 17, 1680, in Kahnawake, Canada

Feast Day: July 14 in the United States, April 17 in
Canada

Declared Blessed: June 22, 1980

Canonized: October 21, 2012, by Pope Benedict XVI

Patron: Native Americans, ecology and the environment, orphans, purity

Notes on Her Life

⟨❀⟩ Born of a Catholic Algonquin mother and a Mohawk
father, she was orphaned at age four.

⟨❀⟩ She began instruction in Christianity in 1675, when she
was nineteen years old.

- She was baptized Easter Sunday, April 18, 1676 (in her home village).

- Because she wouldn't work on Sunday, her family wouldn't allow her to eat all day.

- She tolerated the ridicule and abuse of her family and the village because she knew they couldn't understand her conversion.

- Kateri traveled more than 200 miles on foot and by canoe to the Mission of Saint Francis Xavier, a settlement of Christian Native Americans where she could safely live her faith.

- She received her First Communion on Christmas Day, 1677.

- On March 25, 1679, she made a vow of perpetual virginity—the first Native American woman known to consecrate her virginity to God.

- She died at the young age of twenty-four, her poor health weakened by her fasting and other penances.

Lesser-Known Facts

- Kateri Tekakwitha was a small woman, probably only about four and half feet tall.

- Left scarred and partially blind by smallpox, Kateri Tekakwitha suffered from poor health all her life.

- "Tekakwitha" means: "one who moves things," which some have assumed means that she put things in order. But most likely her name was given to her by her uncle, because smallpox left her partially blind and she used her hands to feel her way. One possible translation of her name is: "she who pushes with her hands."

- ⚒ "Kateri Tekakwitha" is correctly pronounced: Gah-dee-lee Deh-gah-quee-tah.

- ⚒ Because it was so unusual for a young woman not to marry, she was accused at least twice of sleeping with the husbands of jealous wives, but both times her accusers were persuaded that she was innocent.

- ⚒ She wanted to found a community of religious sisters for Native American women, but the Jesuits discouraged her from doing so.

In Her Own Words

"Who will teach me what is most agreeable to God, so that I may do it?"

Blessed Marie-Clémentine
Anuarite Nengapeta

Sister Among Sisters

Sister Marie-Clémentine Anuarite smiled as she passed the fruit salad to Sister Andrée. Today her community, the Sisters of the Holy Family, were celebrating a feast day for Sister Andrée and herself, and it was so good to see the other sisters laugh. Earlier in the month, they had heard troubling rumors that Simba rebel forces were on the move. Since the Congo had gained independence four years earlier, violence and destruction had spurted unpredictably. Times of celebration such as these had become even more precious.

The noise of a truck suddenly drowned out the sisters' laughter. At first, they were not alarmed, but then drunken soldiers invaded their convent, armed with guns, sticks, and machetes. Their leader assured the sisters that they would not be harmed, but that they would be brought to Wamba, some fifty kilometers away, for their own protection. He told the sisters to gather whatever they needed to travel.

Sister Anuarite shakily threw some clothes and food into a bag, including a *pagne*, the all-purpose cloth that many African women wrap around their waist as a skirt, but also use for a variety of other purposes. Then she joined her sisters as they were loaded onto the truck: eighteen professed sisters, nine novices, and seven postulants. They could hear the raucous laughter and vulgar comments of the soldiers, who were planning to forcibly violate the sisters' vows of chastity. The sisters realized that the promise of safety had been false. They encouraged one another with glances and whispered prayers.

In her pocket, Sister Anuarite clutched the little statue of the Virgin Mary that she always kept there. Her other hand held her rosary, and she prayed for the courage to remain faithful to Jesus, no matter what happened.

After many stops where the soldiers drunkenly pillaged whatever they could find, they finally stopped at Ibambi late at night. The priests of the mission had already been murdered. The soldiers smashed through the door of the rectory, then herded the sisters into one room where they were all told to sleep on the floor. Sister Anuarite pulled out the old *pagne* she had packed and offered it to Sister Hélène to soften the ground for her head and shoulders. She gave the place she had found to sleep to another sister, finding a smaller space for herself. As the sisters uncomfortably tried to settle themselves to sleep, Sister Anuarite also tried to lighten the atmosphere. But all night long the soldiers harassed them with threats, insults, and vulgarity. Terrified, not one of the sisters closed her eyes.

Through the long night, Sister Anuarite's heart beat with anxiety. Would she be strong enough to give the ultimate witness to her Spouse if she was called upon to do so? Almost since she could remember, she had wanted to be a sister, even though her mother and even some of the sisters had discouraged her. It was a decision that many of her own people couldn't understand.

Anuarite had been born November 29, 1939, the fourth of six girls. Her father, Badjudu, was a soldier who was often away from home, and Anuarite grew up cherishing his presence, even though he was very strict. When she was four years old, her father's travels took him to the Holy Land. He was so impressed with the life of Jesus that he wrote to Anuarite's mother, Julienne, to advise her and the children to be instructed and baptized in the Catholic Faith.

When Badjudu finally returned home, he decided that, since Julienne had given him no sons, he would take another wife. But Julienne, who was now Catholic, did not believe polygamy was right and separated from him. Anuarite never got over this separation, praying even on her profession day for her parents to be reunited.

At age nine, Anuarite started going to the mission school. She had to study harder than some of the other children if she wanted to pass. When she told her teacher—a sister—that she wanted to become a religious sister, her teacher responded that she couldn't be a sister with such low grades. When Anuarite told her mother that she wanted to enter the convent, her mother told her it was too soon.

Anuarite had to repeat a grade in order to qualify for secondary school, but with a great deal of hard work, she finally succeeded. Then, her mother gave her permission to enter the convent. She was fifteen years old—a typical age for young women to get married.

At first, Anuarite had found some aspects of convent life hard. She especially struggled with obedience, and with being corrected for her faults. Gradually she realized that corrections could help her know herself better. And obedience was not about doing what the superior wanted, but about doing *the will of God*—to whom she was consecrated. Anuarite's lively nature made her an excellent teacher and a joyful presence in the community. On August 5, 1959, Anuarite made her vows. Both her parents were present to celebrate with her, giving the community two goats as a gift.

She continued her studies, then returned to teach the upper primary classes. She was a beloved teacher who paid attention to the needs of the students who didn't fit in or who were known to be troublemakers. She gave herself so completely to her sisters and her duties that her health broke down and she had to take time off to rest. But Anuarite loved her students so much that she couldn't stop at half-measures.

An extrovert, Anuarite was a warm and welcoming presence in her community. But she also could be too quick and abrupt in her speech. She struggled with her sharp impetuosity all her life, but tried to make up by apologizing right away. The villagers and the sisters who lived with her would remember her most for her great generosity and kindness. With her favorite expression, "Jesus alone," she gave voice to her deepest desire: to be faithful to Jesus in everything.

Now, in the darkness, Anuarite whispered in prayer. "O Jesus, give me the grace to die, even at this moment, rather than to abandon you."

The next day, the soldiers herded the sisters back onto the truck. As they approached a village near Wamba, they stopped. One of the chiefs of the Simba rebels, Yuma Deo, ordered all of the sisters down from the truck, to be stripped of all religious articles. Their crucifixes were torn from around their necks. A rough hand grabbed Sister Anuarite's rosary. She clung to it, but it was wrenched away. The soldiers stamped on the pile of sacred objects, then tossed them into the forest.

Then the men forced the sisters back onto the truck, which now took them to Isiro, another eighty kilometers away.

As Anuarite climbed back into the truck, she felt she would choke on the thick silence. Then spontaneously, the sisters started to pray the Rosary—and continued praying it throughout the rest of the trip.

When they arrived at Isiro, the sisters waited to be taken by van, group by group, to a house. One of the rebel soldiers, Colonel Ngalo, eyed Sister Anuarite. Becoming uncomfortable under his gaze, Sister Anuarite turned to the sister next to her, Sister Elizabeth Kahenga, and whispered, "I should run away."

Sister Elizabeth had also noticed the colonel's attention. She encouraged Sister Anuarite. "But you don't know this area, and it's nighttime. Ask Mother Leontine what to do."

Mother Leontine took Sister Anuarite by the arm, and together they climbed into the van for the second trip. "Don't worry," she told Sister Anuarite, "we'll go together." But one of the officers pulled Sister Anuarite out. Mother Leontine kept a firm grasp on her young sister's arm and followed her, insisting that they stay together. The two sisters were then brought to Colonel Ngalo's residence. He told Sister Anuarite bluntly, "You are to become my wife."

Mother Leontine immediately interposed, "This sister has made a vow of chastity; she is consecrated to God. You cannot take her as your wife."

Infuriated, Chief Deo slapped Mother Leontine in the face. "Do you dare to refuse me? I will call my soldiers and we will assault all your sisters. Then I'll tie you up in a sack myself and throw you into the river." Mother Leontine did not give in. She refused to be separated from Sister Anuarite— even when Anuarite was forcibly taken to another room, she made sure the door was left open so she could hear her.

In the room, Colonel Ngalo repeated his demand. "You will be my wife, or I will kill you."

Heart pounding, Sister Anuarite stood silent but firm, refusing to even acknowledge his offer. Finally he added, "If you refuse, we'll kill your superior, too," he said.

Shocked, Sister Anuarite finally answered with a plea. "Why would you kill her? Just kill me."

At this verbal proof of her resistance, Colonel Ngalo tore off her veil and started hitting her.

At the other house, the sisters were given rice and sardines. But they refused to eat until Sister Anuarite and Mother Leontine were returned to them. Colonel Olombe came to Ngalo's residence, bringing word that the sisters were refusing to eat. Ngalo asked Olombe to help him seduce Anuarite, and Olombe confidently agreed. He then reunited the two sisters with the other sisters so that they could eat together.

Sister Anuarite, bruised and shaken, tasted her food, but couldn't eat. Inside, she was terrified. Would her fear betray her? When the other sisters comforted her, she simply said, "I am so troubled. Please pray for me. I am willing to die to preserve my vow of chastity, but pray for me!"

After the meal, Colonel Olombe started to separate the sisters into different rooms, but the sisters refused to go, saying they would sleep in one room. Finally, the drunken Olombe agreed. He pulled Sister Anuarite and Sister Jean Baptiste outside and forced them into the van. As he stepped away, the two sisters jumped out of the van and tried to escape, but the Colonel caught them. Sister Anuarite told him, "I do not want to commit sin. If you want, kill me."

Crazed with rage, Olombe beat one sister then the other with his rifle butt. After he broke Sister Jean Baptiste's arm in three places, she fell unconscious. Despite her beating,

Sister Anuarite remained upright on her knees. "I forgive you," she said, "because you do not know what you are doing."

He hit her again and again, but she made no sound. Finally, she murmured, "Just as I wanted," and collapsed to the ground. The two sisters lay there, unconscious, for about fifteen minutes.

Some of the rebel soldiers who witnessed the ferocity of Colonel Olombe's drunken attacks on the sisters took his rifle, in case he decided to kill all the sisters, as he was loudly threatening to do.

Becoming more enraged because he couldn't find his rifle, Olombe called for more armed soldiers. Two more Simba rebels arrived, and he told them to stab Sister Anuarite in the chest. Each time, Sister Anuarite groaned softly with pain. Then Olombe shot her in the chest with a pistol.

Only then did he allow the sisters to take her tortured body into the house. She was barely breathing. One of the sisters cradled Sister Anuarite's head in her lap, calling her name. Without awakening, she died at about one o'clock in the morning.

Sure they would die soon, the sisters prepared themselves. They asked forgiveness of one another for any lack of charity, then started to sing the Magnificat, thanking God for the grace to follow in Sister Anuarite's footsteps. The singing unnerved the colonel, and he ordered them to stop. Finally, his drunken rage calmed.

The sisters were left the rest of that night at the mercy of the soldiers who threatened, hit, and kicked them. Only Sister Anuarite died that night, but the entire community underwent a true martyrdom.

Sisters in Christ, their sisterhood gave them the strength to resist the soldiers' unwelcome advances, threats, and beatings. Finally, in the morning, the sisters were allowed to leave. They asked for the body of Sister Anuarite, but the soldiers refused their request. Eight months later, her body was discovered in a common grave. A tiny statue of the Blessed Mother—who must have given Anuarite courage and strength in those last minutes—was found in her pocket.

Prayer

Blessed Anuarite,
radiant martyr of purity, pray for us!
Drawn to the consecrated life at a young age,
you shared a joyful life of prayer and service,
as a sister among sisters.
In the hours of crisis, your mutual faith and sisterly
    prayers strengthened you
to once again offer your whole self to God, body
    and soul.
Today, the world still cannot understand
the choice for chastity and a radical fidelity to
    the Gospel.
Protect us, as you protected your sisters in life and death,
so that we, too, can offer our whole selves to God. Amen.

About Blessed Marie-Clémentine Anuarite Nengapeta

Born: November 29, 1939, in Wamba, Belgian Congo
Died: December 1, 1964, in Isiro, Zaire (now Democratic
    Republic of the Congo)

Feast Day: December 1

Beatified: August 15, 1985

Patron: the well-loved patron of young people in Africa

Notes on Her Life

✿ Anuarite was not born into a Christian family, but was baptized with her mother and sisters when she was about four years old.

✿ Anuarite has many names:

— Her parents named her Nengapeta, a family name that refers to riches.

— She was baptized Alphonsine.

— When she started school, one of the sisters made a mistake and gave her the name of her sister, Anuarite, which means "one who laughs at war."

— At her profession, she was given the name Sister Marie-Clémentine.

✿ Anuarite had a stammer that made it difficult for her to speak when angry or tense.

✿ Anuarite is best remembered by the sisters she lived with for her great generosity and kindness, her cooking in the kitchen for feast days, and her lively ability to make the other sisters laugh.

✿ Anuarite had a special love for the wayward girls in the school, and gave them extra encouragement.

✿ Her favorite saints were Saint Cecilia, Saint Agnes, and Saint Maria Goretti.

Lesser-Known Facts

- Anuarite had average intelligence and struggled with school, having to repeat at least one grade.

- Many of the young women who entered the convent with Anuarite later left. Anuarite prayed often for the grace of fidelity to her vocation.

- On her profession day, Sister Anuarite prayed that her parents would be reunited.

- Later, her mother tried to persuade her to leave the convent to come home and help her family.

- Sister Anuarite suffered from fragile health, especially migraine headaches.

- Sister Anuarite's Marian devotion was nurtured by the well-loved book, *The Glories of Mary*, written by her baptismal patron, Saint Alphonsus Liguori.

- She kept a small notebook that included short prayers and personal reflections, recipes, dates, and her favorite passages from spiritual reading.

- After the rebellion, having served several years in prison, Olombe showed up at the convent, asking for food. Mother Leontine gave him something to eat, saying, "Sister Anuarite forgave you, we must follow her example."

- In 1985, at Sister Anuarite's beatification, her murderer asked the Pope to forgive him, and Pope John Paul II publicly assured him of the Church's forgiveness.

In Her Own Words

"My resolution: To love the Lord, because he has done great things for me; how great is his goodness!"

— From her notebook

Saint Elizabeth of Hungary

The Princess Who Found True Love

Elizabeth knew that, at first glance, they must not have looked like a royal couple. Sitting contentedly next to her, Ludwig was working his way through the most recent dispatch, while she was stitching a blanket for her soon-to-arrive third child. She allowed her eyes to linger on her husband's strong hands, then impulsively reached over and intertwined her fingers with his. A smile broke his serious attention, and Elizabeth reveled in his tender glance. "My dark beauty," he murmured.

Elizabeth felt so blessed. She enjoyed every moment with her beloved Ludwig—whether she was sitting beside him in the great hall or they were riding together. She wore beautiful clothes because he enjoyed seeing her in them, although she wore a hair shirt underneath. When Ludwig was away and it was impossible for her to go with him, she dressed in mourning clothes until his return, when she would be the first to hurry out to meet him. For a while, she had worried that she loved her husband *too* much, but her confessor had assured her that her path to union with God was with and through her husband. She had finally realized this and had told him, "It is in God that I love my husband: may he who sanctified marriage grant eternal life."

Their love for each other was God's gift to carry them through the many challenges they faced, not just as a family with little Herman and Sophia, but as the rulers of Thuringia (in those days the ruling couple were called the landgrave and the landgravine). Their responsibilities were heavy: rulers of a large territory, they were also obligated to serve the king of Germany, Frederick II.

Elizabeth reminisced happily as she stole another glance at her husband's handsome profile. She had first met Ludwig when she was only four years old. Her father, King Andrew of Hungary, had sent her to Wartburg Castle near Eisenach, Germany, to be raised with her betrothed, Landgrave Herman I's eldest son. She was accompanied by two ladies-in-waiting and a large dowry. It was a customary political arrangement, but as a four-year-old, she knew only that she was homesick and fearful. The boyish kindness of eleven-year-old Ludwig and his father had comforted her on her arrival, and then again two years later, when she had learned of her mother's murder.

As the little princess matured into a young woman, her friendship and respect for Ludwig grew. But she endured difficult times when Ludwig was away, especially after his father had died. With Hungary's power waning, his family no longer saw Elizabeth as a good match for Ludwig. They criticized her for her piety and her generosity to those who were less fortunate. When Ludwig became landgrave after his father's death, he publicly renewed his intentions to marry her. "I would more willingly part from a mountain of gold than from my betrothed!" he confided to a friend. Finally, when he was twenty-one and she fourteen, he married her in a magnificent wedding—the church packed with royalty, knights, and ladies. Yet, it had not been too extravagant: Elizabeth had set aside a portion of the money intended for the wedding banquet to give to the poor.

What she remembered best from her wedding was his striking figure, and the way his eyes lit up when he saw her approach the altar. But her Ludwig was much more than handsome. He was courageous and true, a chivalrous knight devoted to God and his people. He shared in her life of prayer, encouraged her in her many works of charity, and supported the decisions she made while he was away—even when she practically emptied their treasury to feed the families starving in the recent famine. Her husband helped her to build a hospital for lepers, and didn't object that she herself nursed those who were in the hospitals and fed the hungry who came to the castle gates.

Now, as they sat together, Ludwig tried to get through all the messages quickly, so he could snatch a few undistracted minutes with his Bett. He knew his wife was still sometimes hurt by his family's criticism. Her lifestyle was a challenge to the aristocracy of their feudal world, even provocative at times. Many lords and ladies were generous, but Elizabeth gave of herself in the most natural, direct, and complete way possible. Many of the aristocracy were too busy with politics, society, and their own lives to stop to think of the suffering of the desperately poor people of the land. His wife's generosity was her way of serving the people and drawing closer to God. The more others criticized her, the more he admired and loved her.

In addition, Ludwig knew that some of the court continued to dislike Elizabeth, not only because she was Hungarian, but also because she was so faithful to him. Such fidelity in courtly circles was uncommon at the time, partly because so many marriages were prearranged. To the amazement of the sophisticated court, Ludwig and Bett were a very happily married couple. Truly, their union had been blessed by God! Until now . . .

Elizabeth suddenly noticed that Ludwig's frame had frozen. He was reading intently, his brow furrowed.

"What is it, Ludwig?" she asked. "Another trip?" She recognized the seal of Frederick, who had now assumed the title of emperor.

"Frederick is preparing for the next Crusade, to keep his promise to the Pope," Ludwig said. He turned to her, his eyes filled with regret. "I won't be here for the birth of our next little one," he said softly. "I am called to go with him."

To the Holy Land! Elizabeth felt her world crumble around her. For a moment, blackness overshadowed her vision. The darkness cleared and Ludwig's concerned face filled her eyes.

"Don't go, darling! It's too dangerous! You'll be away for at least a year, maybe much longer! Please for my sake, for the sake of our child. Don't leave me now!"

Ludwig's face grew more troubled. "I have to go, Bett; it's my duty to Frederick. God would not want me to neglect my duty."

"But your duty is also here, to your children, to your people. Even to me!" Elizabeth knew she wasn't being fair. Ludwig did have a duty to his king. But she couldn't let him go. Not so easily. Not when he might not come back.

"Let's pray about it," Ludwig urged. "I'm sure God will make my path clear."

Elizabeth felt sick with fear. She tried to listen in her prayer, but instead found herself pleading with God to keep her husband safely by her side. Finally, worn out with her pleas and prayers, she spoke with Ludwig again. Ludwig was convinced that his going on crusade was God's will for them. In the face of his conviction, and her desire to do God's will, Elizabeth accepted his decision. "I will not hold you back. It is the will of God. I have given myself entirely to him, and now I must give you too!" Despite her pregnancy, she accompanied him on the first part of his journey. Their parting broke her heart, but Elizabeth choked back her tears. Her last glimpse of him was his upright figure saluting her as his horse pranced, eagerly leading the way. It was June 24, the feast of John the Baptist.

In the months that followed, Elizabeth anxiously awaited news of Ludwig while also preparing for the birth of their third child. Finally, in October, she gave birth to their second daughter, Gertrude. A few days later, the news arrived. On September 11, her husband had died in Otranto of a plague that had swept away many of the crusaders.

Elizabeth was devastated. Unable to contain her grief, she shrieked out, "The world and all that gave me joy is dead to me!" After hours of uncontrollable sobbing, Elizabeth found her way to a large crucifix. Exhausted, she prayed simply, "You know, O Lord, that I loved him more than anything in this world, because he loved you, and because he was my husband. But you have taken him to yourself. I commend him and myself to your mercy. May your will be done in us."

She was a widow at twenty. Her five-year-old son, Herman, should inherit his father's title when he came of age. But Heinrich, Ludwig's brother and Herman's regent, assumed all authority as landgrave and banished Elizabeth from the castle in the middle of winter. He further ordered that no one was to give the family any aid, accusing Elizabeth of squandering the family's wealth.

Driven out with nothing, Elizabeth took shelter that cold night in a pig shed, with her baby in her arms. Her faithful ladies-in-waiting joined her and, together with Elizabeth's children, they made their way to a nearby Franciscan monastery, where they asked the monks to sing a hymn of thanksgiving to God. Elizabeth wanted to thank God for the opportunity to experience some of the poverty and suffering he had endured on earth.

For some time, Elizabeth and her children were among the poorest of the poor. Daily she walked the streets, begging scraps of food. Fortunately, news of what had happened reached her aunt, the abbess at Kitzingen, and she gave them shelter. Elizabeth's father and Ludwig's soldiers threatened Heinrich with severe action when they found out what he had done. Finally, when Ludwig's body was brought home to rest, Heinrich expressed his remorse to Elizabeth, who reconciled with him. The kingdom and its title were returned to little Herman (although he never actually ruled; he died at age nineteen), and Elizabeth's properties were restored. She went to live at Marburg, where she established another hospital.

Elizabeth's uncle tried to pressure her into a new marriage. Emperor Frederick even inquired about her. But Elizabeth had made a sacred promise not to remarry and wanted to devote her life to the care of others, especially those who were poor and sick. A great admirer of her contemporary, Saint Francis, she had joined the Third Order of Saint Francis before her husband's death, and now wore the Franciscan habit. Under the strict direction of her confessor, Father Conrad, she grew steadily in sanctity.

Worn out with her unceasing service, Elizabeth fell ill and died at the age of twenty-three. The cup of her short life had been very full: princess, wife of a powerful ruler, mother of three children, widow, and religious. She had suffered grief, calumny, loneliness, and betrayal, as well as the physical sufferings of hunger and penance. Yet to Elizabeth, only one thing had mattered: that the cup of her life overflow with love. In every circumstance, whether joyful or sorrowful, Elizabeth had responded with love—drawing ever closer to God, the true Love of her life.

Prayer

Saint Elizabeth of Hungary,
in your love for your husband and family
you lived God's will.
As leader of your people,
you didn't allow the luxuries surrounding you
to distract you from responding to God's call
to serve him in those who are poor.
Teach me how to live my vocation to love:
that my family may grow in love and forgiveness
    of each other.
May I recognize God's call to serve others
with the same generosity and compassion you had.
Help me to see the face of Christ everywhere,
especially in my family and those who are suffering.
Amen.

About Saint Elizabeth of Hungary

Born: 1207, Hungary
Died: November 16, 1231, at Marburg, Germany
Feast Day: November 17

Canonized: May 28, 1235, by Pope Gregory IX

Patron: brides, bakers, widows, Catholic charities,
   Franciscan Third Order

Notes on Her Life

⚜ Elizabeth's family includes several saints: her aunt was
   Saint Hedwig, her daughter is Blessed Gertrude of Al-
   denberg, and her great-niece, Saint Elizabeth of Portu-
   gal.

⚜ As a youth, when Ludwig went on a journey, he always
   brought back a gift for Elizabeth—such as gloves or a
   coral rosary. When Ludwig was gone, Elizabeth would
   yearn for him, then overflow with joy on his return.

⚜ Elizabeth and Ludwig encouraged each other on their
   journey to holiness. After his death, Ludwig was considered a saint by his people. Although he was never canonized, he is recognized as blessed.

⚜ Ludwig would hold his wife's hand when she rose at night
   to pray.

⚜ Elizabeth asked one of her ladies-in-waiting to wake her
   at night by tugging on her foot. One night, the lady
   accidentally pulled on Ludwig's foot instead. Startled
   awake, he did not yell at her but patiently motioned her
   to wake Elizabeth instead, and pretended to go back to
   sleep.

⚜ Elizabeth was drawn to Franciscan spirituality and lifestyle, and helped establish the Franciscans in Thuringia.
   Later, she would become the first Franciscan Tertiary in
   Thuringia (Franciscan Tertiaries are now known as Secular Franciscans).

Lesser-Known Facts

- Elizabeth's mother was murdered when Elizabeth was six years old.

- We know so much about the details of Elizabeth's life because of the testimony of four servants, particularly her two ladies-in-waiting, Isentrude and Jutta, who had been with Elizabeth since her childhood.

- It is estimated that, while she was landgravine, Elizabeth fed more than 900 people daily. She also provided work, donating tools to men who needed them, and teaching women how to spin.

- After her husband's death and without his protection, Elizabeth fought to regain her property, not for herself, but so that her children would be provided for. She then gave her children to the care of those she trusted and dedicated herself to charitable service.

- One form of penance that Elizabeth practiced was to refuse to eat any food that had been obtained unethically.

In Her Own Words

"How can I, a creature, wear a crown of gold when the Lord bears a crown of thorns, and bears it for me?"

Saint Catherine of Siena

Woman Afire

The twenty-year-old mystic recluse Catherine Benincasa sat stunned on the bench in her little room. What was she supposed to do? For three years, as soon as she had been allowed to dedicate her life to God, she had devoted herself to a life of prayer and contemplation while living at home with her family. She left her bedroom—her "cell" as she liked to call it—only to go to church, and spoke to no one but her confessor. Jesus, who had first appeared to her when she was six years old, had told her this was a time of probation, a time to grow in self-knowledge and prepare for Catherine's deepest desire—mystical union with him. And finally, just days ago, Jesus had espoused her to himself, giving her a ring she could see but which seemed invisible to everyone else.

This morning, she had begged Jesus to deepen her union with him, and he had hinted that he was sending her out into the world to do good to others. Now, his clear directive so surprised her that she didn't know what to think. Jesus had told her to go join her family for the midday meal!

Catherine hadn't eaten with her family for three years. She had been called to retreat from the world, and it had taken her family—especially her mother—several long years and painful conflicts to understand Catherine's desire for a life of solitude and prayer.

Catherine was the twenty-fourth of her parents' twenty-five children, many of whom died in childhood, including a twin sister who had died after birth. Her father was a dyer, and her mother the daughter of a poet. Catherine had been a lively but plain child. When she was only six years old, she had her first vision of Christ, and her childhood and adolescence were filled with visions and a deep life of piety.

When Catherine reached the marriageable age of twelve, family pressure, especially from her oldest sister Bonaventura, succeeded in getting her to dress up, even to color her hair to make herself more attractive. But Bonaventura died giving birth, and Catherine suddenly realized that she was no longer on the path to her true vocation. She asked the advice of a Dominican friar who was also a friend of the family. Initially he tried to persuade Catherine to obey her parents' wishes. But when she finally convinced him of her vocation, he had advised her to cut off her hair—a decisive gesture that would make her mother angry. Finally, after some hesitation, Catherine did it to show her parents that she was serious.

But instead of giving in, her family decided that she needed firmer persuasion. To "help" her change her mind, they assigned Catherine to the tasks of the servants. Since she wanted solitude and silence above all, they even took away her bedroom. But the Lord had helped Catherine to find refuge within herself, to create an inner sacred space so she could still speak to him and be at peace, even in the midst of the heavy chores.

Finally, Catherine had called her family together and explained that she had vowed her virginity to Christ and wanted to join the Dominican Tertiaries. Also known as the Mantellate, these were laywomen who shared in the Dominican spirituality and mission while living at home. Catherine's father, who had always been more understanding of his daughter's ways, joked that he could have a worse son-in-law. He and his wife gave her a room of her own and the peace to follow her vocation. Her mother even helped persuade the Dominican Tertiaries to allow Catherine to join them at the age of sixteen. Since joining them, Catherine had dedicated her life to prayer. It was not easy. She lived the ascetical practices of her times very strictly—going with barely any sleep, disciplining herself with chains and scourging, and eating only bread and water. Yet, Catherine had been very happy.

Now Catherine pondered these new words of Jesus, which she found so unsettling. Was he sending her away? Had she done something wrong? All Catherine cared about was being with him! God knew how distracted she had been before she had "left" the world only a few years earlier. If she went back, she would not only be distracted and lose her sweet conversations with God. She would fall into sin!

Then, Jesus spoke again to reassure her. "Do not be afraid! I will not remove myself from you; rather, I want to draw you even closer to me through your charity for your neighbor."

Catherine had meditated on the words of the Gospel many times: *Whatever you do to others, you do to me.* Could she draw closer to her God through active charity? Still, she struggled with the idea of returning to an active life. She protested one more time. "But how can I, a woman, be useful to others? It is not fitting for women to teach and preach." And Jesus replied once more, "I pour out my grace where I will."

It was midday. Catherine suddenly realized that it didn't matter if she didn't understand. Doing God's will was most important, and what Jesus wanted was clear. So she got up from the wooden bench that also served as her bed, left her cell, and joined her family at table. As she entered, all conversation fell away. In the surprised silence, her mother's eyes narrowed as she contemplated her youngest daughter, emaciated from fasting and penance, standing in the doorway. Then she nodded toward a place at the table and immediately started talking to one of Catherine's brothers. Catherine's father was pleased, welcoming his daughter back with a smile.

Catherine gradually reentered the swirl of life, but what she had feared did not come to pass. Instead, the world around her was transformed because she saw it in a new way—through God's eyes. She discovered a special joy in serving those who were least fortunate or despised by others—criminals, those who suffered from leprosy or in hospitals, those who were troubled in mind and spirit. Catherine started to feel the force of the wisdom of the Dominican ideal: to communicate what one contemplates. And Jesus didn't disappear from her life. Instead, he seemed to delight in making his presence felt when she was out among the people—for example, causing her to fall into ecstasy while she was praying at church. The public signs from God earned deep respect from some, ridicule from others, and jealousy or hatred from still others. It also drew doubters, who, once they got to know Catherine, were likely to experience a profound conversion. Catherine was unperturbed by all this. She remained deeply humble, rooted in her real relationship with God and aware of her unworthiness. (When Catherine went into ecstasy after Communion and became unaware of her surroundings, some people who thought she was a fraud would actually throw her out of the church onto the street, beat her, and then abandon her there. Catherine never complained about this ill-treatment.)

As controversial a figure as Catherine initially was, she came to earn the trust and respect of many people of Siena and of some local Dominicans. A group of disciples gathered around her, and Catherine came to consider them her spiritual family. Catherine's charity, which had been initially focused on her family and the sick (including nursing victims of the plague that struck Siena), now seemed to shift toward teaching, advising, and spiritual guidance. She became known as a peacemaker, mediating family and territorial feuds. (At one point, Catherine supposedly kept three priests busy ministering to the people who had been converted in their encounter with her.) The general chapter of the Dominicans called Catherine to Florence in 1374, wanting to meet and probably also interrogate this young Dominican tertiary whose controversial reputation was spreading. Impressed by her responses to their questions, the Dominicans assigned Father Raymond of Capua as her confessor and spiritual director. He quickly became her friend, adviser, and follower. He also provided the trusted support of the Dominican Order for her important mission.

As Catherine grew more aware of the deep tears in the fabric of the unity of the Church and the harm that the discord was doing to the People of God, she became quite disturbed. Because politics and Church policy had become so deeply intertwined, the actions of Church officials were often politically driven and contrary to the Gospel. At the same time, many civil leaders sought to control the affairs of the Church using force and threats from the outside or corruption from within.

The feuds between the various regions of Italy grew more and more violent. While these touched Siena, Florence was in a particularly fierce struggle with the Papal states (areas under papal rule). Catherine's growing advocacy for peace and unity led her to begin a correspondence with Pope Gregory XI, who lived in Avignon, France. The Pope invited her to Avignon to mediate the feud between Florence and the Papal States. Catherine accepted, but she did not succeed in bringing peace at this time, because the Florentine representatives were insincere. However, she met with Pope Gregory XI many times that summer and persuasively urged him to return the papacy to Rome. The papacy had been in Avignon for most of the fourteenth century and suffered from corruption, a loss of independence (it was subject to the threat of the French monarchy, as well as other French influences), and alienation from much of the Church in western Europe. Devout Christians everywhere wanted the Pope to return to Rome, to the See of Saint Peter and the place of the martyrdom of both Saints Peter and Paul, thus unifying the Church.

In her short time with the Pope, Catherine convinced him to return to Rome, although he wavered when he faced the resistance of the mostly French cardinals. Finally, however, he left for Rome, and Catherine kept up her correspondence with him, encouraging him and pressing him to have the courage to do what was right. During this time, she again went to Florence to make peace. Violence broke out and attempts were made on her life, but Catherine did not flee. She actually regretted that she was not murdered, wanting to become a martyr for peace, until her spiritual director pointed out that her death could have been used as an excuse for more violence. Yet, Catherine finally succeeded in her mission for peace for the Florentines when Pope Gregory's successor, Urban VI, asked her once again to mediate.

Catherine returned to Siena, aware that her time on earth was coming to an end, and dictated her great spiritual work, *The Dialogue.* By this time, Catherine's friends would describe her as a "bag of bones." Yet, despite the great physical pain she must have always suffered, she remained lively and cheerful.

Pope Urban VI rapidly became very unpopular due to his harsh ways. Certain cardinals declared his election invalid and elected a new pope, setting him up in Avignon. Catherine had foreseen and predicted this great schism, but it broke her heart. Pope Urban VI called Catherine to Rome for desperately needed support. Despite her ill health, Catherine went to Rome and labored tirelessly for the unity of the Church. She received a vision of the Church as a great ship crushing her, and her fragile health really started to fail. After three months of intense suffering that she willingly offered for the unity of the Church, Catherine finally left this earth to enjoy the uninterrupted wedding banquet with her Spouse. It was April 29, 1380.

Prayer

Saint Catherine of Siena,
your vision of the world was transformed by your
    contemplation.

And what you contemplated in your prayer, you shared
    with the world.
You strove unceasingly for peace and for unity in the
    Church.
Your relationship with the Church was both faith-filled
    and practical:
you revered priests and bishops in their sacred office,
and you both supported and challenged them to live up
    to their responsibilities.
Today the Church still suffers:
wounded, disillusioned, fractured by disunity.
Ask Jesus to set me alight with the fire of his love.
Guide me so that I can live the Gospel
and become a voice for unity and peace
in the midst of diversity. Amen.

About Saint Catherine of Siena

Born: March 25, 1347, in Siena
Died: April 29, 1380, in Rome
Feast Day: April 29
Canonized: 1461 by Pope Pius II
Declared Doctor of the Church: 1970
Patron: Rome, Italy (with Saint Francis of Assisi),
    Europe, Dominican Tertiaries, nursing

Notes on Her Life

❧ Catherine had her first vision of Christ when she was six
or seven years old, while walking home with her brother
Stephen.

❧ Catherine vowed her virginity to Christ when she was
very young.

- Near the end of Catherine's seclusion from the world, she reached the heights of the spiritual life with a mystical marriage with Jesus. She was just twenty years old.

- Although Catherine was not beautiful, she was very persuasive. In violent times when a feud could destroy a village or ravage a countryside, her tireless efforts to bring peace saved countless lives.

- Catherine wrote 372 letters, which we have today, as well as *The Dialogue*, and some prayers.

- Despite her visions, Catherine was quite practical. As a penance, she started to wear a hair shirt, but replaced it with a chain she wore around her waist because she had discovered the hair shirt wasn't hygienic.

- She died at the age of thirty-three, possibly of a stroke.

Lesser-Known Facts

- Catherine was very intelligent, but received no schooling. With effort, she taught herself to read the Liturgy of the Hours as a teenager. Much later, she learned to write. But she dictated most of her letters and *The Dialogue*.

- Catherine's spirituality was centered on Christ and included an emphasis on self-knowledge, devotion to the Eucharist and Christ's passion, and to Christ's presence in the Church.

- In 1375 in Pisa, Catherine received the stigmata, but she begged Jesus to keep it invisible. After her death, both the stigmata and her wedding band became visible.

- At the end of her life, Catherine felt that she was a failure for not being able to prevent or heal the schism caused by two men both claiming to be Pope.

    Catherine's holiness and influence in the affairs of her time have always been recognized, but recently the depths of her spirituality and mysticism have gained more attention.

    When he named her Doctor of the Church in 1970, Pope Paul VI called her "Doctor of Unity."

In Her Own Words

"O Abyss! O eternal Godhead! O Sea profound! What more could You give me than Yourself?"

— *The Dialogue*, 167

Blessed Isidore Bakanja

Member of Mary's Family

Isidore Bakanja walked uneasily away from the house, fingering the scapular he wore around his neck. His back was mostly healed from the recent flogging by his boss, Andre Van Cauter, the Belgian supervisor of the rubber plantation. He could hear Van Cauter laughing and shouting drunkenly, even though Isidore had walked some distance away. Better to stay out of sight for now, at least until he had decided what to do.

Isidore had known before he came that the bosses in this part of the Congo were not fond of Christianity. But he had never thought it would mean outright persecution for such a simple thing as wearing a scapular. Plus, he had thought that his previous boss, Reynders, a fair-minded employer, could protect him. But Reynders wasn't in charge here, and the plantation was run in a way that any decent Christian would have deplored. Although it was 1909, the European owners still treated the Congolese laborers as slaves. They could be beaten and harassed at the whim of the boss.

Why wearing his scapular and praying the Rosary were so abhorrent to the boss, Isidore wasn't sure, but it was clear that living his faith publicly was quickly becoming dangerous. Isidore suspected that Van Cauter's hostility to Christianity had something to do with its teaching that, in the eyes of God, all people were equal. His brothers and sisters might have to put up with being treated unfairly, but they didn't have to give away their dignity. In the sight of God, Isidore stood as an equal, next to Van Cauter.

This was one reason Isidore was so proud of his new-found faith and eager to share it. The clash between European culture and the lifestyle and traditions of his Congolese people was turbulent and fraught with violence and oppression. The Church had an answer, if only people would listen!

Isidore crouched on the ground. What was he going to do? Van Cauter's rule here was absolute. Isidore considered his options: he could go back to the heavy masonry he had been doing since childhood. But he wanted to improve himself, maybe even provide for a family someday. Being a domestic servant was much easier than masonry, and offered opportunities for the future. And when he wasn't so tired at night, he could pray or talk to other people about Jesus.

Another option was to stop wearing his scapular and to pray in secret. But he didn't want to do that, either. One of Isidore's greatest joys was to share his newfound faith with others. Many people here were just like he had been a couple of years ago—they had not even heard about the loving God who sent his Son to save all God's beloved children. The other workers were curious about what he was doing when he knelt down to pray, and sometimes they asked him to tell them stories about this God who loved them. Although Isidore wasn't trained as a catechist, he had learned the stories well, and he loved to retell them, especially stories about Mary.

He remembered what the Trappist monks had told him before he received Baptism just three years ago. "When you wear the scapular, you are part of Mary's family." ("Scapular" translated to "Mary's habit" in Isidore's native language.) At his First Communion, he had promised himself that he would always wear the scapular.

But if he lived his faith openly, he might be beaten again. Or worse. Isidore had heard rumors about the violence at other plantations. But the hatred in Van Cauter's eyes, and the way he expected Isidore to shrivel up in front of him didn't just make Isidore afraid. It also stirred up something deep in Isidore's soul. He straightened with decision. He would *not* deny God, nor his own dignity and manhood. He was a child of God! It would be dangerous, but he would stand up to this oppressive boss on behalf of all his people, affirming their human rights, even the right to practice their faith.

As Isidore walked back toward the house, he found himself on alert, but at peace with what he had decided to do. "Mary will protect me," he thought. "I don't need to be afraid, no matter what happens."

Isidore went back to his duties and prudently stayed out of Van Cauter's sight. But he soon heard Van Cauter calling his name from out in the yard. A feeling of foreboding clutched at Isidore's gut, but he walked out of the house toward his employer.

"Yes, boss!" he said, expecting a vitriolic verbal attack.

"Take off that thing!" growled Van Cauter in a drunken voice, gesturing at Isidore's chest.

Isidore said nothing, simply stood straight and tall. His heart was beating rapidly. This was the showdown he had been dreading. "Holy Mary, Mother of God, pray for me!" he prayed silently.

Van Cauter's rage erupted. He attacked Isidore, ripped at his shirt and tore off the scapular, knocking him to the ground. Shocked, Isidore lay there for a moment. Before he could rise, a blinding series of blows exploded on the side of his head and his neck, stunning him. He tried to curl up to protect his head, but couldn't.

"You there, get the whip!" Van Cauter shouted to the other domestic servants watching. One of them ran to get it and handed it to Van Cauter. "Keep it!" Van Cauter shoved it back. "Whip him with all you've got!"

Isidore opened his eyes and tried to focus. He had worked side by side with these men—his countrymen. Then he saw the whip made from animal hide—with nails firmly fixed at the ends. Isidore feebly tried to get up. Van Cauter savagely kicked him in the face. "You two, hold him face down. Now!" he screamed at the laborers. "Or I'll beat you in his place!"

One frightened man stood over Isidore and started whipping. The pain ripped through Isidore's back, the nails tearing deep furrows on his back. Isidore kept silent at first, but then the nails struck through to the bone. Overwhelmed by the pain, Isidore screamed.

The young man stopped whipping him, perhaps frightened by the blood or the screams. The other two let him go. Isidore was too weak to do anything but try to roll over onto his side. "My God!" Isidore cried. He begged Van Cauter for mercy. "You're killing me!"

But Van Cauter was blinded by rage. He kicked Isidore all over his head and neck, then ordered another laborer to continue whipping. The laborers lost count. Over 250 times, the nails ripped through Isidore's body. He endured the excruciating pain long past what he thought humanly possible. His loud shrieks dwindled to whimpers as he simply struggled to keep breathing. Finally, the laborers were too exhausted to continue. Van Cauter ordered them to drag Isidore into a hut of the plant, where he chained his legs together so that he couldn't even relieve himself, and abandoned him to his agony.

A day or two later, Van Cauter unchained Isidore and dragged him out to the bush, ordering him to walk to the next village. An inspector named Dorpinhaus was coming to inspect the plantation. He had a reputation for fairness, and Van Cauter didn't want any trouble. But Isidore wasn't able to walk; his back was one open wound. He hid in the bush until he saw the inspector nearby. Then, supporting himself with two sticks, Isidore managed to drag himself toward him. When Dorpinhaus saw his condition, he was horrified. He had his staff bring Isidore by boat to a nearby plantation. But infection set in, and despite the care he received, it was soon clear Isidore would not recover. He asked his caregivers to send a message to his mother, to any priest they could find, and perhaps a judge. "Tell them I have been attacked because I am a Christian. The white man did not like Christians; he did not want me to wear the scapular."

Isidore tried to unite his sufferings with Jesus in his passion, especially with his scourging. Two missionaries heard about what happened and visited him. After he told them his story, they gave him the sacraments and encouraged him to forgive Van Cauter. "I already have," he told them. "If I die, I'll pray for him in heaven."

Isidore suffered in agony from his wounds and infections for six months. Finally, he succumbed to septicemia. It's unknown exactly how old Isidore was when he died, but he was probably in his early twenties. Friends testified to his humble industriousness, and to his joy in sharing his faith with others. Isidore Bakanja was buried as he had lived and died: with his scapular around his neck and his rosary in his hand.

⟨❖⟩

Prayer

Blessed Isidore Bakanja,
you grew up in the midst of injustice and oppression.
Discovering the history of God's love for us,
especially in sending us his Son Jesus,
your whole life was transformed.
You stood up to oppression with courage and dignity.
You refused to betray your faith, your relationship with
    God, your very identity,
even when it cost you your life.
And when you were dying, you forgave the man who
    murdered you.
Help me to treasure the grace of my Baptism.
In these times troubled by prejudice, terrorism, and op-
    pression,
free me from bitterness so that I can forgive those who
    are blinded by hatred.
Help me to stand up for the dignity of every human
    person,
and unite all my sufferings to Jesus's passion and death,
sharing with you in the hope of his glorious resurrection.
Amen.

About Blessed Isidore Bakanja

Born: ca. 1885 in the Belgian-controlled Congo, now the
    Democratic Republic of Congo
Died: August 9 or 15, 1909
Memorial: August 15
Beatified: April 25, 1994, by Pope John Paul II

Patron: While he has not yet been declared a patron
   of particular causes or groups, Isidore could be a
   patron of those who suffer acts of violence and racial
   hatred, who live in Africa, who need to forgive or
   to be forgiven, who suffer persecution for their faith
   in the workplace, who wear the scapular, and who
   want to unite their sufferings to the passion of Jesus.

Notes on His Life

- In 1904, Bakanja left his home village and was employed
  as a stone mason by the government, where he met a
  Christian for the first time: his foreman, Linganga, a recent convert.

- Bakanja received instruction from the Trappist monks,
  who encouraged great devotion to Mary, including wearing the scapular and praying the Rosary.

- Bakanja was baptized May 6, 1906. He was between seventeen and twenty-two years old. His baptismal name was
  Isidore.

- The simple way he lived and witnessed to his faith attracted friends and those he met to the Christian faith.

- Isidore had been a Christian for about three years when he
  was brutally beaten and died for witnessing to his faith.

- After Isidore Bakanja's death, Andre Van Cauter was arrested and spent several years in jail.

Lesser-Known Facts

- The first written document about Bakanja is his baptismal certificate. He was already in his late teens or early
  twenties.

❧ Isidore is often listed as a "catechist and martyr," but he received no training as a catechist. His joy prompted him to share his faith with others.

❧ The process for Isidore's beatification was delayed almost immediately because the Belgian government didn't want negative publicity about its conduct toward Isidore Bakanja, the Church, or the Congolese people.

❧ In 1976, a group of lay catechists in Zaire (now the Democratic Republic of Congo) raised the possibility of Isidore Bakanja's beatification.

In His Own Words

"If the white man beat me, that's his problem, not mine. If I die, I'll pray for him in heaven."

Saint Mary MacKillop

A Bit of Heaven

One of the Sisters spoke emphatically, "But, Mother, what shall we do? You have certainly heard the rumors about the priest. It is said that he is abusing children."

"*It is said. . . . There are rumors. . . .* We must be careful, Sisters. Remember, he is a priest of God."

"Yes, but Mother, the children are *our* main concern."

"You are certainly correct, Sister. The children are foremost. I will go to Father Woods. He will know how we should proceed."

Mother Mary of the Cross went directly to speak with Father Julian Woods, her confidante and cofounder of the Sisters of Saint Joseph of the Sacred Heart. He received her immediately.

"Thank you, Sister Mary, for coming to me. I will inform Bishop Sheil and leave the matter in his hands."

Bishop Laurence Sheil of Adelaide, Australia, took action, and after an investigation had the accused priest sent back to his home diocese in Ireland. However, a backlash would certainly be felt. The priest in question had many friends, and they were determined to make the whistle-blowers pay. As it was, some persons resented Father Woods, who held the office of director of Catholic schools in the diocese, for his strict management of the schools. How better to impress on him their indignation at his intervention than to strike out at his Josephites?

Although he had done the right thing by banishing the abusive priest from Australia, Bishop Sheil now had to endure the wrath of that priest's friends. *Something must be done,* he thought. *I can't deal with all this dissention and keep the diocese running smoothly.*

Mother Mary received notice of the bishop's summons. "Well, His Excellency is requesting my presence at once. He says there is an urgent matter to discuss."

"Do you suppose it is in reference to the exile of the priest?" one of her collaborators suggested.

"Oh, no, that matter is closed. I am sure His Excellency wants to discuss something to do with our various schools. I will set out in the morning."

Any preoccupations Mother Mary might have had were allayed by the cordial welcome she received at the bishop's residence.

"Please, Mother, have a seat. Let me get right to the matter at hand. I would like to see some minor changes in the Josephite rule. . . ."

Immediately uncomfortable, Mother MacKillop sat forward as if to object.

"Mother, please, hear me out. It has come to my attention that difficulties have arisen from your handling of finances. Most of the schools are in considerable debt . . . and disrepair, I might add. And do sit back, Mother. Listen carefully to me. The priests in a number of locations are asking me to intervene in this matter. To assist you, Mother."

"But, Bishop Sheil, I have Father Woods, a very competent man. Why, you yourself have appointed him to various posts of responsibility in the diocese. I'm sure he. . . ."

"Mother, Mother! We both know that Father Woods is a fine man, competent in many areas, but we all know he is somewhat of a visionary, an idea man. I've also heard that he allows a pseudo-mysticism to grow among the Sisters. It is common knowledge that you are the true founder and former of the Sisters of Saint Joseph, and this is why I have called you here, not Father Woods."

"Your Grace, I cannot agree to anything without the approval of Father Woods. We have done this work together."

"You need not consult him, Mother. You will only need to inform him of what I am telling you. As of today, I am assuming direction of the finances of the Josephites and of all their schools and institutions."

"But, Your Grace, you know we mainly serve the poorest students from the poorest families. Certainly it is clear that little money is available in most of our schools. We have chosen to serve the poor, the neediest of God's people."

"And I am sure, Mother, that it is clear to you that I have made a decision. From now on everything will go through me."

"With utmost respect, Your Excellency, I must insist that things remain in our hands. God has entrusted this work. . . ."

"The diocese and its institutions are my responsibility, Mother Mary, and I will be obeyed. You are dismissed. I will expect your letter of compliance."

In dismay Mother MacKillop returned to the sisters' home. She considered and reconsidered the bishop's demand, but could not reconcile his words with what she knew God was asking of her. So she did the only thing she could do, and that was delay. She simply put her trust in Divine Providence.

Soon enough, however, she received not a letter, but a visit from the bishop himself, with several priests. "Call the community together, Sister Mary," the bishop demanded. When the sisters had assembled, the bishop directed Sister Mary to kneel before him. As everyone looked on in dumbfounded silence, Bishop Sheil pronounced the terrifying words. "Because of your disobedience and spirit of rebellion, I excommunicate you from the Church. You are to have nothing to do with the Sisters of Saint Joseph. You are no longer a member of this institute, but are to return to the world simply as Mary MacKillop."

How can this be? She prayed. *My good Lord, how can this happen?* However, in obedience Mary quietly stood up and left the convent. She took up residence with a Presbyterian family with whom she had been friends. Because of this sad event many of the Sisters of Saint Joseph of the Sacred Heart opted to be re-formed into diocesan communities rather than be forced to give up their vocations altogether.

While Mary continued to pray and suffer her fate silently, several other priests were petitioning Rome on her behalf. Meanwhile, God was unfolding his own plan. Bishop Sheil became ill and was not expected to recover. That led him to rethink what he had done, and he lifted the excommunication of Mary MacKillop. Joyfully she was reunited with her sisters. She did not hold a grudge against anyone involved in her suffering, and neither would she allow any of the sisters to speak badly of the bishop or of the priests who had conspired against her. "I feel only a very great love for those who persecuted us," she admitted. Sister Mary did not take her religious name lightly. She was Sister Mary *of the Cross*, and to her this meant she would willingly accept whatever came to her as a share in the saving action of Christ.

Sister Mary busied herself with the work of God. She visited the various schools, hospitals, and homes she had founded. She wrote constantly to the sisters, encouraging them to be prayerful and generous in whatever work they were doing for God's people. She was a person of great hopefulness and perseverance, as well as a gracious and kindly woman. She always had an excuse ready for those who offended her, and a loving motivation for those who exhibited personal failures. It wasn't that Sister Mary was blind or unobservant of those around her, but she preferred to always show the love of God. Once she admitted, "Yes, at present I do have some enemies. God has allowed this. But, they are beloved enemies whom I am sure would rather be my friends if they could only see how things really are."

In the years that followed her great trial, Mary was elected as superior general of her institute. She traveled extensively throughout Australia and New Zealand, beginning many schools and other charitable works. In 1873, Mother Mary MacKillop traveled to Rome to ask for papal approval for the Sisters of Saint Joseph. Pope Pius IX appreciated all she had accomplished and gave his blessing. The constitutions of the congregation were slightly modified regarding poverty, and full authority was placed in the hands of the superior general.

Many young women asked admittance to the Josephites, and everything seemed to be moving ahead. However, in 1885 new conflict arose. The bishops of Australia decided that despite Rome's approval of the new institute and its rules, the religious in their dioceses must be under the direct control of the diocesan bishop, and not of a superior general. Once more Mother Mary MacKillop was removed from any position of governance. After another few stressful years, Rome again set things straight. However, by this time a new superior general had taken office. Mother Mary became her willing and valued assistant. They made great strides in meeting the needs of the Australian people, especially regarding the education of children. No sacrifice was too much for Mary or her beloved sisters.

Over the years, Mother Mary began to have health problems, first with crippling rheumatism and then with a series of strokes that left her hands impaired. Despite these infirmities she was again elected superior general, and she continued in that position until her death in August 1909. As long as she could manage to do so, Mother Mary wrote encouraging letters to her sisters. "Let our life together be like a bit of heaven on earth. No matter what swirls around outside, no matter the humiliations and sufferings, among us there should be only love and charity."

Prayer

Saint Mary of the Cross,
you were a woman of great fortitude and
    heroic charity.
A true daughter of the cross, you willingly bore
    humiliations
and endured injustice in order to accomplish God's will.
You were well aware of the strength that accompanies
    righteousness
and of the graces that flow from persecution.

Now in blessedness, continue your care for all those
who suffer abuse.
Help them turn to the Lord for help and lift up their
hearts in love. Amen.

About Saint Mary MacKillop

Born: January 15, 1842, in Fitzroy, Victoria, Australia
Died: August 8, 1909, in North Sydney, New South
Wales, Australia
Feast Day: August 8
Canonized: October 17, 2010, by Pope Benedict XVI
Patron: Australia, abuse victims

Notes on Her Life

❧ She was born Mary Helen MacKillop, the eldest of eight
children of Scottish immigrants to Australia.

❧ Her family was poor and survived mainly on the wages
made by the children.

❧ Well-educated by her father, at fourteen Mary began work
as a governess.

❧ She met Father Julian Tenison Woods at Portland, Victoria, where she opened a boarding school for girls in
1864.

❧ With two of her sisters, she joined Father Woods to open
a free Catholic school in Penola, South Australia, in
1866.

❧ In 1867 with Father Woods, she founded the Sisters of
Saint Joseph of the Sacred Heart, the first religious order
native to Australia.

- By 1871, 130 sisters were working in forty schools and other works of charity throughout South Australia and Queensland.

- She was buried at Gore Hill in North Sydney.

- Due to popular devotion, her remains were transferred to a memorial chapel in Sydney in 1914.

- The Church accepted as a miracle the cure of Veronica Hopson, who in 1961 was dying of leukemia.

- Mother Mary was beatified by Pope John Paul II in Australia in January 1995.

- In 2009 the cure of Kathleen Evans of lung and brain cancer in the 1990s was recognized as a second miracle, leading to Mother Mary's canonization.

- She is the first Australian canonized saint.

- When she was canonized, there were 1,200 Sisters of Saint Joseph of the Sacred Heart.

Lesser-Known Facts

- Her mother, Flora, drowned on route to help the sisters in Sydney in 1886.

- In 1985 Australian rose growers developed the Mary MacKillop rose.

- The Royal Australian Mint issued a commemorative one dollar coin honoring her in 2008.

- Several films and stage productions have depicted her life.

In Her Own Words

"See how God has protected his work and brought good out of all our crosses. Thus he will ever do if we but put our trust in him and humbly distrust ourselves."

Part II

The Sacraments

Saint Paul

Apostle of Christ Crucified

The young Saul of Tarsus decisively strode through the temple precincts. Stephen, a vocal follower of the New Way, had just been brought before the Sanhedrin, and Saul didn't want to miss the confrontation. He needed to know more about this New Way so he could understand its hold over the minds and hearts of the less educated.

"What right have they," he thought, "to replace the Law that God himself has given us with the claims of some crazy preacher who ended up crucified?" The scandal of it infuriated Saul. These people tarnished the messianic expectations with a false messiah who didn't establish the Kingdom of God, but instead suffered the shameful death of crucifixion. Saul couldn't understand how devout Jews could find the teachings of such a disreputable rabbi compelling.

Originally from Tarsus, Saul had been drawn to Jerusalem by his desire to deepen his knowledge and love for the one true God. He had delighted in studying the Law and had dedicated his life to a close observance of the Law as a Pharisee. He found the claims of this false messiah so disturbing that he even disagreed with his mentor, the revered and wise Rabbi Gamaliel, about what to do. Gamaliel wanted to let the movement die out on its own. Couldn't he didn't see how fast the errors were spreading? Some action should be taken!

Saul shouldered his way through the crowd so he could hear and see everything. Stephen was forcefully making his case, quoting the Scriptures. A part of Saul's mind admired his logic and eloquence. Finally, Stephen shouted, "I see the heavens open and the glory of God revealed, and the Son of Man on the right hand of the Father!"

Saul felt his gut clench at the blasphemy—Stephen was claiming that this rabbi Jesus was equal to God! He shouted out his indignation. "Blasphemy!"

Cries of "stone him!" filled the courtroom. The angry energy of the mob swept away Saul, and even the Sanhedrin.

Some of the younger men took hold of Stephen and led him away to be stoned outside the Temple, which could not be defiled. Saul followed, fiercely glad that something was finally being done to stop these insults against God by those who claimed to believe in him.

When they arrived at the pit, the mob threw Stephen down into it. Everyone scrambled to pick up a rock, to take part in this purge of heresy. The doubts that Gamaliel had planted in Saul prevented him from taking active part, but he showed his approval by watching over the cloaks of his companions.

Saul watched as Stephen fell to his knees and prayed aloud, "Lord, forgive them, for they do not know what they do." And Saul kept watching until the rocks found their mark and Stephen prayed aloud one last time, "Lord Jesus, receive my spirit!" That name again—Saul wanted to eradicate its haunting power from the earth. Yet as Stephen sank to the ground, something about the confident peace on his face disturbed Saul.

He pushed his misgivings aside as he returned his friends' cloaks. "These people are blasphemers, putting this Jesus at the side of God! We need to keep our momentum going. Destroy this New Way!"

Since only the Roman authorities could legally put someone to death, Saul didn't try to re-create Stephen's illegal stoning. Instead, he looked for ways to persecute the followers of Jesus—harassment, prison, physical punishment. For a while, it seemed to work. The name of Jesus was no longer spoken so openly in the Temple, and his followers scattered. Unwilling to see the New Way spread, Saul asked the elders for their unofficial approval to take his campaign against the New Way to nearby Damascus. He joined a caravan and set out on foot. They drew close to Damascus after several days. It was near noon, the sun's hot glare slowing even Saul's grim determination. He *knew* he was right in stopping the spread of this New Way, but during the night Stephen's last cries echoed through his dreams.

Suddenly from out of nowhere, a burst of brilliant light stunned Saul. Eyes dazzled, he lost his balance and fell to the ground. He tried to peer up at the glowing radiance. A figure stood in the sky, at the center of the radiant light, but his eyes couldn't make out the details. And then, the figure stepped forward and Saul glimpsed the face of the man looking down on him. Dark, liquid eyes full of wise compassion looked deep into Saul, past all his fears and defenses. *Those eyes knew him, knew who he was, all he had done, all he longed to be.* A divine gaze, not of justice, but of love. But a gaze tinged with sadness. And then, the light overpowered his sight as the figure spoke. "Saul, Saul, why do you persecute me?"

The words crushed Saul. "Who are you, Lord?" he dared ask.

"I am Jesus, whom you are persecuting."

The world spun around Saul. Gamaliel had warned him, and he had still gotten everything wrong! He lay on the dirt shattered by his own blindness. *Jesus* was the true Messiah, the very Son of God! And he—Saul—had opposed him! For a moment, despair wrestled with Saul's memory of that powerful gaze of love. Then, suddenly, Saul knew that there was one thing he could do.

He raised himself onto his knees. "Lord, what would you have me do?" he asked, looking up to the bright silhouette.

"Get up and go into the city, where you will be told what to do," Jesus replied.

Then the sky darkened; it grew so dark that Saul could see nothing at all. He stayed on his knees—stunned by the revelation he had received. He could hear the voices of his companions, and finally, when one of them tried to lift him to his feet, Saul realized that it was not really dark. He was blind! He had become blind physically, as he had been blind spiritually.

The soul-shattered Saul had to be led by the hand into the city of Damascus. His companions didn't understand what had happened. They hadn't seen Jesus, and they didn't know what to do with this broken man. They brought him to a place where he could stay and left him there.

For three days, Saul struggled to understand his encounter with Christ on the road to Damascus. Saul couldn't eat or drink. His blindness forced him to look closely at the new truths that Jesus had revealed. The Law had been replaced with a Person—the Son of God. That meant his life as a

Pharisee was over. All that Saul had thought important was meaningless in the light of a God who had become man, then died to save all of humanity. Saul hadn't just made a mistake; his whole life was a mistake. Saul was a total failure.

Despair haunted Saul as the meaning of Jesus's words became clearer to him. "I am Jesus, whom you are persecuting." Every time he had harassed and imprisoned a follower of Jesus, he had chained and persecuted Jesus himself. Stephen's death—and his own part in it—would haunt him the rest of his life. The only thing that gave Saul hope was his memory of the glimpse of the face of the Lord Jesus. That timeless, understanding gaze would remain etched forever on Saul's heart.

On the third day, his host interrupted his blind solitude to tell him that a man named Ananias wanted to see him. Saul had had a strange dream of Ananias the night before, but his ordeal had taken so much out of him that he trembled as he stood to greet his visitor.

Ananias laid his hands on Saul's head saying, "My brother Saul, the Lord Jesus who appeared to you has sent me to help you recover your sight and receive the Holy Spirit."

Saul felt something like scales fall from his eyes. He blinked in the dim light—the first light he had seen in three days. An older man stood before him, cautiously waiting. In his desperate need, Saul reached out and grasped Ananias's hand, stiff with reserve. "You are his follower! Will Jesus ever forgive me? What am I supposed to do now, so that the Lord will not abandon me?"

Ananias relaxed his stiff shoulders. "Jesus himself sent me to you. I think he has already forgiven you. He has chosen you to bring his name to both Gentiles and Jews. You know," Ananias added as he looked closely at Saul's gaunt face, "I didn't want to come here. I thought you'd do me harm. But the Lord insisted. He said that your mission will not be easy, and that you will suffer for his name."

A great weight lifted from Saul's chest. "What should I do?" he asked. "How can I begin to follow his Way? I have heard that you baptize new followers with water. Can I be baptized?"

Ananias released Saul's trembling hand. "Let us talk first. You may have questions about Jesus. And, I think you need a good meal."

"Then will you baptize me?" Saul asked intensely.

Ananias smiled. "Gladly, once I am sure you know what it means. For us, Baptism is more than just a purifying ritual. Jesus himself made the waters of Baptism holy when John the Baptist baptized him in the Jordan. Baptism in Jesus doesn't just take away sin. It's a new birth. We're born into a new life, the life that Jesus gives us, life in his Spirit."

Saul suddenly didn't know which of his many questions to ask, and he found it hard to stay on his feet. Ananias guided him to a seat and he began instructing Saul over a meal.

Saul regained his strength, was baptized, and immediately sought to proclaim his newfound faith in Jesus, the crucified and risen Lord. Yet, all did not go smoothly. At first, Saul seemed better at stirring things up than living in harmony. The intensity of Saul's character and his unwavering, sometimes challenging approach to preaching the Gospel became a source of tension in the first Christian communities he lived in. Even when he went to Jerusalem to hear about Jesus from the apostles themselves, he stirred up resentment by his powerful preaching. Finally, the Church in Jerusalem sent him back to Tarsus.

For several years, Saul worked in obscurity in Tarsus, interiorizing and deepening the foundations of his faith and his relationship with his Lord Jesus.

Then, Saul's friend Barnabas visited him and invited him to help minister to the church in Antioch. At an assembly of prayer, the Holy Spirit spoke powerfully, sending Barnabas and Saul as "apostles" to the Gentiles. This was the beginning of Saul's mission as an apostle—a mission that lasted for the rest of Saul's life. Saul began to use his Roman name, Paul, during his missionary journeys.

It is estimated that Paul traveled tens of thousands of miles on foot and by sea as an apostle of his crucified Lord. Both the Acts of the Apostles and his letters list the many sacrifices and dangers Paul faced during his journeys to bring Christ's name everywhere, including imprisonment, stoning, shipwreck, and scourging. But Paul didn't care about his sufferings. His life had become so centered on Jesus that he would write, "For me, life *is* Christ." His biggest concern was for the churches that he had founded and visited, and he offered his sufferings, his "crucifixion with Christ" for their salvation and holiness. His warm affection for his communities and the intensity of his love for Christ nurtured the early church. His letters express that warmth, his gratitude to his many close collaborators, and a "theology in action," for Paul was an innovative thinker as well as a decisive action-taker.

Finally, Paul was arrested during one of the Roman Emperor Nero's persecutions of the Christians. He was not afraid of death, knowing that nothing could separate him from Christ's love. Instead, he was grateful that he could offer himself completely to the One who had died for him. Worn out with a lifetime of service to the Gospel, Paul bowed his head under the sword of the executioner, finally sharing completely in the death and resurrection of his beloved Master.

Prayer

Saint Paul, your heart was filled to overflowing
with the love of the Lord Jesus Christ.
You fully lived your baptism into his death and resurrection,
testifying to the world about Jesus
not just with words and letters, but with your very life
and death.
May the love of Christ overflow into my life,
so that I, too, may witness to the unfathomable love of
Christ
to all whom I meet.
May the fullness of Christ and the power of his love
and purpose
come to fruition in me,
so that I can say with you,
"For me to live is Christ." Amen.

About Saint Paul

Born: ca. 6 B.C., Tarsus or Galilee

Died: ca. A.D. 67, Rome

Feast Days: January 25: Feast of the Conversion of
Saint Paul; June 29: Feast of Saints Peter and Paul

Patron: missionaries, evangelists, writers, public relations professionals, tentmakers, rope makers, Cursillo
movement, Catholic action, protection against hail-
storms and snakes

Common Questions About Saint Paul

How do we know so much about Saint Paul? We have his letters and the Acts of the Apostles. The Acts give us a valuable framework of Paul's life, but Paul's letters reveal the great heart and passion of the apostle.

Did Saint Paul write all the letters attributed to him in the New Testament? Authorship in the days when the New Testament was being written was different from what we understand by authorship today. It was an accepted practice for writers to associate their words with someone else to give their writing authority. Today, Scripture scholars do not agree on the authorship of all of the letters attributed to Saint Paul. About half of the letters are accepted by all scholars as being written by Paul (Romans, Galatians, 1 and 2 Corinthians, Philippians, 1 Thessalonians, Philemon). The scholars who accept only certain letters as written by Paul consider the other letters to have been written by close collaborators, or as summaries of his thought. Early Church tradition supports the Pauline authorship of all the letters. Scripture scholarship has its limits, and ongoing studies continue to reveal new information and insights. All thirteen letters are accepted as being "in the school" of Paul, and, most importantly, all are considered by the Church to be the inspired Word of God.

How can one best describe Saint Paul, whose influence over the Church has been so great that some people erroneously call him the "founder" of Christianity? Jesus Christ is the Founder of Christianity, but he entrusted the spreading of his Church to Saint Paul, who became the missionary par excellence, responsible for Christianity spreading throughout the then-known world. Saint Paul was also a theologian, pastor, spiritual writer, and martyr. His letters sketch the earliest pictures we have of the Church, and give us the language to describe spiritual and theological realities, such as Baptism and life in Christ. But the best description of Paul comes from his own words: "apostle of Jesus Christ."

In His Own Words

"We proclaim Christ crucified, a stumbling block to Jews and foolishness to Gentiles, but to those who are the called, both Jews and Greeks, Christ the power of God and the wisdom of God" (1 Cor 1:23-24).

Saint Cecilia

Singing God's Praises

In the first three centuries after Christ's death and resurrection, Christianity was illegal. We have very few records of early Christian life. Not only was it dangerous to keep records, but those few that were kept were frequently destroyed in the persecutions by the Roman Empire that flared up so unpredictably. Christians were persecuted with varying degrees of ferocity—sometimes ignored, sometimes fined and exiled, sometimes hunted down and martyred. Unknown numbers of followers of Jesus—whether in the thousands or the millions is still debated today— died as martyrs for their faith in Jesus in those first three centuries. The stories and even the names of most of these heroic witnesses have been lost. The catacombs give us the names of some, like Valerian and Tiburtius. For others, like Cecilia, we have a few clues, including the legends that grew up around some of these holy men and women. Cecilia's legend dates back to the fifth century, although she died sometime in the second or third century.

Cecilia was a young woman of a wealthy Roman family. Her father, a pagan, tolerated his wife's Christian faith. Cecilia's mother brought her up as an ardent Christian. In those early ages of Christianity, martyrdom was always a possibility. Commitment to faith was not taken lightly. Yet, in the privacy of her home, under her father's protection, Cecilia had been able to practice her faith secretly, but in peace. Up until now.

Today, Cecilia was to be married—against her deepest desires. Cecilia's heart pounded within her as a servant fixed her hair. She had tried to explain to her father, but although he loved her dearly, he had not understood. She didn't know if he thought her crazy or misguided, but after two or three conversations, he had forbidden her to speak against marrying again. Three months later, he had sternly told her that she was to be married to a well-respected young man named Valerian. When she protested, Cecilia's father had simply turned and walked away.

Cecilia knew why her father didn't understand. After all, he didn't have the gift of faith. But Cecilia greatly struggled with her mother's resistance. Of all people, her mother, who had shared her faith with Cecilia, should understand! Instead, she too had insisted that Cecilia marry, completely dismissing her secret vow. Her mother obviously thought Valerian was a good match. The handsome young man had a reputation for being kind and fair. He was a pagan, but Cecilia's mother thought that he might eventually allow Cecilia to practice her faith quietly.

These were dangerous times for Christians. Only last year, the Bishop of Rome had been put to death. Both Cecilia's mother and the priest she had spoken to had advised submission and prudence. If she lived her faith quietly, no one would be able to tell that she was a Christian. Valerian's paganism would keep her safe.

But Cecilia was not a person who could do things half-way. And she couldn't tiptoe around her husband forever. At some point, she'd have to trust Valerian and tell him. So why not tonight? Was it even fair to marry him without telling him that she was a Christian? Perhaps he wouldn't care. Perhaps he would convert. Or perhaps he would renounce her as his wife and turn her over to the emperor. Cecilia knew she'd be risking her life, but wasn't her life always in God's hands?

Yet, this wasn't just about her being a Christian. Years ago, Cecilia had given herself completely to God, body and soul, by making a vow of virginity. She promised God that she would remain a virgin forever, dedicating her life to Christ. Despite the marriage, Cecilia planned to keep her vow. But she had no idea how to persuade Valerian to respect her vow. Cecilia hadn't slept the past three nights, trying to find the right words.

The servant finished her hair and helped her to dress. It was time!

The wedding ceremony and banquet seemed to drag on forever. Throughout the day's celebration, every time her fear arose, Cecilia renewed her faith. "My Jesus, my true Bridegroom, help me to be faithful to you!" Then suddenly, the wedding feast was over. In candlelight procession, Cecilia and Valerian walked from the house where she had grown up to her new home. In all the celebratory noise, they couldn't talk. But on the way, Cecilia caught Valerian watching her keenly.

They arrived at Valerian's home and went in. Cecilia's servant had already arranged her things. Finally, Valerian and Cecilia were left alone together.

Valerian held out his hand to his beautiful young bride. He didn't know her well, but her reputation was that of a kind, sensible young woman. *Something is wrong,* he thought. *This should have been a happy day for both of us. She's acting like she is happy, and has shown a proper decorum all day, but her smile never reached her eyes.*

Cecilia reached out hesitantly and took his hand, but before he could draw her to himself, she forestalled him, her words rushing out.

"Valerian, I have to tell you something. Something important for you to know about me."

Valerian tensed. He'd been right about her. "Cecilia, I want to get to know you as my wife. Tell me what's been on your mind all day."

"I am a Christian, and I have made a vow of virginity. I'm already promised to God." She held her breath. *What will he do?*

Valerian was stunned and confused. "You are a Christian? What do you mean you are promised to God?"

Cecilia's eyes lit up. He was giving her a chance to explain! "I believe that Jesus Christ is the Son of God, who came down from heaven to share our human life with us. He *died* to save us, to save me, from sin and despair and suffering. I've been in love with him my whole life, and I promised him that I would dedicate my life to him completely. He is my real 'Bridegroom.' It's not that I don't respect you, Valerian. But I'm already promised."

Valerian struggled to make sense of what she said. He couldn't help feeling hurt and betrayed. Yet, the joy on her face made her radiant! "But how can you choose a God you cannot see, over a husband you can see? Is God's love and presence so real to you? More real than I am, standing here before you?" He took a step forward.

For a moment, Cecilia wanted to shrink back. He was angry. Suppose he decided to force himself on her? She took a deep breath, then stepped closer to this man who seemed so sure of himself. His eyes demanded answers, but she could see an undercurrent of something else in them . . . something she couldn't quite identify.

"Yes, this Jesus is as real to me as you are. Just because I can't see him doesn't mean I can't sense his presence, or see the way he works in my life. I hear the melody of his love every day, even though I cannot see his hands or the instrument he plays. He gives my life meaning and he calls me to share in his work. He sends his angels to protect me. He walks beside me. I have nothing to fear from you because he is with me, right now."

As she spoke, Valerian's heart leapt. What was it like to be so sure of something that you would risk everything? He took her by the hand and led her to a couch. "I am deeply moved. Tell me more," he begged. "Teach me about this God-Man whom you call Jesus Christ."

Cecilia's face glowed with joy.

In the next few months, Cecilia had the joy of sharing her faith not just with her new husband, but with his brother Tiburtius as well. When they were baptized, Cecilia thought her heart would burst with happiness. Together, they worked side by side to alleviate poverty and oppression in the city of Rome. The persecution of the Christians was growing fiercer by the day, and the trio found ways to secretly help the Christians who were suffering—visiting the imprisoned and burying the martyrs.

Cecilia's great joy was shaken when her husband and his brother were arrested as Christians. The emperor was especially eager to eliminate the leaders of the Christian faith, and Valerian and Tiburtius were too well known to be ignored. By order of the emperor, after their arrest the two brothers were brought to the arena to die. Their executioner, an officer named Maximus, was also converted and was martyred with them in the arena.

Cecilia tearfully witnessed their deaths. She knew that despite their sufferings, they happily offered their lives to God. But she keenly felt the pain of her loneliness and separation. She worried that she was not worthy to offer her life to Christ, too.

But her fears proved groundless. Shortly after, Cecilia was accused of being a Christian. Brought before the emperor, Cecilia fearlessly proclaimed her faith. Wishing to make an example of her, the emperor ordered her to be suffocated to death in the steam bath in her own home. Soldiers heated the bath and locked her inside. Hours later, long after she should have died, they heard music. Opening the door, they found her alive and singing a hymn of praise to God.

They reported back to the emperor, who ordered Cecilia beheaded. Her executioner struck her neck with a sword two or three times, but either through nervousness or incompetence, he did not kill her outright. Instead, Cecilia suffered intensely for two or three days. As friends and spectators gathered around her, Cecilia, who was unable to speak, wanted to witness to her faith in God. On one hand, she held up one finger to express her faith in her one, beloved God. On the other hand, she raised three fingers to express her faith in the Trinity—Father, Son, and Holy Spirit, one God in Three Persons. With this simple gesture, Cecilia renewed her baptismal faith until she slipped away to receive the inheritance of that faith—the loving embrace of the Father, Son, and Spirit to whom she had witnessed with her entire life.

Prayer

Saint Cecilia,
the melody of God's love surrounded you
and strengthened you in all your trials.
You fearlessly lived your Baptism
and offered your life as a witness
to the triune love of God—Father, Son, and Spirit.
Help us to hear and join in singing
the melody of God's love
to our world. Amen.

About Saint Cecilia

Born: second or third century
Died: second or third century, martyr, in Rome
Feast Day: November 22
Patron: music

Known Facts About Her Life

- Saints Cecilia, Valerian, and Tiburtius really existed and died as Christian martyrs sometime in the second or third centuries.

- By the fourth century, Saint Cecilia was being honored as a martyr; by the fifth century, she was one of the most venerated of the early martyrs.

- Saint Cecilia was probably a wealthy woman because the Church of Saint Cecilia, built in the fourth century and dedicated to her in the fifth century, was probably built on property Cecilia herself donated to the Church.

Lesser-Known Facts

❧ While there is no doubt that Saint Cecilia was a real person who died as a martyr, the legends about her life are from a mid-fifth century text that is not regarded as a reliable historical source, the "Acts of the Martyrdom of Saint Cecilia."

❧ Saint Cecilia has been associated with music from two events in the legends about her: while the musicians played at her wedding, Cecilia sang to God in her heart, and, as the soldiers were trying to suffocate her, Cecilia sang the praises of God.

❧ In the ninth century, Saint Cecilia appeared to Pope Paschal I, who was rebuilding Saint Cecilia's Church and searching for her remains to transfer them to the church. Saint Cecilia asked him to keep looking, telling him that he had been very close to her. Her remains were found and transferred, along with those of Valerian, Tiburtius, and Maximus.

❧ Excavations underneath the twice-restored church have uncovered Cecilia's third-century home, which can be toured today, including the bath where Cecilia was martyred.

Saint Paul Summarizes Saint Cecilia's Life

"Do you not know that all of us who have been baptized into Christ Jesus were baptized into his death? Therefore we have been buried with him by baptism into death, so that, just as Christ was raised from the dead by the glory of the Father, so we too might walk in newness of life" (Rom 6:3–4).

Saint Helena

The Holy Empress

Helena paced the richly furnished room. She was tired from lack of sleep, the turmoil in her mind, and above all, the heartbreak. She had to stop going over in her head what had been done: what she had said, her anguished pleading with Constantine, the yearning in his eyes for her understanding and approval, her failure to prevent the executions. The family tragedies had caused the first serious rift between her and her son. She'd always supported him unconditionally—this beloved son who had shared the painful days of her husband's abandonment and had grown into such a fine and upright man. He was one of the greatest leaders the world had ever known. Helena knew that though Constantine held tremendous power, he tried to balance it with moderation, prudence, and justice. As emperor and the most powerful man in the world, her son had to act in the best interest of the empire. But he was human, and the pull of emotion could unbalance the best of judgments—even an emperor's.

Could she have prevented the deaths of her favorite grandson, Crispus, and her daughter-in-law? Betrayals had consequences, and she couldn't change the past.

"What can I do," she mused to herself. "Something to heal our family, to bring our focus back to Christ and serving the Church." Suddenly her eyes brightened. She knew exactly what she wanted to do.

That night at supper, Helena dined alone with her son, as she had requested. Though lately Helena felt her age more, the resemblance between mother and son was still perceptible: they shared the same energetic determination and the same upright bearing. But Constantine had his father's fiery eyes and dark, curly hair. His manner was a bit stiff now, their recent sorrows and disagreements lingering.

"Son, I've got an idea," Helena broke the silence casually. "I hope you won't object."

Emperor Constantine looked at his mother uneasily. Then as he saw her smile, he relaxed. "I know I will object, Mother. Your ideas are often . . . startling, shall we say?"

"Unexpected is more precise." Helena's smile was so quick her son almost missed it. "It's been safe for some time to travel across the empire, isn't it? I want you to arrange a trip for me . . . to Jerusalem," she said, trying to sound casual.

"What!?" Constantine looked at his seventy-five-year-old mother in disbelief.

"I want to follow in the footsteps of Christ, to go to the actual places where our Savior, the Lord Jesus Christ himself, walked, preached, suffered, and died. It will be a pilgrimage to thank God for his goodness and to ask his blessing on our family and on the empire. And I want to build churches fit to honor those holiest of places. The world today needs to remember the center and core of Christianity—that a humble, self-emptying son of a carpenter died on a cross to save us. Christians must not forget that *he* gives suffering new meaning."

"But you're—" Constantine swallowed the tactless words. Such a journey would be a great sacrifice, even considering the comforts that a mother-empress would be provided with. Such a pilgrimage would separate them, perhaps for years. But Constantine could see that she had made her decision. If he did not arrange the trip, she would find a way to do it on her own. He made one last try.

"It's a brilliant idea. But such a journey will be long and difficult. What if we send a team of architects and they—"

Helena laid her hand on her son's arm. "I want to go myself. This is a pilgrimage I will make for us, for our family."

Constantine looked in her eyes and knew he could not refuse her—not again. "I must be crazy," Constantine muttered, "but I'll do it . . . I'll arrange the trip. You must promise to return safely." When he saw her smile, he knew that somehow, this pilgrimage would make things right between them.

On her journey, Helena practiced the charity for which she had become so well known in Rome: providing for those who were hungry and poor in the villages she passed. But the solitude of the journey also gave her plenty of time to pray and reflect on the journey of her life.

Helena had been raised the daughter of an innkeeper, a humble beginning to a life that would become wound inextricably with the leaders of the Roman Empire. In her early twenties, she met Captain Flavius Julius Constantius (nicknamed Chlorus because of his pale complexion). They fell in love and were married, and Helena soon bore him a son whom she named Constantine. Constantine spent most of his time with her while his father traveled on campaigns, soon rising to the rank of general. When the youthful general returned, he would relive his military adventures with Helena. She grasped his tactics and rejoiced in his victories. And he loved her for it. Helena didn't complain about his long absences, but she missed him intensely when he was gone.

After a particularly joyful reunion with his family, Constantius received a letter from the Emperor Maximian summoning him to Rome. He was to leave as soon as possible. That evening Constantius and Helena went out into the warm night air and talked for hours. The boat was to sail the next day. Time was short, so terribly short.

"You tell Constantine this time," Constantius said huskily. "I can't."

"I will tell him," Helena replied. "Don't look so glum, Constantius; this is good news! Once you find out your new appointment, you will return to us. It won't take long . . . and we'll be waiting here, Constantine and I."

Months passed—longer than Helena had anticipated. Finally, a messenger from the emperor arrived. He seemed uneasy when he entered the room, and Helena, expecting Constantius rather than a messenger, immediately stood up.

"What is it?"

"I have a message for you," he stammered. "The Emperor Maximian has appointed Constantius his 'Caesar,' to assist him in governing the western part of the Empire—Britain, Gaul, and Spain."

Helena's fear changed to joy, though a part of her mind noted that it was odd that the messenger remained so reluctant and uneasy. "When can I expect Constantius to arrive home?" Her mounting excitement turned to puzzlement as the messenger hesitated again.

"He is not coming alone," he mumbled. "The emperor insisted that, in keeping with his new position, General Constantius marry the emperor's stepdaughter, Theodora. One does not say 'no' to the emperor. The divorce was granted quickly, and Constantius and Theodora are already married." He mumbled his last words. "They'll arrive here in less than two months."

"I must go away," she said, too stunned to say anything else.

"And Constantine must await him here—it's his father's orders," the messenger added.

"I must go *alone*," she murmured brokenly.

How long did it take for the emptiness in her heart to become bearable? Helena herself did not know. She spent the next fifteen years quietly, following from afar the affairs of the new Caesar and those of her son, who was also rising politically. In 305, Constantius become Caesar Augustus— Emperor of the West. He immediately called Constantine to his side to inherit his title. When Constantius died only a year later, Constantine was acclaimed Caesar Augustus by his father's soldiers. But other claimants vied for the imperial throne. Constantine waged one battle after another until he met his biggest rival, Maxentius, who had troops greatly out- numbering his own. The day before battle, Constantine saw a brilliant light in the sky, shaped like a cross. A voice told him, "By this sign you shall conquer." It was the sign of the God of the Christians. The following day, at the Milvian Bridge outside Rome, Constantine won a complete victory. And the new Caesar Augustus became fascinated by Christianity.

For 300 years, Christians had suffered scorn, misunder- standing, contempt, and barbarous persecution . . . and their religion had not only survived, but grown. The Christ of Galilee held a deep fascination for those seeking truth, meaning, and an upright way of life. Finally, the Master's love touched the emperor himself. Constantine published the Edict of Milan, not only freeing Christians from persecution, but also ensuring their legal rights and the return of their property seized in persecution.

Having secured the western empire at last, Constantine invited Helena to join him at Rome, treating her with the same affection that he'd always had for her. Her lonely exile was finally over!

Helena was happy to be reunited with her son, but even the honors he wanted to pour upon her couldn't heal her heart from the loss and abandonment she had suffered all those years ago. At first, she was curious about her son's enthusiasm for Christianity, but then she herself became intrigued. She found something captivating about this Jesus, who taught humility, purity, the dignity of every person, and love of one's neighbor as testimony to love for God. But even more than that, Helena wondered about Jesus's suffering and death, which the recent Christian martyrs so gladly shared in. Was it possible that Jesus could do what no one else could— heal her broken heart and give meaning to all her pain and suffering?

Helena was baptized a Christian at the age of sixty-three, and the city of Rome quickly fell in love with the impetuous, gracious lady. Constantine showered extraordinary honors and privileges on her, even placing the treasury of the empire at her disposal. The Empress Mother dipped into it to give alms, not just from a distance, but personally to the people of Rome who were poor, sick, enslaved, or occupied with hazardous work, such as the soldiers and miners. She also used funds from the treasury to build magnificent churches in Rome. Helena focused on doing good and avoided politics, apart from supporting her son. Constantine was extraordinarily capable, even reuniting East and West into one empire.

But then the worst crisis of all had come. After reuniting the entire empire, Constantine had to deal with factions within his own family who attempted to tear it apart. The victims included not only those who had been executed, but the truth itself. Heartbroken, Helena feared above all the harm it had done to her son. This pilgrimage was as much for him as for her.

Finally arriving in the Holy Land, Helena herself directed the efforts to find and restore the holy sites. She took great comfort walking in the footsteps of Jesus. Perhaps she didn't realize how closely she was following the crucified Master— she carried her sorrows with her to Jerusalem. But there she finally found peace, uniting her sufferings to those of Christ on the cross.

Working with Bishop Macarius of Jerusalem, she restored the holy sites that she could, honoring their sacred history by building at least two magnificent churches. She continued to give of herself to those in need, often serving others with her own hands. After several years in the Holy Land, Helena started her return journey, but she traveled slowly, building churches or providing for their construction wherever needed.

The frail Mother Empress finally rejoined her son, but she had greatly aged. She died in A.D. 330, with Constantine at her side. Helena joyfully went to meet her crucified Lord, who had filled the emptiness in her life with overflowing peace.

Prayer

Saint Helena,

you came to know Christ late in your life,

yet you decisively embraced the Christian life,

allowing the Holy Spirit to lead you to follow in the footsteps of Jesus.

You discovered how to unite your sufferings to Jesus on the cross.

Grant me a deep appreciation

for the mysteries of the suffering, death, and resurrection of Jesus.

Help me to become as you were:

a fearless witness to Christ in the world,

whether I am in a position of power or vulnerability.

Amen.

About Saint Helena

Born: ca. 246–250, possibly at Drepanum in Bithynia, Asia Minor

Died: ca. 329, possibly at Constantinople (now Istanbul, Turkey)

Recognized as a saint not only by the Roman Catholic Church but also by the Eastern Orthodox, Oriental Orthodox, Anglican, and Lutheran communities.

Patron: archeologists, converts, difficult marriages, divorced people

Saint Helena is remembered especially on September 14, the Feast of the Triumph of the Cross, because she built churches at sacred sites in the Holy Land, and for the legend that she discovered the true cross.

Facts and Legends:
Discovering the True Helena

- We know little of Helena's life until her sixties.

- Helena was most probably the humble daughter of an innkeeper, although she has sometimes been confused with another Helen, the daughter of a king of Colchester in Britain.

- We don't know how or where Helena met Constantius. His divorcing her for political purposes was not unusual at the time.

- Before the Edict of Milan, both Constantius and Constantine were kindly disposed toward Christians and avoided persecuting them.

- While some legends speak of Helena converting Constantine, earlier sources affirm that Constantine introduced his mother to Christianity, who embraced it more enthusiastically than her son. Constantine grew in his faith throughout his life and was baptized shortly before his death.

- It is not known why Constantine executed his own son Crispus (son of his first wife), and his second wife, Fausta—whether for political or moral reasons. One source indicates that Helena may have indirectly caused Fausta's death because she told Constantine that Fausta had falsely accused Crispus. Two in-laws were also executed, most likely for political reasons.

- The earliest sources about Helena record that she visited the Holy Land and restored several sacred sites, building at least two churches: the Church of the Nativity in Bethlehem, and the Church of the Ascension on the Mount of Olives. They do not mention her discovering the true cross.

⚜ The true cross was discovered during Emperor Constantine's reign. About sixty years after Saint Helena's death, two sources name her as the discoverer of the true cross.

⚜ Whether Saint Helena or her son discovered the true cross, it is certain that Saint Helena's personal devotion led her to restore several sacred sites. It is possible she gave her son the idea to search for the true cross.

Saint Paul Expresses Helena's Devotion to the Cross

"May I never boast of anything except the cross of our Lord Jesus Christ, by which the world has been crucified to me, and I to the world" (Gal 6:14).

Saint Lorenzo Ruiz

"Accidental" Martyr

Lorenzo's heartbeat hammered so hard he thought it would push through his chest. *That would put an end to my terror,* he thought irrationally. He tried to turn away from the horror of the water torture Father Antonio was enduring, but the Japanese soldier at his side forced Lorenzo to watch.

His panicked gaze met Father Antonio's. Pain gripped the priest's face, yet all he could do was grunt in agony after the water had been forced out of him. Was this the fourth or fifth time they had put the tall, frail priest through the inhuman torture? A year in prison hadn't improved any of the prisoners' health, but Father Antonio, the superior of their mission, had weakened most. He wouldn't survive much longer.

And then it would be his turn. They hadn't bothered to question him, just assumed Father Antonio spoke for him as well. *I am not a priest, nor a missionary! I didn't want to come here! I was not planning to convert anybody. I was just trying to avoid being executed. I don't want to die like this!*

Another companion, Lazaro—a layman like himself—huddled in a corner, unable to watch. He had already said that he would renounce his faith to save his own life. Lorenzo desperately wanted to join him, despite the shame. Physical terror made every nerve in his body scream for him to flee. *What can I do?*

Looking around, Lorenzo beckoned to one of the translators, a Portuguese man named Carvalho. As Lorenzo waited for him to come closer, his soul twisted with a combination self-loathing and fear. But he couldn't help himself. He had to know. *Was there a way out of this?*

"I want to speak to you privately," Lorenzo said. Carvalho waited impassively. Lorenzo took a deep breath, and over the pounding of his heart, whispered the terrible question. "If I apostatize, can my life be spared?" He looked down, hating the cowardice that prompted him even to ask such a question. Finally, he glanced up to see Carvalho studying him.

"You'll have to ask the judges," Carvalho said, no pity in his voice. A soldier called him away, and without a backward glance, Carvalho walked away out of the room. The terrible weight of fear, and the choice being forced upon him, pressed Lorenzo so heavily that he backed up against the wall.

Lorenzo had been preparing himself for this moment since they had first been captured a little over a year ago. But witnessing Father Antonio's torture horrified him past reason, past anything! How could he not give in to the demands of the Japanese that he renounce his faith, his Church, his God? What good would he do by choosing death? His wife and children would never know why he didn't come back to them; they would never even know he'd died. Surely, it would be better to pretend to renounce Christianity and stay alive. Didn't he have a duty to his family?

The pounding in Lorenzo's heart eased slightly. Staying alive was all he wanted. There was nothing wrong with that.

Then Lorenzo looked back at Father Antonio, lying stripped and helpless on the ground, and his heart broke. *I am not brave enough to suffer and die for Christ, but am I really capable of such a betrayal? They are my brothers . . . Christ is my Brother!*

Until recently, Lorenzo would never have questioned himself or God. He had been born near the beginning of the seventeenth century in the Philippines in Binondo, a village designed to keep the Chinese Christians outside the wall the conquering Spaniards built around Manila. His father was Chinese, his mother Filipino. Lorenzo had been raised as a Catholic and served as an altar boy and later, as a member of the Holy Rosary confraternity. Educated at the Dominican schools, Lorenzo took on the profession of a scribe, writing out official documents by hand, a much-needed service when the majority of the population couldn't read or write.

Lorenzo had been blessed not just with a good trade, but also with a beautiful wife and three children—two sons and a daughter. How much he missed his family now! But there was no way to go back. Lorenzo had fled his home because he had been accused of being involved in the murder of a Spaniard. As a mestizo—a son of both the conquered Filipino people and the suspect Chinese—Lorenzo had doubted he would get a fair trial from the Spanish authorities. Certain that he would be convicted and hung, he felt his only chance to avoid execution was to flee the country and any other place where the Spaniards could find him.

The superior of the Dominicans, Father Domingo Gonzalez, had offered him the opportunity to flee on a ship secretly leaving the Philippines. Lorenzo had been so grateful for an escape, he had not pressed for information about the ship's secret destination. Only after they embarked had he discovered that their boat was on a forbidden missionary expedition to Japan. They were making no stops on the way where it would be safe for Lorenzo to disembark—all the territories were occupied by Spaniards who could be looking to capture him. Lorenzo had chosen to put his future in the hands of the uncertain Dominican mission to Japan, rather than almost certainly be put on trial and hanged for murder.

His companions on this clandestine mission knew what they were getting into, but Lorenzo had not known how risky it was. All of them, however, were surprised by the quick vigilance of the Japanese. Within a week of their arrival in Okinawa, they had been picked up and imprisoned by the authorities on suspicion of being Christian. They had languished in prison for over a year, where Lorenzo had grown close to his companions.

Tall and gentle, Dominican Father Antonio Gonzalez was the group's superior. The French priest, Father Guillaume Courtet, was in his mid-forties; Father Miguel de Aozaraza, a few years younger, was from Spain. Both were Dominican priests who had volunteered for this mission. Father Vincente Shiwozuka de la Cruz was a Japanese priest who had volunteered to guide them in Japan. During the mission he had joined the Dominicans and taken his vows. The other layman in the group was also Japanese, Lazaro Kyoto. Lazaro had been expelled from Japan for being a leper, but he had risked returning so that he could help guide the missionaries in their efforts to minister to the persecuted Catholics in Japan.

A few days ago they had been split into two groups, with Fathers Guillaume, Miguel and Vincente taken to Nagasaki

ahead of them. Just this morning Lorenzo, Lazaro, and
Father Antonio had arrived here in Nagasaki, and Lorenzo
had caught a glimpse of the infamous Nishazaka Hill where
thousands of Japanese Catholic martyrs had died, witnessing
to their faith in Jesus.

Immediately, they had been taken before several judges,
who told them that their other companions had already apos-
tatized. Lorenzo suspected that the judges were just trying to
put more pressure on them, but Lazaro had immediately
given in to the threats. He said he would reject his faith if his
life was spared. The judges had been pleased and Lazaro
relieved. But he had been kept there to witness Father
Antonio's terrible torture.

Now, the soldiers dragged a collapsed Father Antonio
away. Lorenzo waited for them to seize him, but instead, they
forced Lazaro into position, telling him bluntly that he would
not be spared the terrible torture because they wanted any
information he might have. Lorenzo shuddered at Lazaro's
screams.

Lord Jesus, Lorenzo prayed. *I am weak and afraid. Free
me from my fear. I still don't understand why you have brought
me here, but give me the strength to choose to stand witness to
you, to proclaim you not only through my life, but also through
my death, if that's what you will.* Lorenzo's heart was still
pounding, but a sudden deep conviction filled his heart with
peace. He was no longer torn by indecision.

The soldiers finally believed Lazaro's babbling and took
him to the next room to question him. The soldiers turned to
take Lorenzo just as Carvalho returned. Without allowing
Carvalho to speak, Lorenzo said, "What I asked you before,
I said without knowing what I was saying. I am a Christian,
and I profess it until the hour of my death. For God I shall
give my life." Then he added, "Although I didn't come to

Japan to be a martyr but because I could not stay in Manila, as a Christian and for God I shall give my life."

Carvalho watched as the soldiers forced Lorenzo to undergo the same torture as Father Antonio. They repeated the agonizing procedure time after time. During a break, a guard stood over Lorenzo and looked down on him—naked, soaked, and seizing up with pain. "Renounce your faith, and we'll stop! You can save yourself from all of this if you apostatize!" Lorenzo did not have the strength to speak but slowly shook his head. They propped him up and began again.

Finally, they dragged Lorenzo to a prison cell near Father Antonio and Lazaro. Separated only by thin walls of wood, they could speak to each other. The other three priests were also imprisoned there. All of them suffered terribly—the three priests who had arrived first had already endured several days of torture. They were too weak to stand and could barely speak, but they encouraged each other through the long night and following day. The other prisoners, the guards, and the translators caught parts of their conversations and were amazed at their courage and joy—they even teased one another wryly about their sufferings. That night, Lorenzo pondered in a new light the meaning of the sacred words he'd so often heard: "I live by faith in the Son of God, who loved me and gave himself for me" (Gal 2:20).

A day later, Father Antonio, Lazaro, and Lorenzo were tortured again. Father Antonio was soon sent back to his cell because of his weakened state. Lorenzo was brought to speak before the judges one last time. If he had any desire to escape torture and death, this was his chance. But the grace of God had transformed Lorenzo from a man who fled from accusations to one who fearlessly defied his judges.

They pressed him. "If we grant you life, will you renounce your faith?"

Without any hesitation, Lorenzo answered, "Never! I am a Christian, and I shall die for God. For him, I would give a thousand lives, if I had them. Do with me as you please."

Lorenzo's complete commitment of his life to God did not ease the physical pain he underwent, but gave him the strength to endure it. That night, Father Antonio died. Lazaro, who had once again been tortured and imprisoned with them, begged for forgiveness from his companions. They gave it gladly.

The rest of the week passed in a blur of suffering, except for Lazaro publicly renewing his profession of faith. Not one of them wavered again, despite their severe sufferings.

On September 27, 1537, the five men were publicly paraded on horseback to Nishazaka Hill, gagged so they couldn't preach. Five gallows had been raised with five pits dug beneath them. They were hung upside down from the gallows, faces just above the foul bottom of the pit. This excruciating form of execution could last for days, but after three days, the authorities decided to hurry their deaths. On September 29, they were taken down. The three priests were found still alive and were beheaded. Lorenzo and Lazaro had already entered eternity.

At the supreme moment of crisis, the grace of God transformed the seemingly unremarkable Lorenzo Ruiz into a heroic witness who freely offered his life for Christ.

Prayer

Saint Lorenzo,
you were an ordinary husband and father
whose life seemed unremarkable.
But at your moment of truth,
the graces God had showered on you throughout
    your life
bore fruit.
Instead of giving in to fear,
you generously offered your life to God
a thousand times over.
Give us the spirit of faith
to recognize there are no "accidents" with God.
Like you, may we discover the love God offers to us
in our ordinary lives and in the sacraments,
so that, freed from fear,
we can witness at every moment
to Christ's love for us and for every person. Amen.

About Saint Lorenzo Ruiz

Born: ca. 1610, Binondo, Manila, Philippines
Died: September 1637, Nagasaki, Japan
Memorial: September 28
Canonized: October 18, 1987, by Pope John Paul II
Patron: the Philippines, Filipino and Chinese youth

Notes on His Life

✿ Lorenzo may have been born as early as 1600, but certainly by 1610; he was born of a Chinese father and Filipino mother, and raised Catholic. We know little about him because most of his life was so ordinary.

❧ The few facts we know about Lorenzo come from the eyewitness accounts of his trial and death, or from the testimony of the Dominicans who knew him in Manila.

❧ Did Lorenzo commit murder, or witness it, or was he falsely accused? At his trial, he simply speaks of a quarrel. Whatever the case, Lorenzo probably feared injustice because he was a member of the conquered Filipino people. His Chinese heritage would have only made the situation worse, since at the time, the Spanish saw the Chinese as rivals and potential enemies.

❧ Lorenzo's fidelity to his faith is all the more astonishing because he did not seek to be a missionary or a martyr, but was simply running from trouble.

❧ The kinds of extreme torture that Lorenzo and his companions underwent were so horrible that simply the threat of them caused many Catholics to renounce their faith.

❧ Lorenzo Ruiz is the first canonized Filipino saint.

Lesser-Known Facts

❧ We don't know whether Lorenzo died on September 28 or 29.

❧ One of the translators at Lorenzo's trial was the Jesuit priest Cristobal Ferreira, who had renounced his faith several years earlier after lengthy torture. Almost twenty years later, Father Cristobal Ferreira publicly reclaimed his faith and underwent extreme torture again, this time dying as a martyr.

 The two translators present at their trial and torture—Antonio Carvalho and Pedro Rodrigues—were so impressed with each martyr's courage and faith that within two months they secretly wrote eyewitness accounts and smuggled them to the outside world.

 Within three months, the Dominican priests in Manila and Lorenzo's family found out about the martyrdom of Lorenzo and his companions.

His Last Words

"I am a Christian, and I shall die for God. For him, I would give a thousand lives, if I had them."

— To his judges before his martyrdom

Saint Thomas Aquinas

Humble Giant

The solid, well-built man with slightly balding head and gentle eyes sighed as he put down his quill and stood to his full, imposing height. He looked down on the parchment he had finished. Thomas Aquinas was one of the most respected and acclaimed scholars of his day. Yet his was a humble genius, and today it was troubled. The prestigious University of Paris had asked him to answer a scholarly question about the mystery of the Eucharist, a question that divided students and faculty. Thomas was a serene man whose depths were stirred in his meditations and prayers, but rarely by the conflict and upheaval surrounding him—whether political or academic. Yet, now he was troubled by such strong feelings of inadequacy! He was well aware that, despite his years of study and gifts of intellect, he could never really understand this divine mystery. Had he done the question justice? How could he write worthily of Jesus's presence in the Most Holy Eucharist? He knew only one way to resolve his inner turmoil.

Decisively, he picked up the parchment and carried it with him to the chapel. There, Thomas laid it at the foot of the crucifix and went to his usual place of prayer. He always offered his studies and teachings to the Divine Master, but today, he offered his writing with a special intensity. "Lord Jesus Christ, I humbly beg of you, if what I have written of this most holy Mystery is true, say so. But if it is not, please stop me from going further."

As Thomas fell deeper into adoration, he didn't notice Friar Reginald follow him into the chapel. Reginald was Thomas's confrere, companion, confessor, and collaborator. He knew that Thomas was troubled by the university's request. Thomas of Aquinas had one of the finest minds the Church would ever have, but he was also the humblest man Reginald had ever known. How had the second cousin of the emperor, raised in privilege and academia, remained so humble? Reginald thought back on what he knew of Thomas.

Thomas was born to Count Landulf and Countess Theodora of Aquino, and sent as a young boy to study with the monks at Montecassino, a nearby Benedictine monastery. It was always understood that one day he might become not only a Benedictine monk but also the abbot of the great monastery, wielding not just spiritual authority but political power as well. The monks must have recognized his great intellect, because they recommended to his father that he continue his studies at university. At fourteen, Thomas began studying at the University of Naples, but unlike many of the students, Thomas continued to live a simple, devout life. There he eventually met the Dominicans and felt drawn to enter their order, but they told him to wait because they suspected that he'd have to face great resistance. It would be considered a disgrace for a nobleman of Thomas's stature to enter such a humble order.

For three years Thomas waited, continuing his studies and nurturing his vocation. At the age of nineteen, he finally entered the Dominican order and was overjoyed to receive the rough white woolen tunic and black cloak that distinguished the followers of Dominic. His family, however, were dismayed by the disgraceful news. His mother sent two of Thomas's brothers to waylay him and bring him back to the family's castle. There, they forcibly removed his treasured habit and imprisoned him for more than a year, trying to convince him to leave the Dominicans.

But Thomas proved true to his vocation. Despite the isolation, physical hardships, and unrelenting pressure from his entire family, he was an unruffled prisoner—except when his brothers stooped to the low tactic of bringing in a prostitute to tempt him against chastity. Thomas picked up a burning brand from the fireplace and chased her out. Gradually, he persuaded several family members to his side. His imprisonment grew easier when his sisters started smuggling books to him, and Thomas could continue his theological and philosophical studies as if he were at university. His family finally caved in—whether because of Thomas's stubbornness or pressure from the Church, Reginald would never know—and allowed him to escape. Thomas was let down in a basket from his prison tower.

Reginald smiled to himself as he tried to picture the solidly built Thomas crammed into a basket. How eagerly the Dominicans welcomed Thomas back! But even after Thomas made his vows, influential family members continued to insist that this young man leave the Dominicans. But Thomas remained firm in his conviction that God had called him to be a Dominican. Thomas then began his studies under the great Dominican teacher Albert the Great. Although Thomas advanced quickly, outpacing the other students, he continued to be so quiet that he gained not only the reputation of being stupid, but also the nickname, "the dumb ox." Albert didn't immediately recognize the treasure studying under him until a student slipped him some of Thomas's notes. The next day, Albert gave Thomas a rigorous oral test in front of the class, attacking his arguments from every possible direction. At the end, marveling at Thomas's responses, he said publicly to the class, "I tell you, the lowing of this 'ox' will be heard around the world." After that, Albert took Thomas aside to tutor him personally. He also pushed Thomas to start teaching the other students, and to speak out. The other students quickly discovered that Thomas's summaries were not only shorter, but often better thought out and more easily understood than the lessons of their teachers.

At the Dominican friary, Thomas stood out as much for his simple, unaffected humility as for his intellectual gifts. He clearly put others ahead of himself and carried his conviction into both action and attitude. Once, when he was reading aloud for the community in the refectory, another friar "corrected" his Latin pronunciation. Immediately accepting the observation, Thomas repeated the faulty pronunciation, making what he knew to be an obvious blunder. Asked later why he had done it, Thomas answered, "It matters little whether a syllable is short or long—but it matters much . . . to obey."

Of all Thomas's brothers, Reginald knew how impressive Thomas's scholastic achievements and writings were. He not only carried out the role of teacher at the university—demanding in itself—but was usually writing and working on several other projects as well. He was in the middle of the greatest synthesis of the Catholic faith ever written, his *Summa Theologiae*, and he eagerly listened to the questions of the day so he could respond to them. In addition, Thomas was frequently called on to consult with the great men of his time—the pope, King Louis IX, and other scholars.

And yet, Reginald mused, here he was, wondering if he was worthy to write about the Eucharist. Reginald shook himself, clearing his head of the distracting riddle of his friend's character so he could pray. Suddenly, he heard a voice. Looking up, he saw a vision of Jesus standing on the manuscript that Thomas had placed at the foot of the crucifix. Jesus spoke to Thomas, "You have written well of the sacrament of my Body." Thomas's absorption in prayer deepened, and his body slowly levitated—lifting several feet from the ground. Reginald glanced at the other friars praying in the chapel. From their bewildered expressions, he knew that they were seeing what he was.

Reginald had suspected that Thomas received extraordinary experiences in prayer, but he was astonished to witness one. Some time later, Thomas sank gradually to the ground. Eventually he finished praying, and, as if nothing had happened, walked over to the crucifix and picked up the parchment. Reginald followed him out of the chapel. Thomas was often a bit preoccupied, but today he quickly became aware of Reginald's footsteps.

Thomas turned back and held out the parchment. "Doubts resolved?" Reginald probed. Thomas flashed a glance at him. For all his purity of heart and frequent abstractions, Thomas could be very perceptive. His curiosity changed to dismay as he read Reginald's expression, and he flushed.

"Please," he begged Reginald, "don't tell anyone."

Reginald nodded. "A couple other friars were there. I don't think they'll keep quiet, even if I ask them to. But, Thomas, aren't you happy?"

"I'm at peace," Thomas admitted. "Now I can focus my attention on other concerns."

"But Jesus *said*—"

"It's all grace, Reginald. It's all gift. Everything I do—it's because God has blessed me. There's no special merit in it. I am happy and relieved that I've been useful."

"Useful!" sputtered Reginald. But Thomas smiled and sped his steps, leaving Reginald behind holding the precious parchment.

Thomas continued to tirelessly respond to the needs of the Church and of his beloved Dominican Order. His entire life was spent praying, teaching, preaching, and writing. He frequently traveled to settle difficult questions or disputes. A close adviser to several popes, he served at the papal Curia, as well as universities all over Europe, including Naples, Paris, Cologne, and Bologna. When Pope Clement IV appointed him archbishop of Naples in 1265, Thomas begged to be excused, desiring always to remain a humble Dominican friar and to dedicate his energies to wrestle with the great questions of faith.

His preaching regularly drew large crowds, as his homilies were known to be simple, lucid, and eloquent. He devoted all his energies to seeking to understand and explain always better the Catholic faith.

One day after Thomas had completed the section of the *Summa Theologiae* on the Eucharist, Jesus spoke to him again in prayer. "You have written well of me, Thomas; what reward can I give you?" Thomas answered, "Yourself, O Lord; nothing but yourself!"

Thomas's untiring service gradually took its toll on his health. Then, on December 6, 1273, Thomas had a profound, life-changing experience in prayer. He never revealed what happened, but he stopped writing—something he had never done before. The friars, concerned about him, urged Reginald to approach Thomas. After some days, Reginald encouraged

Thomas to continue his writing. Thomas told him simply, "I can't." Reginald pressed him. "But you haven't finished your *Summa Theologiae*! Your work is for God's glory and the world's—"

Thomas interrupted him. "I can do no more. Such secrets have been revealed to me that all I have written and taught seem to be just a handful of straw." He never offered any further explanation, but began preparing for death.

Early in the year 1274, Pope Gregory X summoned him to the general council at Lyons, and despite his great fatigue, Thomas set out for Lyons. He never made it. On the way, he suffered a head injury in an accident, which may have caused a blood clot on his brain. He stopped at the house of his niece, then, when he realized he was dying, he sought shelter in the nearby Cistercian abbey of Fossanova.

Though he knew he was dying, Thomas honored the monks' request to comment on the Song of Songs from his bed. Finally, he had no strength to continue. He asked Reginald to hear his confession and give him Viaticum. At dawn, on March 7, 1274, while praying aloud one of his hymns to Jesus in the Eucharist, Thomas surrendered his soul to God.

Thomas had finally received the reward he had asked for: "Nothing but Yourself, Lord."

Prayer

Saint Thomas,
you humbly remained true to your vocation to preach
the Gospel
through family opposition, imprisonment, and misguided
admiration.

Your fidelity bore fruit in your prayer and your writings.
Your reasoned and faith-filled approach to philosophy
    and theology
still guides the Church today.
Share with us your own gratitude for the Eucharistic
    mystery:
a sacred banquet
in which we receive Christ himself,
renew our memory of his suffering and dying for us,
and rejoice in the promise of future glory of everlasting
    union with God,
which you now enjoy. Amen.

About Saint Thomas Aquinas

Born: ca. 1225, at his family's castle Roccasecca, near
    Aquino in what is now Italy
Died: March 7, 1274, Fossanova, Italy
Feast Day: January 28
Canonized: July 18, 1323, by Pope John XXII
Declared Doctor of the Church: 1567, by Pope Pius V
Patron: students, schools and universities, thunderstorms

Notes on His Life

- Thomas was born into nobility around the year 1225. He had several brothers and sisters.

- During the time his family tried to prevent him from becoming a Dominican by imprisoning him, Thomas influenced at least two of his siblings: his worldly sister Marotta became a cloistered nun and eventually abbess of her community; his married sister Theodora, a countess, became known for a holiness unusual for her status.

- Later, Thomas wrote about the importance of a young person's freedom to follow his or her vocation to religious life.

- When asked what was the greatest grace he had received, Thomas said that it was to have understood every page he ever read.

- Thomas's early mentor, Albert, became Thomas's close collaborator and friend throughout his life.

- Friar Reginald of Piperno became his friend, confessor, and collaborator around 1260.

- Thomas dictated most of his works, sometimes to four secretaries simultaneously. His writings fill more than twenty volumes today.

- He wrote beautiful Eucharistic hymns that are still used today (such as the *Tantum Ergo*).

Lesser-Known Facts

- Thomas was not a boring or isolated academic; he used new resources and an innovative style of teaching and writing to address the questions of his day brilliantly.

- Accuracy, brevity, and completeness best characterize the style of Thomas's works. One of his great accomplishments was to systematize theology.

- One of the ways Thomas Aquinas shaped theology and philosophy is his teaching that the true relationship between faith and reason is not one of opposition, but of a natural harmony.

- If Thomas had accepted Pope Clement IV's appointment as archbishop of Naples, we probably wouldn't have the *Summa Theologiae* today.

- Even during his life, a few academics had questioned the orthodoxy of a small portion of his writings. But he was so humble, he wasn't drawn into controversy—he submitted to the authority of the Church without question. Some disputes continued after Thomas died, but later his writings were declared free of error, and he is considered the greatest theologian of the Church.

- At the Council of Trent, the council fathers used only three books: the Bible, the decrees of the popes, and Thomas's *Summa Theologiae*.

In His Own Words

"Lord Jesus Christ, I pray that the fiery and honey-sweet power of thy love may detach my soul from everything under heaven, so that I may die from love of thy love, who, out of love for mine, did'st die upon the tree of the cross. Amen."

Saint Elizabeth Seton

"God Is With Us"

The raw November wind whistled through the cracks in the damp stone walls of the quarantine building as the gracious woman sat in a corner and wrote in her journal, watching over her husband and daughter. Elizabeth smiled at eight-year-old Anna as she started to jump rope, using the piece of cord that had tied her belongings together. She skipped over to her father, who lay coughing on his bed. Elizabeth's smile faded. She was finding it harder to hide her anxiety for her husband, whose cough had grown so much worse in the past few days.

Elizabeth and her handsome husband had come to Italy hoping that the warm Italian sun would heal—or at least slow—his tuberculosis. Instead, officials in Livorno had quarantined them in a dank, unheated building because they feared Will might be carrying yellow fever. The unhealthy conditions had sped her husband's decline. His good friends, the Filicchis, provided a bed and sent food, but it wasn't enough.

Will coughed again and called, "Betty!" Instantly Elizabeth was at his bedside. "Let's say our service," murmured the sick man. "I'll feel less chilled afterward."

As she took up her worn prayer book and called Anna to kneel with her beside the bed, the young wife marveled anew at the religious transformation that had taken place in her husband. Will had hardly ever gone to church until just a few months ago. His lack of interest in religion had been the only real cloud in their joyous and devoted relationship. Elizabeth's faith had sustained her through their recent difficulties, and she had grieved that Will didn't share the strength and peace of faith. Now that Will Seton had truly turned to his Savior, Elizabeth's deep sorrow at his illness was mixed with a deep joy—even while suffering the privations of quarantine.

Devoutly, the little Episcopalian family held their daily prayer service, while the wind continued to howl through the fissures in the old stone walls. November merged with December as the dying husband and father waited for clearance. In her diary, Elizabeth took comfort in her husband's newfound faith, and rejoiced that she could "wait on God" in nursing and cheering her husband. The officials shortened the quarantine, but by the time he was released, it was too late. William died in Pisa only two weeks later.

Philip and Anthony Filicchi and their wives welcomed Elizabeth and little Anna into their own home, as first Anna and then Elizabeth fell ill after Will's death. The Filicchis grew to admire Elizabeth greatly. Her devotion to God, her silent grief, her care for her little daughter, and her longing for her children across the ocean impressed them. They openly lived their own faith and shared it with her, hoping to comfort her.

At first polite and curious, Elizabeth gradually found herself truly intrigued by their Catholicism. She was amazed to discover the Catholic belief in the Real Presence of Jesus in the Eucharist. When she saw how ardently her newfound friends believed, she too fell to her knees before the Blessed Sacrament on procession in the streets. Her yearning for a deeper, sacramental communion with God, and her gradual recognition that the Catholic Church linked directly back to the apostles, set off a storm of inner conflict. She felt drawn to enter the Catholic Church, but she knew the tremendous resistance she would face from family and friends when she returned home.

Home for Elizabeth Bayley Seton was New York. She was born two years before the American Revolution into a prominent New York family. Her early childhood was overshadowed by the War of Independence and her mother's untimely death, followed by her younger sister's passing. Elizabeth grew up close to her father, a busy physician who took time to guide her education. He remarried when Elizabeth was four, but Elizabeth's stepmother rejected Elizabeth and her older sister. Finally, when Elizabeth was in her teens, Elizabeth's father and stepmother separated, and for a while Elizabeth struggled with a deep depression. Later, she would thank God for saving her from doing anything desperate. Even at a young age, Elizabeth had a deep faith that she nurtured by reading Sacred Scripture and praying the psalms.

At the age of nineteen, Elizabeth had met and fallen in love with William Seton, a young man from another prosperous, distinguished family. The fashionable young couple had several years of married bliss and social prominence, hosting a party for George Washington and being neighbors to such famous people as Alexander Hamilton. They were blessed with five children.

But a series of challenges faced the young family. The death of Will's father left the support of his large family (including the raising of the smaller children) to the young couple. The family's importing business declined to the point of bankruptcy; and then their own children became ill, one after another. Next, Elizabeth had been devastated by the death of her own father. Now she had lost Will after ten beautiful, unforgettable years. An impoverished widow at age twenty-nine, Elizabeth had five children under the age of nine to raise and support. Her desire to convert to Catholicism would deeply disturb her family and friends. Elizabeth could rely on only one person—her sister-in-law and "soul sister," Rebecca Seton, in whose care Elizabeth had left her other children during her trip.

Accompanied by Anthony Filicchi, Elizabeth and Anna returned to New York in early spring. Elizabeth's sorrowful heart was eased by her joyful reunion with her children—Bill, Dick, Kitty, and baby Bec. But another sorrow immediately marred her joy. Rebecca was gravely ill. Only a few weeks after Elizabeth's return, Rebecca, her confidante, died of tuberculosis.

The grief, insecurity, fears for the future, and doubts became a storm raging inside Elizabeth—a struggle that she shared with her Episcopalian pastor and spiritual director, the Rev. John Henry Hobart (who later became a bishop), and Catholics she came to know through Anthony. She corresponded with both Bishop Jean-Louis Lefebvre de Cheverus of Boston and Archbishop John Carroll of Baltimore. After months of internal debate and prayer, Elizabeth made an act of faith and entered the Catholic Church on March 14, 1805. A few days later, she received Holy Communion, and wrote in her journal, "At last God is mine and I am his!"

Now one of the loneliest periods in the young widow's life began. Family and friends could not understand her conversion. Fearing that she would try to convert them, most shut her out of their lives. The Filicchis remained good friends, providing financial help as well as counsel, which the struggling family desperately needed. Anti-Catholic prejudice made Elizabeth's efforts to attain financial independence very difficult—whether she tried running a boarding house or teaching.

Finally, Archbishop Carroll of Maryland invited Elizabeth to come to Baltimore to open a Catholic school for girls. Elizabeth accepted his invitation. With her children at her side, she began the school under extremely poor conditions. The poverty and obscurity of those first years would have discouraged anyone—anyone, that is, but Elizabeth. Somehow Elizabeth's faith gave her the courage she needed. In addition, she was highly educated, refined and well mannered, a practical and balanced woman who accomplished much.

One of her deepest joys was that, unlike in New York, it was now easy to shape her life around prayer and daily Mass, since the chapel was next door. Ever since she had been in Italy, Elizabeth had longed to dedicate her life to prayer and service. Her daughters were inspired by their mother's ideals and joined in her efforts even as children. Two of Elizabeth's younger sisters-in-law, Harriet and Cecilia, not only converted to Catholicism, but also came to join Elizabeth. Other young women were similarly inspired and joined her to work at the school. Without realizing it, only three and a half years after her conversion, Elizabeth had not only begun a new religious community, but also launched what was to become a vast undertaking of the Catholic Church in America: the parochial school system.

In 1809 the community received a generous donation to found a school for poor children. They moved to a farm nearby in Emmitsburg, where the little community continued to live with great physical hardships, yet in a Christ-centered joy under Elizabeth's inspiring leadership.

Under the guidance of Archbishop Carroll, Elizabeth and the other women gradually formed themselves into a religious community, with exceptions being made for Elizabeth to continue her responsibilities as a mother. They first took the name the Sisters of Saint Joseph, but a few years later, they changed the name of the growing congregation to the Sisters of Charity, basing their spirituality on Saint Vincent de Paul, whose writings Elizabeth translated. Their very name—Sisters of Charity—underscored their way of life. The long black dress, elbow-length cape and characteristic black bonnet soon became a familiar sight in schools, hospitals, and orphanages. The sisters went any place spiritual or corporal works of mercy were needed.

Against her will, and despite the fact that she had to balance the additional responsibilities of motherhood, the sisters always kept Elizabeth as their superior. "Mother Seton" as she came to be called, wisely guided the community through the hardships of its early days and throughout its early expansion.

Elizabeth was also a prolific writer, using the distinctively feminine writing forms of her day: letters, journals, and memoirs. Her writings are full of spiritual gems, and they trace an incredible journey of trust in God's will and in his love for her in each and every moment, no matter how painful the circumstances.

Elizabeth's writings also reveal one of her greatest strengths and inner beauties: her ability to build deep and abiding friendships. Yet this also was one of her greatest sources of suffering, as again and again she lost her dearest, closest companions—members of both her "families." Within a year of joining her, her young sisters-in-law, Harriet and

Cecilia, died. Next her own daughter Anna, who was a novice at the time, died. Later, her youngest daughter, Bec, would die at Emmitsburg, too. Of the nearly 100 women who joined the community, Elizabeth would bury eighteen.

Elizabeth's great consolation in these sorrows was her friendship with Jesus in the Eucharist. She wrote, "What can shut us out from the love of him who will ever dwell within us through love?"

The last three years of her life, Mother Seton grew increasingly ill and felt God inviting her to live more deeply the paschal mystery, sharing in Jesus's sufferings and death so as to share in his glorious life. On January 4, 1821, at the age of forty-six, Mother Seton slipped away to enjoy the perfect union with God that she had so joyfully anticipated every day in Holy Communion. She urged her sisters in her last words, "Be children of the Church. Be children of the Church."

Prayer

Saint Elizabeth,
many of the great joys of your life—
your family life, your conversion,
the fulfillment of your deep desire to dedicate your life to
    Christ as a religious sister—
were interwoven with great sorrow:
deaths of loved ones, rejection by family and friends,
physical hardships, and the challenges of founding a new
    way of life.
For you, these sorrows could be borne, accepted,
    and turned into treasures
by your love for Jesus in the Eucharist

and his love for you.
Help us to accept the challenges in our own lives,
trusting in God's loving presence.
Amen.

About Saint Elizabeth Seton

Born: August 28, 1774, New York

Died: January 4, 1821, Emmitsburg, Maryland

Memorial: January 4

Canonized: September 14, 1975, by Pope Paul VI

Patron: those who have difficulties with in-laws, children
near death, loss of a parent, widows, Catholic schools,
those persecuted for the Catholic faith

Notes on Her Life

- Elizabeth was extremely close to her father, who, despite his many responsibilities as physician and health officer, guided Elizabeth in more than her education.

- As a couple, Elizabeth and William belonged to the fashionable Trinity Episcopal Church, where Elizabeth also received spiritual direction from the pastor, the Rev. John Henry Hobart. With her sister-in-law Rebecca, Elizabeth organized other women to alleviate poverty.

- Tuberculosis ravaged the Seton family. Two of her daughters, Anna and Bec, died in Elizabeth's arms. In addition to her soul sister, Rebecca, her other two sisters-in-law, Harriet and Cecilia, also died of tuberculosis.

- Elizabeth and sixteen women pronounced their vows as Sisters of Charity for the first time in 1813.

A year later, Elizabeth sent three sisters to Philadelphia to found the first orphanage in the United States.

Lesser-Known Facts

Elizabeth's life was filled with lonely periods of loss. Her stepmother rejected her and her older sister. Later, when her father and stepmother separated, Elizabeth's depression may have led her to contemplate suicide.

Elizabeth's first question to the Filicchis about the Catholic faith stemmed from her curiosity about the words of a prayer, the "Memorare." Elizabeth became greatly devoted to the Blessed Mother after her conversion.

Elizabeth's fourth child, Catherine, was the only daughter present at her mother's death, and her only daughter to survive her. Catherine eventually became a Sister of Mercy and devoted herself to prison ministry.

As she was dying, Elizabeth had her bed repositioned so she could see the tabernacle at all times.

Elizabeth Ann Seton's writings are full of spiritual gems that are still not widely read.

In Her Own Words

"The greater my unworthiness, the more abundant is his mercy."

Saint Rita

Saint of the Impossible

R ita finished baking the bread and setting the table for supper, then looked out the door to see her if her husband, Paolo, was approaching. Not yet, so she didn't need to call her sons in from outside. Rita took a deep breath and looked up to the mountains. Despite the peaceful evening, her heart was not entirely at peace.

The endless feuding that tore medieval Italy apart had recently flared up in Cascia and its neighboring villages. Paolo's family had been involved for generations. Though Paolo himself had a fiery temperament, he'd never directly engaged in the feud. Cherishing this rare free moment, Rita knelt in front of the crucifix in their home. "Keep him safe, Lord. Don't let our family suffer from this feud. Bless us with peace. Bless Paolo with peace."

Rita suddenly realized it was growing dark. She had lost track of time in her prayer, and now real anxiety hit her. Paolo should have been home by now! She banked the fire, wrapped her shawl around her, and started to walk to meet her husband. On this beautiful evening she was too worried to stay home waiting.

On the path, Rita heard sounds of angry voices ahead. Stomach churning, she ran toward them. A neighbor tried to hold her back. "Rita, wait! You don't want to see him like this—we were just coming to get you . . ." But Rita shook him off and ran past him toward the awful scene awaiting her.

Paolo's body lay still on the ground, his chest covered in blood from stab wounds. One look at his face and Rita knew he was already gone. She fell to her knees, grasped his face in her hands, and kissed him. "Paolo! My Paolo!"

Tears streaming down her face, she looked up to the small circle of men. "Did you find him like this? Was he alive? Was there a priest here? Or did he die . . . alone?"

When the men could not meet her gaze, she knew the answer. Paolo had died alone. Suppose he had been afraid? Suppose he had fought? Suppose he had died with anger in his heart? Rita's fear for her husband's salvation pressed on her, choking her. Her husband, with whom she had struggled to build a life, a family, a safe circle in this mad world of violence, was gone in an instant. Grief and fear robbed her of breath and clear vision. All she could see was Paolo's frozen, empty face.

More footsteps were heard on the path. Feeling a thousand miles distant, clutching her husband's cold hand, Rita recognized first the voices, then the faces of her husband's family. Screams of grief, roars of "Who did this?" echoed around her but didn't touch her. Then, one sentence jarred her back to herself.

"When we find out who did this, they will pay for it in blood," promised an angry voice.

"No!" Rita's horror pushed her to her feet. "Stop talking like that! How many more wives must become widows? How many more children, orphans?" She gasped for breath. "Help me bring him home. I must get back to my sons before they hear from someone else," she pleaded.

The men carried Paolo's body in a respectful, silent procession behind her as she made her way home. Rita pulled her mind away from her own grief and horror. How could she break this news to her sons without igniting the understandable desire for revenge? Her impetuous teenage sons would be easily influenced by their relatives.

They were waiting inside for supper, eating some bread at table when she walked in. "My sons," she said, "Father was attacked on the way home and hurt very badly. He's in the hands of God now." Rita held out her arms, and Gian Giacomo and Paolo Maria rushed into them. She held them close, heart pierced anew by the sorrow and confusion that had filled their eyes.

Somehow, Rita made it through the next couple of days. She tried to be attentive to Gian Giacomo and Paolo Maria, not leaving them alone with her husband's family, yet respecting their need for space to grieve. Rita focused her grief by praying insistently for Paolo's entrance into heaven. But her sons grew increasingly withdrawn and seemed very tense with each other. Rita pulled them aside individually and talked to them. She invited them to come to church and pray for their father and his murderers—that was the word her sons insisted on using. With her mother's instinct, she could tell that her sons were being drawn into the negative cycle of revenge and violence—they seemed obsessed by it.

Rita visited her husband's family and begged them to forgive Paolo's murderers, or at least to stop speaking to her sons about revenge. When they indignantly dismissed her as weak and disloyal to Paolo's memory, the accusations wounded her deeply.

That evening over supper, Rita raised the subject with Gian Giacomo and Paolo Maria. "Do you think I am disloyal to your father's memory if I don't want to take revenge on his killers?"

Gian Giacomo looked away and didn't answer. Paolo Maria responded, "That's okay, Mamma. We know it's not disloyalty. We'll be strong for you."

Rita leaned forward and laid her hand on her son's. "Do you think it's easy to ask God to forgive those who killed your father and left him to die alone on the road? Forgiveness takes more strength than revenge does. I'm not being weak. I'm respecting your father's love for justice and Jesus's call to be peacemakers. Revenge is not the answer, boys. If you try to take revenge for your father's death, you will be unjust to someone else. The violence will never stop unless we take a stand and are strong enough to forgive."

Paolo Maria snatched his hand away at her words. "No! It's not fair! We lost our father! They should suffer for it!"

Rita turned to Gian Giacomo. "Don't do this! Only God can make things right! Violence isn't the answer—it just brings more violence, more death!"

Gian Giacomo shoved his half-empty plate away. "All we want is justice for our father." He stood up. "C'mon, Paolo, don't let her talk you down."

Paolo stood up with his brother and they left the house, slamming the door behind them.

Dry-eyed, Rita cleared the table. She had no tears left. She had just lost her husband, and still feared for his eternal salvation. Now it seemed her sons were lost to her—and perhaps to God as well. Waiting up for them, Rita offered the most difficult prayer a mother can.

"Lord, you know all things. And you love my sons more than I ever could. But they are all I have left in this world.

You know the goodness in their hearts. Don't let them go down this path of destruction and violence that will destroy them. *Anything* would be better than for them than to lose their very selves in this pit of hate-filled revenge. They won't listen to me anymore, so I entrust them completely to you. Protect them from themselves, guide them to eternal happiness in you."

Shortly after Paolo Maria and Gian Giacomo had revealed their true intentions to Rita, they both fell ill. Fearing that this might be God's answer to her prayer, Rita nursed them with great dedication. *They are both young and strong; they will recover!* she thought hopefully. But their illness grew grave. Both young men came back to their senses. They confessed their murderous intentions and received the sacraments of Reconciliation and Viaticum. But tragically, neither survived. Rita lost both her sons within days of each other, less than a year after their father's death. Rita's only consolation in her great grief and loneliness was that she was sure they would enter the heavenly Father's embrace.

"What now, Lord?" she prayed. After some months, Rita found an earlier desire resurfacing. As an only daughter, Rita had followed her parents' wishes to marry so she could be near them in their old age, and so she could enjoy the protection of a strong husband and family in that feud-riddled area. However, Rita's parents had died soon after her marriage. She found it ironic that her obedience to their desires had left her so vulnerable and alone. Could she now follow her initial desire to enter the convent?

She visited the Augustinian convent in nearby Cascia and requested an interview with the abbess. The abbess listened to the request of the devout woman who was also the victim of such terrible tragedies, but kindly explained that, although widows sometimes became nuns, it was very rare for this particular convent. She told Rita to come back for an answer after she had spoken to the community. When Rita returned, the abbess told her she had been refused.

Greatly disappointed, Rita went home. Although two other convents were in the area, in her prayer Rita continued to feel directed to enter the Augustinians. She went back a second and then a third time. The last time, the abbess told her rather harshly not to return. Rita wondered if the nuns were concerned that her family connections might bring the feud to the convent.

Rita prayed for patience, perseverance, and clarity about what to do. After some months passed, she received a vision of three saints: Nicholas of Tolentino, Augustine, and John the Baptist, who showed her the way past the closed doors of the convent. Rita arranged a reconciliation between the two feuding families. After she succeeded in bringing peace, she was finally accepted into the convent. The sisters quickly discovered that Rita's spiritual maturity was evident in her wholehearted spirit of obedience and deep prayer.

In the convent, Rita's devotion to the crucified Jesus deepened, especially after listening to a famous Franciscan, Saint Giacomo della Marca, preach about Jesus's sufferings and death. She begged God for the grace to share everything with Jesus, even his sufferings. She felt that only in this way could she *really* become one with her divine Bridegroom. Jesus granted her desire in a singular way. While she was gazing at the crucifix, Rita felt one of the thorns from Jesus's crown pierce her forehead. The thorn created a painful, gaping wound that refused to heal. It soon festered and became repulsive, making it difficult for the other sisters to even approach Rita. Even if they could overcome their repulsion, the sisters still feared contagion. From this mystical wound, Rita suffered terrible pain and the burden of living as a virtual hermit within the community for the last fifteen years of her life. Yet, she rejoiced to share in Jesus's sufferings so directly, and she was happy to spend her life completely dedicated to prayer.

On May 22, 1457, when Rita was about seventy-six years old, she went to meet her beloved Bridegroom. The moment she died, stories of miracles started to surround this humble woman. The convent bell began to ring without anyone touching it. The room where she lay glowed with a heavenly light, her wound was healed, and her face became fresh and youthful. A dozen miracles attributed to her took place within weeks of her death. And although Rita's body was never embalmed, her body lies still incorrupt in the chapel of the convent in Cascia.

Rita is now called the saint of the impossible, because in her own life she faced so many impossible situations and in each, she found that with God, all things are possible.

Prayer

Saint Rita,
faithful disciple of Christ
in every circumstance of your life, no matter
    how painful,
you trusted in God.
Teach me to trust in God's love,
to be persistent and courageous
in seeking peace and ending violence,
able to see past injury and injustice
to the suffering face of Christ.

For only in making peace with one another
can we live in union with the God
whose love embraces us all. Amen.

About Saint Rita

Born: ca. 1381, in Roccaparena (near Cascia) in Umbria,
Italy

Died: May 22, 1457, in Cascia, Italy

Memorial: May 22

Beatified: 1627

Canonized: 1900 by Pope Leo XIII

Patron: impossible or desperate causes, difficult marriages, infertility, parenthood, victims of abuse

Rita's first biography was written over 150 years after her
death, making it difficult to determine what is fact and what
is legend. Additional, critical research done close to her canonization sheds some surprising light on her life. What
remains clear is that the many miracles attributed through
Saint Rita's prayers to God confirm not only her closeness to
God, but her great desire to help those who face very difficult
situations.

Facts and Legends: Discovering the True Rita

- Cascia is so small a town that few would have heard of it
  were it not for Saint Rita.

- Legends tell us that Rita's parents were elderly when she
  was born and were known as peacemakers in the region.

- Stories that Rita's husband, Paolo, was a violent, abusive
  spouse were based on a mistaken reading of some writ-

ing on Rita's original coffin that was obscured by smoke stains. When the coffin was restored 500 years later, the words originally thought to refer to him were found instead to refer to the great pain she suffered from her mystical wound. If Rita's parents were peacemakers concerned for her future, it is unlikely that they would have arranged for her marriage to a violent, feuding husband. Nonetheless, like every marriage, Rita's required a daily commitment of love, self-sacrifice, and acceptance of her husband's wishes.

- Rita's sons may have been twins.

- A legend recounts that the nuns were persuaded to accept Rita into their community because Saints Nicholas Tolentino, Augustine, and John the Baptist escorted Rita through the convent's locked and bolted doors one night. The next morning, the community found her in the convent chapel, praying, with all the doors still locked and bolted. Another legend says the saints inspired her to reconcile the feuding families.

- Another lovely legend says that when she entered the convent, the superior told Rita to water a dead stick planted in the ground. Rita did so faithfully, and the "stick" became a vine that continues to flourish today.

- Rita is considered a stigmatist because she truly shared physically, as well as spiritually, in Jesus's suffering.

We have no recorded words of Saint Rita. But we know of her commitment to peace and reconciliation, and her immense devotion to Jesus in his passion. Most likely the crucifix was the "book" she meditated on most frequently.

Saint Augustine

Seeker of Truth

A lipius studied his friend's abstracted face while they ate. Augustine was his former teacher, a cherished friend, and a brother on the journey of seeking the truth. Augustine's great mind and heart had led Alipius to follow in his footsteps. And now, it was clear that Augustine's attention wandered far from the fascinating table conversation.

Their guest for lunch, a Christian named Pontitianus, had been describing the life of a holy man, Anthony of Egypt, who was inspiring other Christians—including two of his friends—to dedicate their whole lives to God. Augustine had listened eagerly, until now.

As Pontitianus rose to leave, Alipius said good-bye, then followed Augustine to the next room. As he entered, Augustine whipped around to face to him and almost shouted in agitation, "What are we doing, Alipius? The unlearned are seizing heaven by force and what are we doing? We, with all our knowledge, are heartless cowards, wallowing and sinking in the mire!"

Alipius was astonished, not so much by Augustine's words but by the anguish in his eyes and tone. Augustine turned and went into the garden, and Alipius followed. He could not desert his friend, whom he had never seen so distressed.

For a while, they sat together in silence. Finally, Augustine got up and walked a short distance away. Alipius watched as his friend sank to the ground. Alipius glanced back at the house where Augustine's mother, Monica, was clearing up after their meal. Should he call her? He had never seen Augustine so upset.

Sitting alone under the fig tree, Augustine poured out years of grief and regret through his tears. Even now, when so much had finally become clear, Augustine's doubts tormented him.

His doubts had begun as a youth, when he had left his devoutly Christian mother to study at the university of Carthage. In those days, it was the custom to be taught the faith, but not receive Baptism until adulthood. But the skepticism prevalent at the university made a deep impression on Augustine, and he gradually rejected the teachings of the Church as too simple and impractical to live. At age 19, impressed by the writings of the Roman orator Cicero, Augustine began his lifelong search for truth. Discounting the Christianity in which he had been raised but which he had never truly explored, he found himself drawn to Manichaeism, a religious cult that attempted to synthesize all known religions into one.

A brilliant student, Augustine quickly became a teacher, but he continued to explore various philosophies and religions. Eventually, he grew disillusioned with Manichaeism, but he continued to search. In his need to seek the truth without restraint, he had even deceived his mother and left for Rome without her. Eventually, he had ended up teaching in

Milan. Here, Augustine had begun listening to the preaching of Ambrose, bishop of Milan, because he admired his rhetoric. But soon he found himself agreeing with much of what Ambrose was saying. Augustine started to study Christianity.

Augustine's intellectual doubts finally started to melt away in the light of Christ. He felt he had at last found the truth. But Augustine wasn't ready to embrace Christianity, because he knew he couldn't live the Church's teaching on purity. Augustine had been faithful to one woman for decades—a woman he deeply loved but never married, who had given birth to his son, Adeodatus. At Monica's prodding, Augustine had recently broken up with the woman, but he found he could not bear the solitude, and he had started living with another woman while his mother arranged for his marriage. It was too late, too hard, for him to learn to live chastely.

At lunch, the story Pontitianus told had shone a brilliant light that had cast Augustine in a deep shadow. Augustine felt he finally saw his true self—a self deformed by sin. How could he, with all his studies and intellect, not have the courage to embrace the truth? If others could follow Christ so single-heartedly as to leave everything behind, why couldn't he leave behind his life of sin? In the midst of his tears and self-loathing, Augustine started to pray, "How long, O Lord, how long?"

Suddenly, Augustine heard a child's voice chanting, "Take up and read! Take up and read!" Augustine looked around for the child. Seeing no one, he realized that what he heard was the voice of inspiration. Hadn't Pontitianus said that Anthony of the Desert's conversion had come from reading one line of the Gospels? Rising to his feet and going back to Alipius, Augustine picked up the Letters of Saint Paul that he'd been reading. Eagerly, like a man crazed with thirst, he opened the Scriptures and read, "Let us live honorably as in the day, not in reveling and drunkenness, not in debauchery and licentiousness, not in quarreling and jealousy. Instead, put on the Lord Jesus Christ, and make no provision for the flesh, to gratify its desires" (Rom 13:13–14). As he read the words, a light suddenly filled his entire being, dispelling not only his doubts but his inner turmoil. Closing the book, Augustine joyfully turned to Alipius. "I am abandoning the past and embracing Christianity!"

Alipius read as Augustine had, and found a line that inspired him. Together, Augustine and Alipius went to tell Monica the good news. Monica hugged her son, weeping and sobbing, "Thanks be to God! At last! Thanks be to God!"

An uncontainable happiness finally filled Augustine's heart. He had been so afraid to lose the pleasures of his former life, but now they seemed like trifles compared to the delights of the spirit he enjoyed in God's love. He withdrew from public life to prepare himself for his baptism—praying, fasting, and doing penance. He wrote a prayer that revealed his regret at having waited so long before surrendering to God:

O Jesus Christ, amiable Lord, why did I, in all my life, ever love and desire other things instead of You? Jesus, my God, where was I when I was not thinking of you? Oh, at least from this moment on, may my heart have no other desires than for you. O desires of my soul, hasten and run from now on, you have lingered too long already; hasten to reach the goal to which you aspired. Really seek him whom you seek. God of my heart, Divine Jesus, let my heart consume itself for you. May the glowing ember of your love burst into flame in my breast and be the beginning of a divine conflagration: may it continuously burn upon the altar of my heart, inflame the intimacy of my being and consume my entire soul, so that on the day of my death I may appear before you, consumed by love for you. Amen.[*]

Finally, on Easter in the year 387, Saint Ambrose of Milan baptized Augustine: he died to his former life and began his new life in Christ. Joining him were his good friend Alipius and his son, Adeodatus, who was about fifteen years old. Grateful for the treasure of new life he had received, Augustine still feared his own weakness and constantly begged God in prayer for the strength he needed to resist temptation.

Shortly after his conversion, Augustine's mother, Monica, died. Augustine returned to Tagaste, his hometown, and dedicated his life to God through a monastic life of prayer, chastity, and study. He gathered friends around him who shared in his simple lifestyle. Despite his hesitancy and protests, the bishop of Hippo ordained him a priest, and encouraged him to preach. A few years later, the bishop ordained him a bishop and proclaimed Augustine his successor.

Although he was initially hesitant and remained committed to a simple lifestyle, Augustine became an energetic and prolific herald of the Gospel, tirelessly and enthusiastically explaining, defending, and clarifying the teachings of the Church and the Scriptures. Daily, sometimes twice a day, he preached to the faithful. More than 400 of his sermons are still in existence.

Many of Augustine's writings and sermons focused on the errors and crises of his day. He convincingly addressed the theological or philosophical errors that were popular or seemed particularly deceptive, such as Manichaeism,

---

[*] Prayer of St. Augustine as found in *True Devotion to the Blessed Virgin* (Boston: Pauline Books & Media, 1962), 45. (English translation revised by author.)

Donatism, Pelagianism, and Arianism. As the Roman Empire collapsed around him, Augustine wrote *City of God* to address the relationship between the kingdom of God and earthly kingdoms.

The most widely read of all his books is his *Confessions*, which Augustine wrote to share his experience of the mercy and goodness of God. He wanted others to know him as he truly was—and, in his humble opinion, to stop giving him too much credit. In his own words: "The caresses of this world are more dangerous than persecutions. See what I am from this book: believe me and not what others say of me. Pray for me that God may complete what he has begun in me and that I may never destroy myself through pride and vainglory. I have written this book to incite myself and others to praise God who is ever just and good and to raise our minds and hearts to him." Ironically, in writing his *Confessions* Augustine was not only one of the first to write a true autobiography, but he actually created a new genre of literature: the spiritual autobiography.

At the age of seventy-six, after forty years of intense service to Christ and the Church, Augustine was stricken with a fever. Despite his fears of temptation and his own weakness, Augustine had faithfully lived his dramatic baptismal commitment to Christ, maturing to the fullness of life in Christ. Afire with the love of God, as he lay dying, he could hardly bear the vehemence of his love. What a desire he had to go to heaven, to see face to face the gracious God who had sought him out and won him, showering him with mercy and forgiveness; that God who had sought him relentlessly and to whom he had finally surrendered.

When he became too ill to rise from his bed, Augustine asked for the penitential psalms to be written out and hung on the wall in front of his bed. He also requested that no one visit him except the doctor and those who brought his meals. The last ten days of his life became a kind of retreat, in which he prayed the psalms continually and was moved to an even greater sorrow for his sins and more profound gratitude for God's goodness and mercy. He died peacefully on August 28, 430.

Augustine had no material goods to bequeath, for long before he had given everything away. Yet, in bridging the gap between the early Church Fathers and later Church Doctors, he left a profound legacy to the Church: his example of conversion and holiness chronicled in his *Confessions*, and his profound theological and philosophical preaching and writings (about forty volumes' worth), which undergird the understanding of all Christians up to the present day. Because Augustine's personal experience of God's gracious embrace shapes all of his writings, he is known as the Doctor of Grace.

Prayer

Saint Augustine, you sincerely and fearlessly
sought to discover and live the Truth,
no matter where it led you.
May we listen as attentively to the Word of God,
and respond to God's invitation
as fully as you did.
Help us to celebrate God's beauty, love, and goodness in
    our own lives,
to trust that God has a plan for us
and that God gives us the grace to live it every day.

May we live as you did, in continual conversion,
seeking to live always more fully
the grace of our Baptism. Amen.

About Saint Augustine

Born: November 13, 354, in Tagaste, Numidia
  (now Algeria)

Died: August 28, 430, in Hippo (now Annaba, Algeria)

Feast Day: August 28

Canonized: Augustine was canonized by popular acclaim,
  and later recognized as a Doctor of the Church in
  1298 by Pope Boniface VIII.

Patron: brewers, printers, theologians

Saint Augustine is considered one of the greatest Fathers
  and Doctors of the Church, often called the Doctor
  of Grace.

Notes on His Life

- In Augustine's day, it was the custom to wait for baptism until becoming an adult, so although Augustine was raised Christian, he was a catechumen until he rejected his faith as a teenager.

- Augustine speaks disparagingly of the sins of his youth, but he was known to be a man of good manners and principles. He was faithful to the one mistress he loved—who was also the mother of his son—for many years.

- His conversion journey was lengthy, but his immediate inspirations were the example of the life of Saint Anthony of Egypt and a passage from the Letter to the Romans (13:13–14). The reading from Romans occurred on August 15, 386; he was baptized the following Easter, April 25, 387, at age thirty-two.

- Augustine was ordained a priest in 391, although he was very reluctant; he preferred monastery life. As a priest and later as a bishop, he continued living the monastic life.

- Literary milestones: his *Confessions*, published in 401; *The Trinity*, published in 420; *The City of God*, completed and published in sections from 413–425; his *Retractions*, (426–428), which are a revision of his previous writings.

Lesser-Known Facts

- Augustine was not an eager student in his youngest days—his parents and teachers had to force him to study.

- Augustine listened to Saint Ambrose because he was interested in his rhetoric. Gradually, he became intrigued with what Saint Ambrose was saying.

- Upon returning to Africa, Augustine settled in Hippo partly because it already had a bishop and Augustine didn't feel called to priesthood or pastoral ministry.

- Augustine not only lived a monastic lifestyle himself but, as a bishop, he asked his priests to live the monastic lifestyle as well. He wrote a rule of life for his priests and for the community of women he founded.

In His Own Words

"Late have I loved you, O Beauty ever ancient, ever new; late have I loved you!"

— *Confessions*, Book X

Saint Alphonsa of the Immaculate Conception

The Lord's Own

Sister Alphonsa moved restlessly on her cot. Her many ailments often made it difficult to sleep, so she had devised her own nocturnal pastime for the sleepless, dragging hours: to express her love to the One to whom she belonged. Although the sores on her legs caused her great discomfort, she focused her inner gaze on Jesus on the cross. *For you, my Jesus,* she offered silently. *All I want is to be united to you. I am happy to suffer for you and with you.*

But something was missing from her prayer. Sister Alphonsa needed to be entirely honest with her Spouse. So she went on. *I want to ask you about my novitiate. If I don't get well, I can't continue. Father has told all the novices to pray for me, that I be healed through the intercession of the servant of God, Father Kuriakose Elias Chavara. I would like to make novitiate so that I can belong here with you forever! But even more, I want to do your will.*

Satisfied with her prayer, Sister Alphonsa wondered what God would do. God had brought her here, to the Franciscan Clarist community, but not always by the most direct path.

Sister Alphonsa was born Annakutty Muttathupandathu on August 19, 1910, in a small village in India. The youngest of four children, she'd lost her mother only weeks after her birth. Raised in turns by a loving father and grandmother, and more strictly by her aunt, her "second mother," she had received a deeply spiritual upbringing. Her family were Syro-Malabar Catholics, who trace their origins back to Saint Thomas the Apostle. (Syro-Malabar is an Eastern rite that is in communion with the Catholic Church.) "Annakutty" (or "little Anna"), as she was called, had suffered severe eczema when a young child, but she eventually recovered. At school, as a Syro-Malabar Catholic, Annakutty was a member of a respected religious minority. She easily made friends, and one of her best friends at school was Lakshmikutty, a Hindu girl.

Annakutty's aunt didn't understand her niece at all. Thinking of the future, she raised her to be an excellent housewife and to make an advantageous marriage. But from the age of seven, Annakutty considered herself as "given" to Jesus. She was no longer her own. She often visited the Carmelite monastery near her home, and felt called to religious life. But her family wouldn't hear of it. Annakutty determinedly resisted every effort her family made to persuade her not to follow her call.

Finally, her aunt began arranging a formal marriage for her. The pressure mounted so high that thirteen-year-old Annakutty came up with a desperate and misguided plan that had been prompted by her reading the lives of several saints. She would destroy a part of her beauty, so no one would want to marry her any more. One night, she purposefully put her foot into the hot embers of the fire pit to scar it. But she slipped and fell. Instead of receiving a superficial burn, Annakutty painfully burned both feet and legs, so badly that the toes of one foot had to be surgically separated and bound. Her recovery took over a year and left her permanently disabled. Her family gradually recognized that they would not be able to change her mind about her vocation.

Her confessor guided her to the Franciscan Clarist community at Bharanganam, whose mission included teaching. On Pentecost, 1927, Annakutty arrived at the school intending to continue her education and eventually enter the community. She entered the postulancy the following year, taking the name Sister Alphonsa of the Immaculate Conception, in honor of the saint of the day, Saint Alphonsus Liguori.

For the next five years she endured an unending succession of illnesses. Sister Alphonsa had completed her schooling, received her government's license to teach elementary school, and had taught for a full year. But recurring illnesses forced her to take on the smaller roles of assistant teacher, parish catechist, or secretary. The hardest thing of all had been the delay in entering the novitiate. Perhaps some of the sisters even doubted that she had a vocation!

A few months earlier, she had become a novice. Only days later, she became so ill that her death seemed close. Maybe Jesus was calling her to heaven?

The blanketing darkness of the pain pressed down on Alphonsa. She thought about Jesus's agony that dark night in the garden and didn't feel so alone. She thought she might doze for a few minutes when, suddenly, a bright light shone in the room.

The brilliant figure of a man dressed in a Carmelite habit appeared—the servant of God Kuriakose Elias Chavara, to whom the other novices were making a novena! Father Chavara blessed her, touched her, and spoke. "You are cured of this illness, but you will bear other sufferings." When he left, Alphonsa could feel that she was healed. The next morning, the novices and entire community rejoiced in her miraculous recovery. Alphonsa told no one about the apparition.

Sister Alphonsa was able to complete her novitiate. The day of her perpetual profession—August 12, 1936—was one of the happiest days of her life. She vowed to always live chastely, poorly, and obediently. Then she joyfully returned to her teaching duties at Bharanganam. But only weeks later, Sister Alphonsa fell ill, this time with a severe fever. The doctors suspected tuberculosis, and she suffered with it for six months. Once again, the community made novenas to Father Chavara and Saint Thérèse of Lisieux. And once again, Sister Alphonsa was miraculously cured. When her superiors pressed her for details, she reluctantly described the apparitions of both Saint Thérèse and Father Chavara, who had healed her.

During the next nine years, Sister Alphonsa suffered a series of serious illnesses, including double pneumonia and typhoid fever. She also suffered a severe nervous shock one night when a thief invaded her room while she was ill. She was so traumatized that she lost her memory and certain basic abilities, such as reading and writing, for more than a year. Even in this fragile state, she offered her sufferings for others. Her health continued to deteriorate until September 29, 1941, when it was feared she was dying. She received the Anointing of the Sick in preparation for her death, but with the grace of the sacrament and the prayers and care of her community, she recovered her memory and started to recover her health.

Sister Alphonsa was a favorite of the schoolchildren for her kindness and cheerfulness, though she only had the strength to teach them occasionally. Her room was near one of the schoolrooms, and she enjoyed watching and visiting with the children, often giving them treats of fruit.

Sister Alphonsa's frequent illnesses were misunderstood, but she bore the misunderstandings as silently as the physical pain. She often spoke of the Gospel image of the grain of wheat that falls to the earth to die and give life, or of the grain of wheat being ground to become the bread of the Eucharist. She also compared herself to a leaf that falls to the ground and becomes a part of the soil to nurture other plants. Her "work" was to suffer with joy.

Despite her many illnesses, she was always smiling and patient, even joyful. No one ever suspected how much she was suffering, and she preferred it that way—she did not want to receive special treatment. Those who visited to comfort or encourage her when she was ill found themselves comforted by her joy. Alphonsa was convinced that for her, suffering was her path to union with Christ. She treasured every step on that path because he not only pointed it out to her, but had first walked it himself. She sincerely believed that the crosses that she received were signs of Jesus's love for her, writing in her journal that a day without suffering was a day wasted. Her motto was: "I want to suffer for my Lord, who suffered for me." When her sufferings were severe, Alphonsa's deep devotion to Jesus in the Eucharist and in his passion and death on the cross sustained her. She would also turn to Mary, "the woman under the cross" for strength and comfort.

In 1945, Sister Alphonsa began suffering seriously from what would be her last illness. Tumors had spread throughout her organs, and she suffered from violent convulsions and vomiting—sometimes as many as forty times a day. On July 28,

1946, fully aware that she was dying, she passed away with several sisters at her bedside. She was only thirty-five years old, and could finally rejoice forever at being the Lord's own.

Her funeral was very small—only the sisters and a few friends and family members gathered to remember and pray for her. But her spiritual director predicted that her tomb would become a place of pilgrimage as people discovered what a holy mystic had lived in their midst. The day after her funeral, some of the schoolchildren started to pray for her intercession. When they received what they were praying for, devotion to Sister Alphonsa began to spread. So many miracles were attributed to Saint Alphonsa's intercession after her death that she was compared to Saint Thérèse of Lisieux, becoming known not as the Little Flower but as the Passion Flower of Bharanganam.

Prayer

Saint Alphonsa,
your one desire was to live God's will for your life.
Suffering and illness did not take away your joy.
Instead, they became your way
to live a joyful self-offering
to the One who gave all for you.
When my sufferings discourage me,
help me to recognize them
as invitations to receive God's love
and to offer my love to God.
Help me to grow in love for Jesus crucified,
who loved me and gave himself for me. Amen.

About Saint Alphonsa
of the Immaculate Conception

Born: August 19, 1910, Kudamaloor, a small village in Kerala, India

Died: July 28, 1946, Bharanganam

Feast Day: July 28

Canonized: October 12, 2008, by Pope Benedict XVI. Saint Alphonsa is the first woman of Indian origin to be canonized, as well as the first canonized saint of the Eastern rite Syro-Malabar Catholic Church.

Patron: those who are ill, those who have suffered the death of parents

She is often called Saint Alphonsa of India.

Notes on Her Life

❋ Saint Alphonsa's entire life was shrouded in suffering from its beginnings. Her mother, eight months pregnant, was awakened by a snake coiling itself around her waist and upper body. The shock pushed her into premature labor, and she died a few weeks later, after entrusting her newborn daughter to her sister.

❋ Sister Alphonsa was remembered by her sisters as a friendly, kind sister who never complained or criticized others.

❋ Perhaps it was Sister Alphonsa's childlike spirit that enabled the children at the school to recognize her holiness and to immediately pray to her with such faith after her death.

❋ Saint Alphonsa's tomb has become a place of pilgrimage for people of all faiths.

- The miracle attributed to Alphonsa's intercession which was recognized for her canonization is the healing of the clubfoot of an infant. Many other healings of clubfoot have been attributed to her intercession as well.

- In 1985, Sister Alphonsa was beatified along with Kuriakose Elias Chavara, to whom she had prayed for healing.

Lesser-Known Facts

- Although her aunt loved her, Saint Alphonsa did not have a typical childhood because her aunt was so severe and demanding.

- Saint Alphonsa was a hidden saint whose holiness lies not so much in what she did as how she did it, much like Saint Thérèse of Lisieux, to whom Alphonsa had a special devotion.

- Saint Alphonsa's best friend from childhood, Lakshmikutty, was ninety-nine at the time of the canonization of her friend. Her family (including her grandchildren and great-grandchildren) consider Saint Alphonsa their "guardian angel."

In Her Own Words

"My beloved Lord dwells within my heart. Nobody can take him away from there!"

Saint Damien de Veuster

Hell Transformed

Hawaii, the land of palm trees, coconuts, and vibrant colored flowers, was a tropical paradise long before it became the fiftieth state. Anyone going to Honolulu on the island of Oahu would find beauty, relaxation, and a friendly atmosphere. However, anyone going to Molokai would find despair!

The northern outcrop of the island of Molokai, in the center of the Hawaiian chain, was a desolate region. On its rugged surface thousands of men, women, and children lived in total isolation. People forced to leave their homes and families came to the village of Kalawao to waste away and die. Society treated them as outcasts, for they had contracted what was then considered the most terrible disease known—leprosy.

The plight of those forgotten people moved the heart of Bishop Maigret. On May 4, 1873, the bishop spoke with several missionary priests at Wailuku, on the island of Maui.

"Fathers, I had decided to grant the requests of the lepers of Molokai to have their own resident priest. But . . . I cannot lay this burden on any of you; it would be like sentencing a man to death."

Several of the priests generously volunteered for what was intended as a temporary assignment on a rotating basis. However, at this point, a rugged young missionary jumped to his feet.

"I . . . I want to go, Your Excellency!"

"Damien, do you realize what kind of assignment you're volunteering for?"

"Yes, Bishop, I do. I still want to go; I am ready to embrace the lot of the lepers."

"Thank you, my son! You've lifted a great weight from my heart. When can you be ready?"

"I am ready now, Your Excellency."

"Good! You can leave on the next boat in six days; and I'll accompany you myself and introduce you to your new children."

When the boat docked, Father Damien told himself, "I am here for life. I am on Molokai forever. I will die here—on this island."

Because of board of health regulations, anyone who contracted leprosy (now called Hansen's disease) was banished to the leper colony, where he must remain for the rest of his life. However, to the thirty-three-year-old priest with only nine years of missionary experience behind him, the future gleamed with brightness. Full of energy, strength, and enthusiasm, Father Damien was willing to sacrifice himself completely, for he was driven by a force greater than a human being's: the force of divine love.

When he arrived in the village, the young priest saw a most pitiful spectacle. The people who greeted him resembled, not human beings, but corpses, devoured by worms. Bloated and covered with sores, their bodies gave off the odor of decaying flesh.

A large wooden door creaked open. When Father Damien stepped into the one-room leprosarium, he reacted with utter shock.

"This is the hospital?" he exclaimed.

They had no doctors, no beds. Suffering from the cold and hunger, dozens of lepers lay on the floor, stretched out on mats. Flies swarmed everywhere, and the sick simply wallowed in filth, with little food or water.

As the young missionary looked over the room, he said to himself: "These unfortunate ones are now my spiritual children . . . and I, in turn, am to be their father."

Immediately, Father Damien began to care for the material and especially the spiritual needs of the lepers. He found it very difficult to carry out his duties, however, for every fiber of his being rebelled against the horrendous conditions.

In performing his priestly ministry—baptizing, hearing confessions, distributing Holy Communion, and anointing the sick—Father Damien often had to hold his nose, or even to run outside periodically to catch a breath of fresh air. The stench of leprous sweat nauseated him, and the fluid that leaked from the open sores caused his legs to itch so badly that he had to wear high boots in order to prevent it. His clothes, too, carried the odor of leprosy, so he tried to counteract it by constantly smoking a pipe.

"Lord, give me strength, courage, charity. . . ." Damien prayed. "Let me help my people more, love them more, and forget myself."

Even though his senses rebelled at the encounter with each ill person, Father Damien persisted in his work among the lepers. He strove to always be cheerful, although his heart filled with sorrow over their sufferings. Every step brought him toward new miseries, but the zealous missionary wanted only to spend himself in serving God and his beloved lepers. His heart ached for their sufferings, and he turned to constant prayer for the strength he needed in his work.

And God answered his prayers. God opened Damien's eyes, hands, and heart to see all the needs of his brothers and sisters. He abandoned himself ever more completely in order to serve them as much as he could.

Father Damien saw that, besides the wounds of the body, these lepers experienced a more tremendous suffering—that of the soul. The people were not only discouraged by the torments of the disease, but many had also lost all hope. They felt they had nothing to live for.

The missionary knew what was lacking in the lives of some of these lepers: faith, hope, and love. Crushed by the rejection they had experienced from other people, many thought that even God hated them. As a result they easily fell into sins such as impurity, idolatry, and even brutality.

By his witness in following Christ, Father Damien's example slowly uplifted the moral climate of the entire settlement. The lepers called him Makna, which means "Father," for he was always pouring himself out as a gift to the people. He built houses for them; taught them to raise crops; gave them food, clothing, and medicine; dressed their wounds; arranged recreational activities and religious celebrations; and even helped them organize an orchestra.

Many of the people began to join with Father Damien in his many acts of kindness to others. As much as was possible to them, men would help in his building projects. The women took food to those in most need, offering them comfort and care. Even the children, who were restored to "liveliness" by his attention, could be found playing together as if their sorrows were suddenly lifted.

Father Damien often taught children their catechism, for he wanted to attend to their spiritual needs most of all. One day when he returned home from an errand, Father Damien found one of the leper girls sitting outside his door.

"Are you waiting for me, Tatila?" he asked.

"Yes, Makna Kamiano," she answered. "Please bring me Holy Communion. Please bring it to me right now."

Without any further question, the priest brought the Blessed Sacrament to the child, which she devoutly received. No sooner had she finished thanking Jesus who had come into her heart than she went to meet him in heaven. The following day, Father Damien made her small coffin and dug her grave, as he did for all the lepers who died.

As months turned into years, the Apostle of Molokai completely gave himself in caring for the lepers. Even when dressing open sores, Father Damien looked as though he were arranging a bouquet of flowers, completely forgetting himself and his own sensibilities. Once a leper in the last stages of the disease looked up to see the priest changing the soiled bandages around his waist.

"Oh, Makna," he exclaimed. "Please be cautious. My wounds are leaking and the fluid will get on your hands."

"That's all right, Joseph," the priest replied. "I don't mind. It's more important that you have clean bandages."

"But you can get leprosy. I'm very contagious now."

"Don't be disturbed. Even if the disease seizes my body, God will give me a better one on Resurrection Day. Isn't one's eternal salvation the most important thing of all? God wills our holiness; that's what we must work for on this earth."

Damien was often chided for being careless in his own regard while dealing with the lepers. But to Damien this ministry of hands-on care he lovingly gave to everyone, whether a believer or not, was the anointing of the sick. Even if he could not administer the sacraments to one of these gravely ill people, he could be a blessing to their body and soul by his touch, his gentle words, and by the respect he showed each one.

On one beautiful evening in his twelfth year on Molokai, Damien prepared some warm water to soothe his tired feet. The work still made many demands on him in every way, but he was content. It had been a long day of visits to his sick. That afternoon he had finished work on the last of many houses he was building and even had time for an extra game with the orphan boys. Now Father Damien was ready to for a few minutes of well-deserved rest. He rolled up his pant cuffs and pulled off his dusty boots. Carefully he removed his socks and lifted one foot into the bucket and then the other. He looked down distractedly and noticed steam rising from the water. He dipped his fingers in the water and exclaimed, "Hotter than I thought!" Quickly he pulled up both feet and swung them over to a towel. Blisters began to appear on his red feet, but he hadn't felt a thing.

"Blessed be the Good God!" he prayed. "I am now most certainly a leper. This is why my feet have been aching for so long. The disease has been incubating. Thank you, Lord." When he volunteered to come to the leper colony, he realized he would probably eventually contract leprosy. To him it would be a sharing in Christ's passion, a way to consummate the sacrifice he had so willingly made. As he prayed, Damien thought of what he still wanted to accomplish at the leprosarium before the Lord called him to heaven.

The disease progressed rapidly. Large blisters appeared on his once handsome face, and his neck became red and bloated. Initially his powerful hands were spared, so he continued directing his many projects. For three more years, Father Damien worked vigorously for the bodily and spiritual well-being of his beloved lepers.

Far from quenching his zeal, the leprosy seemed to make it blaze ever more vibrantly. He still faced many trials, and the fatigue and suffering grew more intense with each new day, yet he bore all for the love of Christ who had died on the cross for him and for all people.

Damien did live to see a cherished dream fulfilled. On November 14, 1888, Mother Marianne Cope of the Franciscan Sisters of Syracuse arrived at the settlement with two companions, ready to take care of the island's children. Another priest also came to Molokai, as did two generous volunteers, Joseph Dutton and James Sinnott. "I can die happy now," Damien said. "You will carry on the work and do it much better than I."

On April 13, 1889, a few days before Easter, Father Damien gave his soul back to God. His work was finished. He had transformed the squalor of Molokai into a haven of God's love. Father Damien did not only die a victim of leprosy. He died a victim of sacrifice because of his love for Christ, and for the souls of God's least ones, the lepers of Molokai.

Prayer

Saint Damien, apostle and martyr of charity,
teach us to value this virtue above all others,

and above all our interests and plans.
You learned love from the hearts of Jesus and Mary
and made it the instrument of your life's work.
Teach this lesson to all priests and ministers of the
   Church,
that before and above all, love is to be poured out as an
   ointment
on the needs of those they serve.
May your example inspire all of us to spend our lives to
   the last drop
in loving God and sharing his love with everyone. Amen.

About Saint Damien de Veuster

Born: January 3, 1840, in Tremeloo, Belgium
Died: April 15, 1889, in Kalawao, Molokai, Hawaii
Feast Day: May 10
Canonized: October 11, 2009, by Pope Benedict XVI
Patron: victims of leprosy (Hansen's disease)

Notes on His Life

- He was born Jozef (Jef) de Veuster to a prosperous farming family.
- In 1858 he joined the Society of the Sacred Hearts of Jesus and Mary (SSCC), or Picpus Fathers (after the street in Paris where they first lived).
- He became a choir brother due to lack of success in school.
- After being tutored by his brother, Father Pamphile, Damien became proficient in Latin and Greek.

- In 1863 he was missioned to the Sandwich Islands (Hawaii) instead of his brother, who was supposed to go there but became ill.

- In 1864 he was ordained a priest in Our Lady of Peace Cathedral in Honolulu.

- He served for nine years on the islands of Hawaii and Oahu, and then, in 1873, volunteered for the leper colony at Kalawao, Molokai.

- He cared for the sick and built houses, a hospital, two orphanages, schools, meeting halls, chapels, roads, and a water conduit.

- In 1884 he was diagnosed as a leper.

- In 1889 he died and was buried next to Saint Philomena Church.

Lesser-Known Facts

- He is recognized as a martyr of charity.

- Kalawao was cut off from the rest of the island of Molokai by sheer cliffs 2,000 to 3,600 feet high.

- The leprosarium received much publicity and financial and material assistance from Catholics and Protestants in Europe and the United States.

- Damien was fluent in Hawaiian, Portuguese, Spanish, French, and English.

- In 1881 he was made a Knight Commander of the Royal Order of Kalakaua, an honor bestowed by Princess Liliuokalani.

- He was buried under the same pandanus tree where he first slept in Molokai.

- In 1936 his body was exhumed and sent to Belgium for burial in Louvain, but his right hand was later re-interred in the grave at Molokai.

- His statue is in National Statuary Hall at the U.S. capitol and at the state capitol of Hawaii.

- Robert Louis Stevenson wrote a famous defense of Father Damien.

- The miracles approved for his cause were both instant cures of fatal illnesses suffered by Sister Simplicia Hue, a French nun, in 1895, and Audrey Toguchi, a Hawaiian, in 1997.

- In Hawaii his feast day is celebrated April 15, his day of death.

In His Own Words

"In tears I sow the good seed. From morning until night my heart is broken by the moral and physical misery here. But I try to always look happy in order to encourage my poor lepers."

Saint Noël Chabanel

God's Zero

In the small wooden chapel of the mission of Sainte Marie, deep in the night of June 19, 1647, a lonely figure knelt at the altar rail. Jesuit missionary and priest Noël Chabanel had come to the chapel to relieve his mental torture, but the choking blackness only made his depressing thoughts clamor louder.

"I don't belong here! I've been trying for almost four years! How can I possibly be called here, to this mission?" Self-loathing at his own failure forced Noël to his aching feet, and despite his fatigue, he paced restlessly back and forth.

"I'm thirty-five years old, and I've got nothing to show for it. If I was back in France, I could be of real use. How can my superiors ignore the waste of my talents, of my life? How can it be God's will that I fail so miserably at everything, that I can't even serve as a real priest to the Huron people?"

The anguish in his soul reached insurmountable intensity. "My God! My God! Why have you abandoned me?" Exhausted by the struggle, Noël collapsed to his knees, his face bowed to the floor. He wept. How had his life come to this?

Noël Chabanel had dreamed of being sent to New France to evangelize the native peoples who had never heard of Christ. But once he arrived, this keenly intelligent and articulate professor of rhetoric had been reduced to silence, unable to learn even the basics of the Huron language. The Gospel that he so urgently wanted to preach was reduced to a garbled stutter. And he wasn't able to adjust to the close communal lifestyle of the native people, either. The smells and noise constantly distressed him; his queasy stomach couldn't digest the simple food; the lack of privacy was torturous to his reticent nature. To pray, he had to get up before dawn or go deep into the woods. An avid intellectual, Noël couldn't even read or study in the smoky, dim, and crowded Huron dwellings.

Many of the Huron people despised him for his apparent ignorance and inability to adapt to their language and customs. They mocked him, calling him the "palest of the pale faces." When he compared himself to the other missionaries, Noël felt ashamed. In his own eyes—and, he wondered, in the eyes of his fellow Jesuits, too?—he was completely useless.

His fellow missionaries suffered the same hardships and raw life in the wilderness, and faced the same dangers of travel or death by the enemies of the Huron people, the Iroquois. Yet, the other Jesuits could preach and minister tirelessly. His heroic companions even desired martyrdom, if it would bring another native to a genuine encounter with Christ! Noël, instead, did not yearn for martyrdom. He feared he would not be worthy of it. He would fail at being a martyr, as he failed at everything else.

A cold sweat bathed his body as Noël battled the tidal wave of depression engulfing him. "I haven't instructed one convert nor heard a single confession. What is my priesthood for? I'm lost in this wilderness. Suppose . . . I could ask to return to France. I'd be able to do some good there. But then . . . what if I was running away from God's will? Despite everything, my superiors haven't sent me back."

The cruelest torture of all was that the one thing that had always sustained him until now had failed him: his prayer had become the source of his deepest anguish. For almost as long as he'd been here, Noël had been drowning in a sea of spiritual darkness. The God to whom he had given his life seemed remote, unreachable.

Tonight, Noël's shattered heart and spirit could take no more. How long he crouched there, he would never know. Finally, one prayer came spontaneously to his lips. Noël looked toward the tabernacle and cried aloud, "My God, what do you want of me?"

A gleam of moonlight revealed the faint outline of the tabernacle. The closeness of the tabernacle, of Jesus in the Eucharist, pierced Noël's soul. He suddenly knew that it didn't matter to God what he could or couldn't do. God simply wanted him, his heart, his life. Grace poured into his broken-open heart. He raised himself up on his knees, and reached for the large crucifix in his robe, pressing it to his lips. "Lord, I'm nailed to the cross with you. Help me. With your grace, I will not come down."

But was this spontaneous prayer enough? Noël searched his heart. How could he strengthen his resolution to never give up, to share in the passion and death of his Lord as long as he was allowed, no matter how much discouragement or suffering he would face? Suddenly, he knew what he could do.

"Jesus Christ, my Savior, you have willed me to be a helper of the apostles in this Huron vineyard. I am most unworthy of this call. But I trust in you and in the designs of your holy will in serving the Huron people. I, Noël Chabanel, vow to remain here in the Huron Mission until the end of my life, if my superiors so dispose. Accept me, O Lord, as a permanent servant of this mission. Make me worthy of so great a ministry. Amen."

It was the morning of June 20, 1647, and the feast of Corpus Christi. The light of dawn chased the night from the village, the chapel, and Noël's heart. He would stay. It didn't matter that he would continue to feel useless and inadequate, physically revolted, and humiliated. His vow didn't remove the natural aversion that he felt until his death, but it made him stronger. Every new day would bring fresh ways that he could offer himself to Jesus Crucified for the sake of the Huron people. He could accept to minister in the shadows of the other missionaries. He could refuse to give up. He could give himself completely to God's will, no matter what he felt.

For the next two years, Father Noël Chabanel faithfully lived his vow. He celebrated Mass and baptized only the sick and dying. He continued to suffer from harsh conditions, demanding physical labor, and the painful lack of privacy. Lack of pure drinking water left him constantly thirsty. The steady diet of boiled corn paste, acorns and roots, indigestible to his weak stomach, left him continually weak. The feelings of inadequacy and his spiritual darkness continued to haunt him daily, but his determination remained unchanged. His ministry, his martyrdom, would be a hidden one.

In the fall of 1648, Father Noël was sent to assist Father Jean de Brébeuf at the Mission of Saint Ignatius. Fully aware of the growing menace from the hostile Iroquois warriors, Noël confided to his spiritual director, "I don't know what is happening to me or what God wants of me, but I feel death is not far off and I am not afraid. This state of mind is not from me, for I have always been afraid."

As he was saying goodbye, his last words to his spiritual director were, "Father Chastellain, I hope to really give myself entirely to God this time, once and for all!"

Later, Father Pierre Chastellain remarked to a passing priest at the mission, "I am deeply moved after speaking with that good priest. Father Chabanel's voice and appearance just now were indeed those of one making an offering of himself. I don't know what lies in God's providence for him, but I do know this: God wants that man to be a great saint."

In February 1649, Father Noël was replaced by Father Gabriel Lalemant and sent to assist Father Charles Garnier in evangelizing the Petuns at a more remote and dangerous mission. Shortly after Noël left, the Mission of Saint Ignatius was attacked and Fathers de Brébeuf and Lalemant were martyred. Noël wrote in a letter to his brother Pierre, also a Jesuit priest back in France:

> As you have already read in our reports, [The Jesuit Relations], Father Gabriel Lalemant merited the honor of martyrdom. Only a month before, I was in the same settlement. (You were robbed of the privilege of being the brother of a martyr.) Father Lalemant had been assigned to relieve me since I was physically stronger, and I was sent to a more difficult mission. I was not worthy of the crown he won. My turn will come, if it pleases God, and if I try to live my own "bloodless martyrdom in the darkness."

Nine months later, the Jesuit superior, Father Ragueneau, not wanting to risk the lives of both priests at the Petun mission, sent word for Father Noël to return to the main mission. But Noël wasn't sure he should leave. He didn't want to abandon Father Garnier or the Petun people at a time of suffering and danger, but Father Garnier insisted that Noël obey. On Sunday, December 5, 1649, Father Noël celebrated Mass and reluctantly embraced Father Garnier in farewell.

"I am going to where obedience calls me. . . . I must serve God faithfully until death." Then he set off with a few Huron warriors, and late in the afternoon reached the mission of Saint Matthias, twelve miles away. He would not know that the warring Iroquois would swoop down the following day and slaughter the people of the Petun mission, including Father Garnier. Father Noël continued on his journey with a party of Hurons, traveling more than eighteen miles over dangerous and difficult trails. Nightfall forced them to take refuge in a heavily wooded area near the river. The Hurons fell asleep right away, but Father Chabanel kept watch in prayer. Despite his spiritual desolation, he was at peace. He clung to his hope and desire that finally, he would be able to offer himself totally to God.

At about midnight, Noël heard noises in the distance—the victorious whoops of Iroquois and the cries of their captives. He woke his Huron companions and they fled, circling around the Iroquois and heading back to Saint Matthias. But Noël was unable to keep up. Not wanting to slow their escape, he told them to go on without him.

The Hurons left him behind and eventually reached Saint Matthias to report what had happened. In the meantime, Father Noël hid in a clump of trees and passed the night alone. At sunrise, he set out again for the main mission, but was unable to cross the river, which was too deep. A Huron, Louis Honareenhax, appeared and offered to take the priest across in his canoe. They had gone just a short way when the Huron suddenly turned on Father Noël and attacked him with his tomahawk, killing him. He threw Father Noël's body into the Nottawasaga River but took his belongings. It was the morning of December 8, 1649.

Father Noël's body was never found. It took two years for Noël's superior, Father Ragueneau, to confirm his suspicions of how Father Noël Chabanel had died. Witnesses heard Honareenhax brag how he had rid the world of the despised priest out of hatred for the Christian faith.

In many ways, Saint Noël Chabanel's martyrdom was unique. Without the spiritual consolations or feelings of accomplishment shared by his fellow Jesuit missionaries, Noël had nothing to sustain his self-offering other than faith and surrender to grace—a grace that he rarely felt. Daily, Noël struggled with feelings of aversion, sadness, disgust, discouragement, inadequacy—perhaps even despair. According to the world's standards, Noël was a failure, a "zero." Even his martyrdom was unwitnessed except by his assassin, and his body was never found.

But Noël's deepest desire, purified in the crucible of desolation, was to fulfill his priestly and missionary calling and give himself completely to God in service of the Huron people. By God's standards and by Noël's, his life was a complete success. This "zero" belonged to God. And that was all that mattered.

Prayer

Saint Noël Chabanel,
you faithfully fulfilled your priestly vocation
in the difficult and dangerous life of a missionary,
despite the interior darkness you continuously suffered.
Help all priests who face difficulties and temptations
to be as open to God's grace as you were.

When I am discouraged,
help me remember and cling to God's faithful love,
so that I may faithfully live my calling to serve,
and give myself to God always more fully. Amen.

About Saint Noël Chabanel

Born: February 2, 1613, in Saugues, France

Died: December 8, 1649, in Canada (New France)

Feast Day: October 19 in the United States, September 26 in Canada

Canonized: June 29, 1930, by Pope Pius XI

Patron: Canada, along with the other seven North American martyrs

Notes on His Life

❧ Saint Noël Chabanael is one of the "little four" of the North American martyrs, often mentioned last.

❧ He entered the Jesuits at age seventeen and was ordained at age twenty-six.

❧ Noël arrived in New France when he was thirty.

❧ Unable to learn the Hurons' language or adapt to their way of life, Noël lived the dark night of the soul for six years while a missionary.

Lesser-Known Facts

❧ Because his superiors in France didn't want to lose him, Noël had to ask twice before he was sent as a missionary to New France.

- His older brother, Pierre, was also a Jesuit.
- Noël admitted to fearing martyrdom.
- Noël was described by his superiors in France as: "Serious by nature; energetic; great stability; better than average intelligence."

In His Own Words

"May it be for good and all this time, that I give myself to God; and may I belong to him."

— Noël's words, shortly before his death,
to his spiritual director

Saint Thomas Becket

All or Nothing

The dawn on this lovely morning heralded a glorious day. Their horses, both well-rested and eager to join the hunt, were snorting and prancing about. "Now, beauty! Remember you are a royal mount," King Henry II of England exhorted as he patted the horse's neck. Poised and turning to his chancellor, Thomas Becket, the king suddenly nudged this horse and it bolted forward. Soon both riders were jostling for position as the horses galloped toward the woods.

Henry was a brilliant, capable ruler and recognized the same intelligence and ability in his friend and chancellor. Thomas was twelve years older than his king, but people declared that the pair had one heart and one mind. At lighter moments they were as playful as schoolboys. But the good of the kingdom was uppermost in the minds of both men.

When they reached the designated spot and were taking a break before the hunt, the young king searched the face of his companion. Yes, he thought, Thomas is in an exceptionally good mood today. I'll just tell him clearly that he must be the new archbishop, and do my bidding. But not right now, I'll wait until we are returning home.

Archbishop Theobald of Canterbury had just passed away. Henry had nominated Thomas, planning to use his friend to obtain full control of the revenues of the diocese and monasteries, and to make his own court supreme in Church matters. But would the people accept Thomas? Despite his lavish display of pomp and ceremony as the chancellor of England, Thomas's character was unimpeachable. Although worldly, he was not licentious like so many others. No one could impugn his integrity. Improper conduct and foul speech angered him, and he often severely punished these failings in others. This versatile and capable administrator would make a fine archbishop. He would do anything for his king. Henry was sure of Thomas . . . or was he?

"Thomas," the king said as they returned from the hunt, "I want you to be the new archbishop of Canterbury."

Thomas whirled half-way around in his saddle and stared at Henry.

"What! What type of man do you think I am to be placed in that holy office? And besides that, I know your plans for the Church. You will assert claims which I, if I were archbishop, would certainly oppose. If such a thing happened through God's designs, I am very sure that you would speedily change your tune. The great love now existing between us would turn to black hatred!"

Without a word, Thomas spurred his horse on and rode the rest of the way home in sullen silence.

Well, thought Henry, *he's always opposed my schemes against the Church anyway. But he'll think twice before he opposes me as archbishop. I'll make him pay dearly.*

Thomas was eventually forced to accept the appointment and was ordained bishop in 1162. Yes, he had been a dazzling, successful young man and always showed a smiling front to the world. But the king, who thought he knew him, didn't know the real Thomas. Henry hadn't witnessed the day Thomas revealed to a friend that his courtly grandeur made him weary of existence and stirred up in him a longing for death and heaven. His friend had been puzzled. How could such a worldly man, surrounded as Thomas was with the grosser vices of court life, escape all these untouched?

One day he received an answer to his unspoken question.

A nobleman who came to London to have an appointment with the chancellor, told Thomas's friend the story:

"I set out for London before sunrise. I reached the cathedral at dusk, and saw a figure lying prostrate at the entrance. This startled me. Just then I got a fit of sneezing and the figure quickly stirred and rose. I couldn't see his face, but noticed his stature. He was tall, and slim, and wore costly robes. The mysterious man intrigued me, and I was determined to find out who he was. All day I kept a close watch on the people I met. In the afternoon, I went to see the chancellor. As Sir Thomas arose to greet me, I knew right away that he was my mystery man. He must really be an extraordinary person."

Thomas's friend smiled and, shaking his head, responded, "He is indeed. He is indeed!"

When Thomas became the archbishop of Canterbury, a great outward change took place. The first thing he did was to resign his chancellorship. He removed all signs of lavish display and pomp. He intensified the severe penances he used to perform in secret. Under his simple cassock, his coarse woolen undergarments irritated and bruised his body as they had done when hidden under his rich robes as chancellor. He fasted and prayed constantly for strength in the struggle with the king that he foresaw as inevitable. Every evening, he invited and personally served the poor of the city who came to his door begging for alms. Anyone and everyone could approach the kindly archbishop, and they were sure of receiving some material or spiritual consolation.

The estrangement from the king came just as Thomas had predicted, for the archbishop constantly opposed Henry's attempts to control Church matters. Henry retaliated by persecuting his once-beloved friend and forcing him to pay fines and taxes. The king intended to settle once and for all his rule over the Church in England, so he called a meeting. After much discussion and cajoling, Henry convinced Thomas that he, the king, only meant to uphold the correct order between the Church and the kingdom. Thomas, believing the king to be sincere, acquiesced. The next day the written details of the king's demands were circulated as the Constitutions of Clarendon. When Thomas read through them he was stunned. It seemed that King Henry had absorbed all the Church's rights in this one act. As papal legate he could not lead the other bishops into this trap. Thomas proclaimed to all present, "By God Almighty, my seal shall never be put to such papers!"

Having no other recourse, Thomas fled across the English Channel to to seek refuge in France. Once there he went to Sens to ask permission from Pope Alexander III (who was in France at the time) to resign as archbishop. It was pathetic to see this holy man, tired and discouraged, pleading to be relieved of his heavy responsibility. The Holy Father looked at Thomas in his moment of weakness and knew what kind of a man he really was.

"No," the Pope responded gently. "You must stay at your post and defend the rights of the Church."

Thomas seemed to gain new strength as he gazed into the understanding eyes of his spiritual father. He would obey at any cost. But for now the struggle for power continued, with the pope attempting to bring about peace. So for the time being, Thomas took up residence in a Cistercian monastery.

Meanwhile, back in England, Henry was fuming with rage. He confiscated all Becket's property and banished his relatives into exile. He even threatened the monks who were sheltering the holy archbishop. The turmoil lasted six years. Finally a truce was made between the king and Thomas, even though neither agreed to compromise.

Thomas returned to England amid jubilant cries and enthusiasm from his flock. The truce, however, lasted about two weeks. Then the king heard that Thomas had clashed with him again. He had censured the bishops who had sided with the king against the Church. He also nullified several appointments and decisions that had been made against his wishes, which worked against the good of the Church. The excommunicated bishops sent persons to the king with lies and accusations against Thomas. In a fit of anger the king shouted, "Oh, the cowards who eat at my table! Isn't there anyone among them to rid me of this troublesome archbishop?"

Four knights took the king's words at face value. They, too, had grievances against the archbishop. They seized their opportunity to wreak vengeance under the cloak of loyalty to the king.

First, they burst into the archbishop's residence and demanded to see him. After searching, they found Thomas praying in his own room. Since they had not come to seek peace with him, the meeting soon gave way to shouting and accusation from the men. Finally the four stormed out, while the archbishop was quickly led into his cathedral for sanctuary.

Leading a well-armed and noisy crowd, the four knights pounded on the locked cathedral doors. Calmly, the archbishop told the sacristan to open them. "The doors to God's house must not be barred," he said. The four men lunged forward and froze in their tracks. The crowd pressed in around them.

"Whom are you looking for?" asked the archbishop from the altar steps.

"For Thomas the traitor," cried out one. "For the archbishop!"

"I am here. Not a traitor, but archbishop and God's priest."

With that, the scoundrels rushed forward, swords upraised. They tried to drag him from the church, but Thomas and the men with him put up a struggle. Being unarmed, they couldn't resist. A sword came crashing down on Thomas. "I commend myself to God and holy Mary," he cried. Then falling to his knees under another blow, he prayed, "Into your hands, my God, I commend my spirit." Then came the final thrust. As he fell his last words were, "For the name of Jesus and for the defense of the Church, I am ready to die."

The king was devastated when he learned of the murder and deeply regretted what his offhand remark had caused. For forty days he fasted and was subjected to public penance. It is said that he made reparation for the rest of his life.

Nine years before, Thomas had told Henry, "I have fully served my king; now as archbishop, I shall serve my Church." The one-time chancellor had become a totally dedicated servant of the Church. Thomas was canonized only three years after his martyrdom.

Zeal for the law of the Lord had inspired Thomas Becket, as centuries before it had inspired the Psalmist:

Princes persecute me without cause
but my heart stands in awe of your words.
I hope for your salvation, O LORD,
and I fulfill your commandments. (Ps 119:161, 166)

Prayer

Saint Thomas Becket,
holy archbishop of Canterbury,
martyr of God's Church, help us to be steadfast
    in our faith.
We do not want to compromise anything of what we
    hold to be true,
but the pressure to bow to the prevailing culture
    is difficult to resist.
Teach us integrity of heart, strength of character, and
    devotion to prayer.
Pray for us that we too may withstand all persecution,
great or small, and remain loyal to God's kingdom,
despite any sacrifice that may entail. Amen.

About Saint Thomas Becket

Born: December 21, 1118, in Cheapside, London,
    England
Died: December 29, 1170, as martyr in Canterbury
    Cathedral, Canterbury, England

Feast Day: December 29

Canonized: February 21, 1173, by Pope Alexander III in
    Saint Peter's Church in Segni

Patron: diocesan priests; Exeter College, Oxford

Notes on His Life

- He was also known as Thomas à Becket, Thomas of Canterbury, or Thomas of London.

- After his studies he became a clerk and was later attached to the household of the archbishop of Canterbury and studied canon law.

- He was named archdeacon of Canterbury in 1154.

- He was appointed lord chancellor in January 1155.

- King Henry II nominated him as archbishop of Canterbury in 1162.

- He was ordained a priest on June 2, 1162, and consecrated a bishop on June 3, 1162.

- Several times he prophesied his own martyrdom.

Lesser-Known Facts

- He was twice exiled and found refuge in the Cistercian monastery in Pontigny, France.

- He is venerated in both the Catholic Church and the Anglican Communion.

- The pilgrims in Chaucer's *Canterbury Tales* are on the way to Becket's shrine: "*the hooly blissful martir for to seke.*"

- T. S. Eliot wrote *Murder in the Cathedral*, a play about Saint Thomas Becket.

- Jean Anouilh's play, *Becket*, was also made into a film entitled *Becket*.

- His parents are buried in Old Saint Paul's Cathedral.

- Later writers affected the *à* before his last name, as also happened with Thomas *à* Kempis.

In His Own Words

"Pray for us that our faith fail not in tribulation, and that we may safely say with the Apostle that neither death nor life, nor angels nor any creature shall be able to separate us from the love of God, which has subjected us to affliction until he comes who will come, and will do with us according to his mercy, and will lead us into the land of promise, the land flowing with milk and honey."

Blessed Peter To Rot

An "Extraordinarily Ordinary" Man

Peter To Rot sat in darkness, puzzling over the sad events of the day. Since the bombing and invasion of the Japanese military forces almost a year ago, his world had been turned upside down. The first time the Tolai people had even seen a plane overhead, it had rained down destruction. The Japanese had completely conquered this part of Papua New Guinea, and had set up their military command center in the nearby town of Rabaul. They focused their attention less on the island than on the war beyond. The Second World War, formerly so far away, now engulfed his home.

At first, Peter gained strength from the faith and leadership of the people's missionary priest, Father Lauffer, who had simply gone about his pastoral ministry, encouraging Peter to do the same.

But today, the Japanese had come and taken away *all* the missionaries in the region. As Father Lauffer was being led away, he had shaken hands with Peter and told him, "To Rot, look after your people. Help them so that they don't forget about

God." As the soldiers led Father Lauffer away, the villagers had turned to Peter with dismayed expressions. He had done the best he could to hide his inner shakiness. He loved being a catechist, instructing others in the faith, listening to others' needs, and helping where he could. So he had put on a brave front for the sake of the village. But now, in the darkness of night, when no one needed his strength and his comforting words, he trembled under the crushing burden of nurturing the faith of all the Catholics in the Rakunai district.

A soft hand rested on the back of his neck in the familiar way. Without turning around, To Rot reached up and grasped his wife's hand in his own. "What will I do?" he whispered. "Everyone is counting on me, but I feel so alone."

Paula's hand tightened around his, as she knelt beside him on the ground. Her lips touched his ear. "You are not alone, To Rot," she whispered. "God is with you, I am with you."

The comfort of her touch and her renewed promise to stand by him eased the band of pressure around his chest. He turned to her, barely able to see her profile in the moonless night. She knew him best of all. In the early years of their marriage, they had often argued. He thought he knew best, and once he had even tried to force her to do what he wanted. How he regretted that! She had seen him at his worst, and yet, she had stayed with him. Their love had grown since that stressful time—even their weaknesses had strengthened their love for each other. Now, Paula seemed to know what he needed better than he did. She held out her arms to him. Peter leaned toward her, finding strength and comfort in her embrace.

The next day, after he and Paula had prayed their morning prayers together, Peter started gathering food. His first duty was to find out exactly where the missionaries were being kept, and what food and supplies they needed. Paula watched him with a half-smile. She couldn't help worrying, but she shared her husband's faith that God would be with them.

But as the months passed and the Japanese military grew more oppressive, Paula started worrying that Peter's faith was showing too strongly. At first, he had been able to work with the authorities. He had carried out his usual rounds of teaching, counseling, serving those who were poor and in need, baptizing infants, and leading the Sunday Eucharistic services, even after the school and church were deliberately destroyed. Although they couldn't celebrate Mass without a priest, when Peter To Rot brought food to the missionaries, they provided him with the Eucharist. He hid the consecrated hosts in a secret underground cave, along with his Bible and some prayer books. On Sunday he would lead the villagers in a service with readings from the word of God, followed by Communion.

But now, the military rapidly grew more hostile toward Christians practicing their faith. The military police imprisoned, beat, and even executed people for things that had been permitted only months before. Some of the local villagers acted as spies for the Japanese military. Peter had been harassed and brought in for questioning several times. Today, they forbade Catholics to worship publicly, discouraging people from praying even in their own homes. What would Peter do?

Once again under the safe cover of darkness, Paula talked to her beloved husband. "We cannot stop practicing our faith," Peter insisted.

"Of course not," Paula retorted. "But you can be more prudent. Please, Peter! I want our children to know their father." And to make her point, she gently rubbed her belly, just starting to show the new life she carried—their third child.

Even in the darkness, Paula could see the proud smile that lit Peter's face. He kissed her. Then his face sobered. "I will try. I think perhaps, if we meet in small groups, we can worship in the underground caves that we dug after the bombings started. And," he added casually, "I've asked Louise, a young girl from the village, to come by every day and look in on you, just in case."

Paula's heart double-thumped at his unfinished thought, "just in case of . . . *what*?" But she knew that Peter could not continue his work as a catechist without risk. With all that he was doing, she knew that he worried about her and the children most of all. She leaned against him, cherishing this moment of safety and closeness.

Peter didn't tell Paula that he'd also asked Louisa, who had no immediate connection to his family, to hide his religious books and the church records, in case he was imprisoned.

The family's greatest trial quickly came. The military police suspected that the Catholics were still worshiping in secret. In their desire to gain the people's good will and simultaneously destroy their connection to the Catholic faith, they legalized and encouraged polygamy. Polygamy had become virtually nonexistent as a result of fifty years of evangelization in the village. But some of the local men, eager for a second wife, started abducting girls—including Catholics—and forcing them into marriage.

Peter couldn't stand by silently. The faith of his people was at risk. He continued his pastoral work in secret, but he publicly disagreed with the legalization of polygamy, openly arguing with his older brother. He affirmed the sanctity of marriage and of marital fidelity. And he tried to assist the

young Catholic women who were being forced into polyga-
mous marriages.

One of the villagers, To Metapa, especially resented Peter,
who had opposed To Metapa's efforts to force a Catholic girl
to become his second wife. One day To Metapa met a young
couple from another village on the road. They were giggling
as they walked, and a few probing questions later, he found
out they had just been married, with Peter officiating. To
Metapa reported Peter to the Japanese military.

Immediately, Peter was taken from his family, and his two
brothers were also arrested. All three brothers were interrogated and beaten. Peter's older brother was accused of
attending church, and assigned to work in the labor camp for
a month, after which he was released. Peter's young brother
was beaten unconscious but then released two weeks later
due to his physical condition. But the military police felt Peter
was the greatest threat. After beating him mercilessly, they
charged him with opposing the officially sanctioned policy of
polygamy, and with leading religious services. They sentenced
him to six weeks in prison. But as his prison term came
toward its end, they refused to tell Peter when he would be
released, despite the inquiries of his village chief and that of
a nearby chief. Peter himself did not believe they would
release him.

Peter's captors informed him that a Japanese doctor
would bring him some medicine the following day. Peter was
not ill—he only had a slight cold. Suspecting something was
wrong, he asked for his shaving kit, his best clothes, his cross,
and his rosary. The next day, Friday, Paula brought what he
asked for, along with some food and their two children:
Andreas, six years old, and Rufina, now three. Paula became
distressed when Peter wouldn't eat much of the food she had
brought. He tried to calm her, telling her it was his duty to

die for his people and for the name of the Father, Son, and Holy Spirit. The little family huddled together as long as they could, the pregnant Paula refusing to leave him. Finally, Peter told her it was time to take the children home.

That afternoon, Peter's elderly mother came to visit, and Peter told her about his suspicions. Earlier in his imprisonment, he had told his friends, "I am in prison because of those who were unfaithful to their marriage vows and because of those who do not want the growth of God's kingdom."

Later in the afternoon, Peter shaved and dressed in his best clothes, carrying his cross and rosary. Unexpectedly, the guards took all of the prisoners except Peter and another man away from the camp, keeping them out overnight— something they had never done before. When the guards saw Arap To Binabak with Peter still in the camp, they sent him away as well. Peter was then forced to lie down, injected with poison and, when he went into convulsions, suffocated. Because he walked away very slowly and kept looking back, Arap To Binabak witnessed Peter's martyrdom. He told a few other prisoners what he had seen, and they found Peter's body as Arap To Binabak had described. Out of fear, none of them told anyone.

The next morning, the returned prisoners found Peter's body carefully rearranged. The prison authorities pretended to be surprised and said that he had died of an infection. They allowed Peter's family to take the body, which on examination showed that he had been poisoned and suffocated. Fear of military reprisal did not prevent a large crowd from gathering to honor this young husband and father, even though his burial was silent, with no religious ceremony allowed.

On January 17, 1995, Pope John Paul II beatified Peter To Rot in his home country of Papua New Guinea. His daughter Rufina was present. Rufina, who had been only three when her father had died defending his faith and the sanctity of marriage, would repeat what her mother told her as she was growing up, "Your father was a good man." But perhaps she remembered her aunt's testimony the best, "He was extraordinarily ordinary!"

Prayer

Blessed Peter To Rot,
Christ was the center of your life and family.
You were a loving father and husband, a dedicated
    catechist,
who courageously and faithfully lived your vocation
in humility amid the ordinary moments of married life.
You chose to witness to the sanctity of marriage
in the face of death.
In these times when the sacredness of marriage
    and family life is frequently denied,
inspire us to a deeper understanding
of the sacrament of marriage and the blessing
    of family life.
Assist all married couples to live their vows
with the same love, respect, and devotion
that you shared with your wife
and with your people. Amen.

About Blessed Peter To Rot

Born: ca. 1912 in Rakunai, East New Britain (part of
    modern Papua New Guinea)

Died: a Friday of July 1945 in a prison camp near his
    village

Memorial: July 7

Beatified: January 17, 1995

Notes on His Life

- Peter was the third of six children, son of the village chief, who converted to Catholicism before Peter was born.

- Peter was an ordinary boy who got into his share of mischief.

- Recognizing his leadership qualities, Peter's pastor wanted him to become a priest, but Peter's father would only agree to Peter becoming a catechist.

- Peter was admired and loved as a catechist not only because he lived what he taught, but also because he was accessible and especially sympathetic for those who were in need or away from the faith.

- Peter was devoted to the Bible, carrying it with him and quoting it frequently. (This was unusual before Vatican II.)

- The only certain date we have in Peter's life is the date of his marriage to Paula Ia Varpit: November 11, 1936. The marriage—arranged by the family—was celebrated not only religiously but with many local customs, including the groom presenting fifty strings of shells for his bride.

- The lack of written records about Peter's life is due to the oral nature of the culture of Papua New Guinea and the destruction of church records during the invasion.

- Peter was the father of three children. Peter's third son, born after his martyrdom, died in infancy. Andreas also died at a young age. Paula lived until 1993. Rufina was the only living member of Peter's family to witness her father's beatification.

Lesser-Known Facts

☞ Although well educated for a man of his village, Peter was a humble man living a simple life. He never traveled more than thirty miles from his place of birth. His sister said of him, "He was extraordinarily ordinary!"

☞ Peter was a keen fisherman and enjoyed eating.

☞ At first, Peter's marriage was far from easy, as the young couple argued a lot. Paula admitted that much of their fighting was due to how hardheaded she was. Gradually, as their love for each other grew, neighbors noticed how devoted the couple were to each other.

☞ When Peter's first child, Andreas, was born, Peter took him with him everywhere he could, which was unusual for a father.

In His Own Words

"I am a catechist and only doing my duty. If I die, I die for my faith."

Saints Zélie and Louis Martin

A Family of Saints

Zélie Martin sat upright in the chair of the doctor's office on that never-to-be-forgotten day in
October 1876. She waited patiently for his verdict.
Without raising his eyes, the doctor cleared his
throat and began writing out a prescription. He
said, "Madame, what you have is a tumor."

"Please be direct with me, doctor. What is the
use of the prescription?"

"Really, no use at all," admitted the doctor.

"Will an operation help me?"

"I'm afraid not, Madame. We have diagnosed
you too late."

Dazed, Zélie stood up, mumbled words of
thanks to the doctor and slowly made her way
home.

Home was a comfortable house in Alençon,
France, where she and her husband, Louis, raised
their five daughters, and from which Zélie ran her
successful lacemaking business. Zélie tried to focus

on finishing an order for lace. She had gone to the doctor by herself, so she alone knew the dreadful truth about her illness.

Exteriorly she remained calm and serene, but anguish tore at her heart. "What will poor Louis do without me?" she thought. "What will happen to Marie, Pauline, my poor Léonie, Céline, and baby Thérèse? How will they manage when I'm not here? I cannot leave them like this. I must remain for a little while longer. I must live!"

Suppertime arrived. Louis led the family in prayer and everyone sat down to the delicious meal. Little Thérèse sat perched on her high chair happily fingering her fork and spoon. Zélie swallowed hard as she looked at her baby.

After supper was over and the dishes were washed, Zélie pulled Louis aside to tell him what the doctor had said. As she choked out the words, Louis dropped his unlit pipe onto his lap. Eyes filling with tears, Louis rose, walked over to her, and embraced her.

"I want to tell the children," Zélie told him. "I may live for years, but it would be well to prepare them . . ." Louis held her close until her tears stopped, and she leaned against him. Finally, Zélie looked up at him. Louis nodded, and together they walked to the living room to join their daughters. Marie, 16, was old enough to run the household and already took care of her little sisters. Fifteen-year-old Pauline was away at boarding school, but Zélie knew how much the news would affect the daughter that she was so close to. At thirteen, Léonie had already been expelled from school three times, despite Zélie's best efforts. Céline was seven and Thérèse was three. They would be too small to understand. Gathering all her courage, Zélie told her daughters the bad news.

The scene was so pitiful, Zélie suffered more for her loved ones than for herself. Poor Louis just looked from Zélie to the circle of children and then back to her. Marie and Léonie sobbed inconsolably. Léonie ran to fling her arms around her mother's neck. She knew her mother would understand her unspoken words. Little Céline and Thérèse looked puzzled and wondered what this was all about. They had never seen everyone so sad before.

Zélie alone remained dry-eyed, although her heart was breaking. After a few moments, she picked up some needlework and quietly set about it. Her calmness and serenity eventually managed to quiet the other members of the family. Zélie would not pain her devoted husband and children by showing them the depths of her own sorrow and fear.

Their little family was no stranger to sorrow. In the past ten years, both Zélie's and Louis's fathers had died. Tragically, Zélie and Louis lost four of their nine children. First, they lost their two little boys within a year of their births. Then their vivacious five-year-old daughter, Marie-Hélène, died suddenly within twenty-four hours of falling ill. Finally, the wet nurse hired to feed their eighth child neglected her, and she died of malnutrition at only eight weeks old in her mother's arms. Zélie had feared that little Thérèse would follow in her sisters' footsteps, but she had survived and grown strong. Both Zélie and Louis had been devastated by their children's deaths, and years later would speak of little Marie-Hélène. They counted on their innocent children being in heaven, and often prayed for their intercession in family needs.

But Zélie knew this news would crush her Louis. They were so close and they shared so much, on such a deep level. He had sold his business to help her run hers, and he never complained. How well they complemented each other—her passion, energy, and intelligence were matched by his strength, patience, affection, and methodic ways. From their earliest days of acquaintance, they had agreed that their marriage was to be a mutual journey to holiness, and they'd prayed together that each of their children would consecrate their lives to God.

Zélie watched anxiously for Louis to collapse under his grief. But after his initial reaction, and a deep seriousness that overcame him, the only changes in Louis were his greater tenderness toward her and that he gave up all his usual activities—even fishing—and refused to leave Zélie alone for any length of time.

At first, the busy round of household tasks and the prosperous lacemaking business continued as usual. Even though Zélie had not felt well for some time, her energetic creativity, combined with her desire to provide for her family, became a helpful outlet. But gradually, her greater preoccupation became providing for her children's welfare and helping to manage the burden that would fall on her beloved Louis's shoulders. Together, they decided to sell her lace business, so Louis could devote himself to nursing his wife and taking care of their daughters.

They both prayed for acceptance of God's will, but still hoped for a cure. Zélie went to Paris to visit her brother Isidore and to seek a second doctor's opinion. But the doctor only confirmed that it was indeed too late for surgery. After some months, as Zélie's strength failed and the pain grew greater, she and Louis decided she should visit Lourdes to pray for a miraculous healing. Zélie took her three oldest daughters on this pilgrimage of faith. It was a difficult trip— two of the girls got train-sick; Marie and Pauline lost their favorite rosaries; Zélie fell and injured her neck. Disappointingly, despite the baths and prayers, Zélie was not cured. During the journey home, Zélie tried to comfort her daughters, who were deeply distraught, by reminding them of

Our Lady's promise to Bernadette, "I will not make you happy in this world, but in the next."

As Zélie stepped down from the train, she could see Louis waiting, holding hands with their two youngest daughters. She saw the hope in his face fade as she walked toward him—she knew the lines on her own face had deepened even in the short time she'd been away. She leaned into his gentle hug, and she resolved to live in the same spirit of faith she'd just witnessed in his eyes. *How could she let go of everything—not just her health and abilities, but her children?* Louis, swallowing tears, whispered in a shaken voice for her ears alone. "Welcome back, my dear. I won't leave your side again," he promised. And he didn't.

Louis became a rock of strength that Zélie clung to as her sufferings rapidly grew worse. She went to Mass for the last time on the first Friday of August. A few weeks later, she lay dying. Louis left her side only to call for a priest, who anointed Zélie and gave her Viaticum. All five daughters knelt silently by her bed, crying. Zélie could no longer speak, so Louis comforted them.

At one point, Zélie fixed a long look of supplication on her young sister-in-law, Céline, who understood immediately and pressed her hand. "I will be there for your daughters," she assured Zélie.

Louis, Marie, Pauline, Léonie, and Zélie's brother Isidore stayed with her through the last agonizing night. Zélie died on August 28, at 12:30 AM, surrounded by their love. The next morning, Louis performed the heartrending task of bringing his younger daughters to kiss their mother for the last time.

That moment almost broke him. He and Zélie had been married almost twenty years, and, though he had been a determined bachelor when he had met her, Zélie's beauty—inner and outer—had quickly attracted him. They had truly become as one. What would he do without his partner on life's adventure? And how could he raise their five daughters on his own?

Louis would have preferred to remain in his beloved Alençon, where he had friends and support. But Zélie had wished him to take the girls to Lisieux, so his daughters could be near their Aunt Céline and Uncle Isidore. They would greatly need a motherly figure in their lives. Louis, now widowed at fifty-four years old, retired early so he could focus on raising his five daughters, ranging in age from four to seventeen. He had never felt so lost.

He knew that his daughters could see the weight of his grief, but he didn't allow it to weigh on them. Daily, Louis took sanctuary in a little attic apartment the girls called "The Belvedere," where he could read and pray. But Louis took tender care of his daughters. He encouraged them to keep their little family customs, such as gathering around the fireplace in the evening to read a carefully chosen spiritual book before going to bed. He still sang to little Thérèse while she sat on his lap. Little Céline chose Marie as her "little mother," and Thérèse chose Pauline as hers. An affectionate and loving father, Louis's attentiveness to his daughters' needs gradually helped heal the family's grief. He'd always had a special relationship with each of his daughters, giving each a pet name. He was closest to his oldest daughter, Marie, whom he called his "diamond." Pauline was his "pearl," Léonie was "Good Léonie," Céline "his dauntless one," and Thérèse, "little Queen." Their home continued to be a tranquil "holy ground" for his daughters to nourish themselves spiritually and prepare for their vocations.

In 1881, Pauline, who had always expressed an interest in becoming a religious, discerned her vocation to Carmel. Four years later, both Léonie and Marie also asked permission of their father to enter religious life. To give permission was a great sacrifice—Céline and Thérèse were still young, even though Céline was ready to run the household. But above all, Louis would miss his daughters. Touchingly, he opened his heart to Marie, the daughter he'd always confided most in. While he encouraged her in her vocation, he also revealed that her going was his greatest sacrifice, because he had thought she would never leave him.

His health gradually began to deteriorate and Louis suffered a minor stroke. His youngest daughter, fifteen-year-old Thérèse, asked for permission to enter Carmel. Not so much surprised, but grief-stricken once again at the thought of such an early separation, Louis picked a little white flower growing nearby and handed it to her, explaining how God had showered it with love. From then on, Thérèse thought of herself as that little flower.

Although Céline also secretly desired to enter Carmel, she decided she would be the one to stay with her father through all the trials of his illness. After Thérèse entered Carmel, Louis began to suffer from the effects of cerebral arteriosclerosis. He started wandering off where no one could find him. Realizing that she could no longer take care of him because she couldn't watch him all the time, Céline sorrowfully brought her father to a psychiatric hospital run by the Sisters of Charity of Saint Vincent de Paul, who only allowed her to visit him once a week. Louis offered to God the humiliation of being institutionalized. Three years later, when his health had declined further and he could no longer wander off on his own, Céline brought him home to care for him.

He continued to gradually decline, visiting his daughters at Carmel one last time. He died a peaceful death on Sunday, July 29, 1894, at age seventy, rejoining his beloved wife Zélie and their four children already in heaven.

Zélie and Louis Martin's deepest desires were granted. All five of their surviving daughters dedicated their lives to God in religious life. The youngest would one day be known as *Saint Thérèse of the Child Jesus*, more popularly called the *Little Flower*, and declared a doctor of the Church. Saint Thérèse would refer to her parents as "holy ground" in which she and her sisters grew up.

Prayer

Saints Zélie and Louis,
hear our prayers for our family.
You tenderly nurtured your littlest ones
into health and holiness,
and you also knew how to encourage the best in your
    loved ones.
You generously entrusted your family into the loving
    hands of God,
not allowing the stresses
of busy commitments to business and loved ones
to fracture your love for each other
nor the peace of your home.
In the difficulties we face as a family,
help us to grow together in love,
so that our family may truly become
the place where we become saints. Amen.

About Saints Zélie and Louis Martin

Zélie Martin (born Zélie Guerin)
Born: December 23, 1831, in Gandelain, France
Died: August 28, 1877, of breast cancer

Louis Martin
Born: August 22, 1823, in Bordeaux, France
Died: July 29, 1894
Canonized: October 18, 2015
Feast Day: July 12
Patrons: married couples, widowers, parents, those facing illness and death

Notes on Their Lives

- Zélie describes her own childhood "as sad as a winding-sheet"; her mother was very strict and wouldn't even allow her two daughters to have dolls.

- Zélie's father provided a very good education for Zélie and her sister and brother.

- Both Louis and Zélie wanted to become religious before they met each other. They didn't because. . . .

- Louis was told he couldn't enter the Carthusians because he didn't know Latin; after some months of studying he gave up.

- Zélie was probably refused because of ill health; her only sister became a Visitation sister and later provided guidance for Léonie.

- Despite her longing for religious life, Zélie would later say that she was born to be a mother, she loved her children so much.

Both parents paid close attention to their children's individual qualities, seeking to help them develop. Zélie's observations can be found in her letters (more than 200 of them remain); Louis nurtured a unique rapport with each of his daughters that grew as they matured.

Louis and Zélie Martin are the first spouses in the history of the Church to be canonized as a couple.

Lesser-Known Facts

Before Zélie had met Louis, she passed him on a bridge and heard a voice telling her that Louis was the one prepared for her.

Despite his mother's concern, Louis was a confirmed bachelor, but within three months of meeting Zélie, he married her. Louis was thirty-five, Zélie twenty-seven.

Louis and Zélie had nine children, but only five girls survived. (They lost two boys and two girls under the age of five.)

Zélie Martin was a working mother who oversaw the work of a number of young women weekly. Louis also ran his own successful watchmaking/jewelry business, but eventually sold it to support Zélie's lacemaking—as accountant, manager, and salesman.

Motto for Their Marriage

"God is served first."

— Motto inspired by Saint Joan of Arc

Reader's Guides

⌒ℰ♣ℐ⌒

Blessed are the poor in spirit,
for theirs is the kingdom of heaven (Mt 5:3).

Saint Francis of Assisi

Francis was like the rich young man Jesus spoke to in the Gospel (Mt 19:16–30), but Francis overcame his sadness, gave everything away, and wholeheartedly embraced a life of radical poverty. The irrepressible joy that shone from his poverty of spirit drew many to the imitation of Christ.

Personal Reflection

❧ Francis heard this urgent request, "Restore my church, which is falling into ruins." Our church today has much need of renewal. How can you personally respond to this call?

❧ Reflect on Saint Francis's reaction to the leper. Think over your relationship with charity. Do you actually perform works of charity? How personal is your touch? Do you see Christ in those you serve?

Group Discussion

🞂 Saint Francis is often quoted as saying, "Let us go preach, and if necessary, we will use words." Discuss what his statement says to the meaning of discipleship.

🞂 We generally admire Saint Francis for his gentle spirit and his reverence for all of God's creation, but he was not a man of compromise or of half-hearted commitment. How can we individually or as a group better "Serve the Master rather than men"?

Read ⟶ Reflect ⟶ Respond

Mark 10:17–31
Luke 14:33
Deuteronomy 15:11
Psalm 41:1–3
Catechism of the Catholic Church 2544–2550

Saint Juan Diego

A simple, uneducated man, but wise and willing, Juan Diego took the evangelization of his people squarely on his shoulders when he accepted Mary's commission.

Personal Reflection

🞂 Juan Diego spoke to our Lady with a familiarity not often seen even among the saints. He was amazed, but not startled to encounter her in his travels. What can I learn from him that would make prayer more real to me?

⁂ Although he thought of himself as an unworthy messenger, Juan Diego seemed disarmingly self-possessed, even in the presence of the bishop and his attendants. Reread his story and look for some basis for this confidence he projects.

Group Discussion

⁂ Discuss the significance to our contemporary Church, your parish or group in particular of the revelation of the Mary as Our Lady of Guadalupe to Juan Diego.

⁂ Reflect on Mary's solicitude for Juan Diego. She said to him: "Am I not your Mother? Aren't you beneath my shadow, protected by me? Aren't you within the folds of my mantle and within the embrace of my arms? Is there anything that you need?" Consider ways to enliven within your parish and your own family devotion to our Lady and confidence in her.

Read ⟶ Reflect ⟶ Respond

Isaiah 40:31
Psalm 91
John 2:1–12
Catechism of the Catholic Church 967–970, 2548

*Blessed are those who mourn,
for they will be comforted (Matthew 5:4).*

Saint Germaine Cousin

A young French shepherdess whose life was one of sickness and neglect, Germaine achieved a high degree of virtue and mystical prayer.

Personal Reflection

- We usually think of mourning as lament for the dead, but as in the case of Germaine, we can also mourn that love is withheld. Do other examples of mourning come to mind? How are all of these similar to loss through death?

- While Germaine's sufferings were obvious, the "comforts" she received in life were not. Look at the "comforts" described and their significance in her life. Think also of God's gifts to you of "comfort."

Group Discussion

- Reflect together on the ministries of comfort that exist in your parish or that your family or group engage in. How can you persuade others to join with you?

- Saint Germaine's story highlights the abuse of children, something so prevalent in our day. In this account we also see spousal abuse, disruption of the normal relations among children in a family, and endangerment of animals. Are you prepared to educate others about the forms of abuse and the ways of prevention and intervention?

Read ·•· Reflect ·•· Respond

Psalm 31:9–24

2 Corinthians 4:7–17

Luke 14:10

Catechism of the Catholic Church 1930, 1936–1937,
2222–2223

Saint Monica

Saint Monica is the patron of wives and mothers because she lived her whole life in the hope of bettering strained relationships and winning for God the hearts of those she loved. Her efforts and tears were rewarded with the conversion of both her husband and her son.

Personal Reflection

⟨⟩ Monica found strength in her mourning through the virtue of Christian forbearance, which led her to a patience marked by gentleness and kindness. In your life can you find a similar chain of virtues? If not, what do you see as the next good step?

⟨⟩ Monica's life was one of constant anxiety and disappointment. Monica brought all of this to prayer, seeking strength and guidance, and she often received a specific directive. And eventually all her prayers were answered. Reflect on your prayer life. Are you constant, persistent, trusting, and grateful?

Group Discussion

⟨⟩ Many Catholics suffer because children, grandchildren, or godchildren no longer practice their faith. In some cases their own young ones are not baptized or instructed. Share ways in which you have addressed this heartbreak in your family or among friends.

   Saint Monica had a very troubled marriage. Not only was her husband irreligious and bad-tempered, but he was also unfaithful. Her mother-in-law caused her much suffering as well. Monica worked very long and hard to win her husband over and to preserve their marriage. In your parish setting or within your extended family there may be persons facing the same sorrow. How can you offer assistance and comfort?

Read •→• Reflect •→• Respond

Luke 11:9–10
2 Thessalonians 2:16
1 Thessalonians 3:10
Ephesians 5:22–25
Catechism of the Catholic Church 1643, 2742–2745

〰

Blessed are the meek,
for they will inherit the earth (Mt 5:5).

Saint Bernadette Soubirous

A sickly illiterate child of an insignificant family is visited by the Blessed Virgin and entrusted with a message of penitence and prayer. Her docility and humility lead to the establishment of one of the greatest healing shrines in the world: Lourdes.

Personal Reflection

🙡 What do you think motivates God so often to choose children or the powerless for great missions? Might this be a "message" within the specific message of the apparition?

🙡 "The beautiful young Lady" who appears to Bernadette irradiates a certain magnetic attraction for the girl. She cannot stay away from the grotto despite her parents' objection. If you are a devotee of Mary you might be able to explain this attraction. If you are not a devotee, how do you picture yourself approaching her?

Group Discussion

🙡 Bernadette's trust in and love of the Lady was tested in many ways, but most dramatically when she was told to drink from and wash in the spring that was nothing but a spot of mud. She was humiliated as she walked through the crowd choking and covered in mud. However, the miraculous spring resulted from her obedience. What miracles or graces have you witnessed coming from some seemingly absurd directive you were asked to follow?

In the convent at Nevers, Bernadette's life continued to be unexceptional. She was subjected to the common trials and misunderstandings that accompany everyone's life. Bernadette was sustained by Mary's promise, not of happiness in this world, but "in the other." Although this kind of happiness is a reality, it still remains a "mystery." Reflecting together find a way to "make sense" of this mystery.

Read ⸱→⸱ Reflect ⸱→⸱ Respond

John 5:36–37
Isaiah 29:19
Psalm 37:11
Matthew 18:4
Catechism of the Catholic Church 490–492, 968–969

Saint Gregory the Great

Although he wished to decline his appointment to the papacy, Gregory accepted and placed himself and his talents so wholeheartedly at the service of the Church as to be truly deserving of the title, "the Great."

Personal Reflection

Abbot Gregory begged God to find a good, capable man to fill the See of Peter. The answer given was unexpected and unwanted. Think of a time that you prayed to find the right person for a position only to find out that you were that person. Remind yourself of how God's grace accompanied your acceptance.

Few persons have had such a storied career as Gregory. Consider your personal career of service beginning with the chores of your childhood to volunteer activities. Do you feel that what you are currently involved in is really bringing on the kingdom, or is there something more you feel drawn to do?

Group Discussion

Often it is difficult for sincere people to work together and remain focused on the common task without falling into the inevitable human foibles that stall or stop the good intended. Is there anything in the example of Gregory that could help us achieve a modest claim on greatness in our service?

We may hear certain persons lamenting that they must stay in this or that situation, or that they are asked to change occupations against their own better judgment or inclination. How would you recommend that such a person go about the process of discernment?

Read ··•·· Reflect ··•·· Respond

Matthew 11:29
Romans 1:5
Hebrews 10:36
Catechism of the Catholic Church 880, 2611

Blessed are those who hunger and thirst
for righteousness, for they will be filled (Mt 5:6).

Blessed Pier Giorgio Frassati

A young man who died in his twenty-fourth year, Pier Giorgio reached a maturity of virtue and grace that was beautifully manifested in his exuberance for life and his generous spirit of hidden service.

Personal Reflection

- The term *righteousness* is often translated as *justice* or *holiness.* Among these three words, do you see any clear distinctions?

- What do you think of Pier Giorgio's radical choices, i.e., giving away his shoes as a child; spending his graduation gift on the poor; clashing with police at a public rally; or suspending his love life out of respect for his parents? Have you experienced radical movements of grace?

Group Discussion

- Often we hear it said that a particular athlete or a team has more hunger for success than their opponents. How is this like the hunger and thirst of Pier Giorgio?

- Reflecting on the obvious interplay of prayer and service in Pier Giorgio's life, evaluate the opportunities within your parish that would allow for such integrated Christian witness.

Read ⟶ *Reflect* ⟶ *Respond*

Proverbs 2:1–11
Isaiah 58:6–9
Matthew 22:37–40
Catechism of the Catholic Church 1810–1811, 2419–2420,
2443–2444

Venerable Teresita Quevedo

Teresita made the Blessed Virgin Mary the model and guide of her life. Through an abundance of small kindnesses and profound prayers, she offered Mary the gift of joyful service.

Personal Reflection

❀ While preparing for a tennis competition, Teresita recognized her motivation as vanity. When she lost, she thanked Our Lady. When she gave alms, she received a very meaningful gift. Reflect on any such "holy" coincidences in your life. Was there a connection between a virtuous act and God's gift to you?

❀ "Love makes all things easy." What proof have you seen of this maxim in your own life or in the life of another?

Group Discussion

❀ Reread the dialogue between Teresita and her father about her vocation. How would you respond if a lively young person confided to you about his or her attraction to religious life? If he or she mentioned a desire for a life of sacrifice, would you know how to react?

✿ Teresita wanted everyone who saw her to see Mary "who was her life." Is devotion to Mary prominent in your own life, in that of your family, or within your community? How could it be enhanced?

Read ·→· Reflect ·→· Respond

Wisdom 8:7
Deuteronomy 6:4–5
1 Corinthians 6:19–20
Luke 1:46–48
Catechism of the Catholic Church 2560–2561, 2660, 2679

⟨❀⟩

*Blessed are the merciful, for they will receive mercy
(Mt 5:7).*

Saint Frances Xavier Cabrini

Mother Cabrini made herself an immigrant among immigrants, embracing, as she said, "everything—labors, joys, and pains—for the salvation of all people."

Personal Reflection

⚜ It is easy to imagine living the life of a saint like Mother Cabrini when we are looking at it from its end and glorification—she was rewarded with mercy because she was merciful in life—but can you feel anything of the stress and struggle of her daily life and labor?

⚜ Reflect on Francesca's attempts to enter religious life and her two early attempts at life within community. What does her journey say to you about your own search for and living out of your calling?

Group Discussion

⚜ Mother Cabrini's sisters did a variety of works—not all led or taught others, administered, or traveled—some did little parts of the whole work. What are some specific actions that we can do together to assist today's immigrants to better their lives in our community?

⚜ Mother Cabrini was an extraordinary woman who in her sixty-seven years accomplished the work of several lifetimes. What do we see as her motivation(s)? How does baptism motivate us to live the beatitude of mercy? How could our parish and community benefit from this realization?

Read ⤞ Reflect ⤞ Respond

Philippians 6:17–21
Matthew 25:31–46
Leviticus 19:33–34
Catechism of the Catholic Church 1718, 1821–1823

Saint Martin de Porres

Known as "Martin the Charitable" because from his youth his life *was* one continual act of gentle and generous service to others, regardless of how he was treated, he saw Christ in everyone.

Personal Reflection

❦ Saint Martin was so known for his charity; why is he offered as an example of the beatitude of mercy? What connection do you see?

❦ Have you ever tried to imagine how saints can think of themselves as so unworthy and yet be such happy people? How do you think of yourself in your relationship with God?

Group Discussion

❦ Do you think of mercy as something coming from a person of means (wealth, power, influence) to someone in some type of need, or could a poor brother bestow mercy on a rich benefactor simply by begging his help? Have you experienced this phenomenon of grace yourself?

❖ It is unlikely that any of us will be wonder-workers as was Martin (of course, neither do we reach the heights of his prayer or the depths of his penance), but in what ways is it possible for us to be men and women of mercy?

Read ⟶ *Reflect* ⟶ *Respond*

Matthew 5:7; 6:1–4; 7:21–24
Psalm 84:10–12
Catechism of the Catholic Church 1823, 1828–1829, 2447

Blessed are the pure in heart,
for they will see God (Mt 5:8).

Saint Kateri Tekakwitha

Known as the "glory of the Mohawks," this young Native American was inspired by the memory of her mother's faith to seek out instructions in the Catholic faith, be baptized, and live as a virgin for Christ.

Personal Reflection

- It is amazing to observe how willingly most newly baptized persons accept the beautiful but challenging teachings of our faith, i.e., the Incarnation, the Real Presence in the Eucharist, the power of prayer, and the value of penance. Too often cradle Catholics appear to have difficulty maintaining a strong faith. What are your personal insights into keeping a strong and active faith?

- Kateri was determined not to marry. In her culture it was expected that parents or guardians would arrange a suitable match for a young person. Kateri was ahead of her time in realizing the right each of us has to choose our own state in life. Think over your own life choices. Do you recognize them as steps leading to the ultimate goal of the blessed encounter with God?

Group Discussion

- What do you understand by "the pure in heart"? In what ways are you able to grow in this multifaceted virtue and promote it within your family and parish, and among your peers?

- In Kateri's story we see the power of prayer at work even before her baptism. She begged "Rawanniio" to send her a priest so that she could know the faith of her mother. What does this say to you about the validity and sincerity of the prayers of non-Catholics, or non-Christians?

Read •→• Reflect •→• Respond

John 14:23
Philippians 4:8
1 Peter 1:22–25
Titus 1:15
1 John 2:17, 24–25
Catechism of the Catholic Church 2518–2519, 2527

Blessed Marie-Clémentine Anuarite Nengapeta

As a young religious, when she was called upon to face the ultimate test of virtue with little time to prepare, Anuarite chose to stand firm and accept death rather than sin. She witnessed to her commitment with her life.

Personal Reflection

- Reading the opening of Anuarite's story we see how quickly things can change in life. For the Sisters of the Holy Family, it was a violent invasion of their evening meal; for us it could be a financial misfortune, a serious illness, a difficult relationship, or some other unforeseen crisis. Reflect on your spiritual readiness for the unexpected.

❧ Sister Anuarite had chosen the prayer "Jesus alone" as her motto. These two words inspired her personal spiritual progress, her dealings with others, and her studies, and they proved her comfort in martyrdom. Do you have a prayer or saying that sustains and inspires you?

Group Discussion

❧ One of the terrible consequences of war is unwarranted violence, particularly the rape of women. In this case the victims were consecrated religious, but rape is never excusable. In our society, this crime occurs all too frequently and often is glossed over or played down. Do you as a group have any insights or strategies for educating the young on the importance of being pure of heart?

❧ It is said that although only Anuarite died, the whole Community suffered martyrdom. Their solidarity and support of one another was their strength and comfort. As a group do you experience this sense of being brothers and sisters? Do you feel that the sharing of spiritual support unites and energizes you to live always a deeper faith?

Read ⟶ Reflect ⟶ Respond

Luke 20:34–38
Romans 6:22–23
Ephesians 5:1–5
Catechism of the Catholic Church 2520–2521

⟨✿⟩

Blessed are the peacemakers,
for they will be called children of God (Mt 5:9).

Saint Elizabeth of Hungary

This young woman, wife and widow of the ruling count of Thuringia and mother of three small children, was a woman of peace. Her home was a haven of peace; she sought peace with her in-laws, in serving the needs of the poor, and in doing the will of God.

Personal Reflection

⚜ Afraid she loved her husband too much, Elizabeth prayed, "It is in God that I love my husband: may he who sanctified marriage grant eternal life." Her love for Ludwig was as intense as any modern relationship, but God was first in her heart. Reflect on this wisdom of Saint Elizabeth.

⚜ Elizabeth lost her beloved Ludwig when she was only twenty. However, her intense grief soon became acceptance. Reread her prayer to see how she made peace with God's will. Are you able to accept God's will graciously even when you find it difficult?

Group Discussion

⚜ Elizabeth of Hungary was a very charitable woman who never denied the poor. She believed that the well-being of a person led to the well-being of the nation. She offered tools and training, as well as alms, to ensure that her people became self-sustaining. How can you tap into this philosophy?

❧ Driven from her home when she was widowed, Elizabeth intensified her charitable works, pausing only to ensure the future of her children. What opportunities are available in your area for the widowed and retired to spend more time serving those in need?

Read ⤳ Reflect ⤳ Respond

Matthew 5:42–6:4
Matthew 6:25–34
John 14:27
Catechism of the Catholic Church 306, 2429–2431, 2433, 2443–2444

Saint Catherine of Siena

Patron saint of Italy and Doctor of the Church, Catherine of Siena was a mystic and true apostle of peace. In her thirty-three years she and her followers brought about a great renewal in the Church.

Personal Reflection

❧ Catherine was privileged to see and converse with Jesus and several saints. She dictated some of her experiences in a book called *The Dialogues*. Consider your own prayer. Are you able to dialogue with God in prayer? Are your prayers conversations?

❧ At a certain point after allowing a few years of solitude and prayer, Jesus told Catherine that she must go out and live what she had contemplated and serve him in others. How does your prayer life lead you to action?

Group Discussion

❧ Some of Catherine's biggest peace missions were within the Church, when trouble arose due to politics and corruption. The pope and the Catholic princes had armies, and the threat of violence always loomed. Even today the Church suffers from feuds and partisanship within parishes and dioceses, among individuals, and even universally. How can each of us be a peacemaker in today's Church?

❧ Mediating peace is not always a source of peace for the one doing the mediating. Emotions are strained, strength is tried, and patience is tested. Share ways in which you have helped bring about peace and reconciliation.

Read ·➛· Reflect ·➛· Respond

Matthew 6:9–10
Philippians 4:6–7
Proverbs 3:17
1 Corinthians 2:6–16
Catechism of the Catholic Church 1831, 2305–2306, 2611

*Blessed are those who are persecuted for righteousness'
sake, for theirs is the kingdom of heaven (Matthew 5:10).*

Blessed Isidore Bakanja

At his death, Isidore was a very young man and a recent
convert intent on bettering himself in a new occupation.
Because of his desire to witness to his faith simply by wearing
a scapular, he was violently persecuted and killed.

Personal Reflection

- Prayerfully reflect to discover reasons for any dislike you
  may feel toward a particular person or group of people.
  Ask honestly if there is something in your mind or heart
  that triggers this feeling. Are you being just?

- Despite such violent reactions, Isidore knew he must stand
  up for his belief and for his personal dignity and his manhood. Consider the importance of standing up for those
  who suffer because of their faith, their convictions, their
  dreams. And what about those whose dignity is violated in
  the womb, in hospitals or prisons, or on a deathbed?

Group Discussion

- The outward demonstration of faith riles many people today (for example, verbal vitriol on the Internet or screaming matches outside places of worship). Motivations
  range from false information and ignorance to guilt and
  malice. How can we best deal with unreasonable displays
  of hostility toward our personal faith or against the teachings of the Church?

How do you apply the fact of our equality before God—as persons, but especially as baptized members of Christ's Mystical Body—to the inevitable cultural clashes that occur in parishes, neighborhoods, and even families because of ethnicity, age, customs, race, background, and so forth?

Read ·➤· Reflect ·➤· Respond

Mark 13:9–13
1 Corinthians 12:12–26
Titus 3:1–11
Catechism of the Catholic Church 618, 2297, 2303

Saint Mary MacKillop

A native daughter of Australia, Mary engaged all her love and energies in the work of education and catechetics, serving the needy, and advocating for prisoners and oppressed laborers. She overcame all odds, including harassment and accusation, by her living devotion to the Sacred Heart.

Personal Reflection

Many people suffer at the hands of others, but for this suffering to be the stuff of heaven certain dispositions are necessary. What stood out for you in Mary MacKillop's disposition?

If you are unfamiliar with what excommunication entails, look up the term. Spend some time considering how unjust such a sentence was to Mother Mary and how disruptive it was to the lives of so many who were dependent on her. Consider her as a special patron in times of injustice and in situations that appear to be beyond resolution.

Group Discussion

❦ Mother MacKillop's advice to her sisters, as cited at the end of her story, is appropriate for all Christian families and groups. How would living by these words help us face the disagreements and stresses that are inevitable as we strive to serve God's people together?

❦ One of the causes of Mother Mary's persecution was her part in the removal of an abusive priest. This sin of abuse has caused the Church much suffering in our times as well. Are you familiar with the guidelines for dealing with situations of abuse in your diocese? Are there also ways you can call down purifying grace upon the Church?

Read ⟶ Reflect ⟶ Respond

Romans 1:16–17
John 16:33
Galatians 5:22–26
Catechism of the Catholic Church 164, 1826, 1832

ᘓ𝐂✿ᘐᗝ

The Sacrament of Baptism: Newness of Life

Saint Paul

A sincere young Pharisee finds himself on the wrong side of truth. His conversion is a living illustration of the power of baptism. His life is totally made new and his energy infused with grace.

Personal Reflection

- In his dramatic encounter with the risen Christ, Saul was rendered blind (symbolic of his inner blindness to Christ's truth). At the word and touch of Ananias, his blindness fell away like scales from his eyes. Have you ever been struck by a moment of truth sent to you through an Ananias?

- After some instruction, Saul was baptized. Yet when he proclaimed Christ, Saul encountered fear and opposition due in part to his reputation, but also because of the force of his character. Is there anything in you that you want to change so that Christ can work through you?

Group Discussion

- Baptism charges each of us with the mission to preach our faith in Christ. Paul brought the message of salvation to many different peoples. We often must present the faith to different types of people with various abilities and backgrounds. In what ways can we imitate Paul in adapting Christ's message to our audience?

- Christianity is marked by joy, peace, and love, yet Saul was told that he would have to suffer for his belief (Acts

9:16). In your collective experience, how do these two things go together?

Read ⟶ Reflect ⟶ Respond

1 Corinthians 10:16–17
Acts 2:38–39
Romans 6:17–18
1 Timothy 1:12–17
Catechism of the Catholic Church 787–790, 1227, 1263

Saint Cecilia

As a young woman of her time, Cecilia submitted to her parents' plans; as a Christian, she was obedient to Christ. She catechized her husband and her brother-in-law, and together with them she gave the ultimate witness of faith.

Personal Reflection

✸ Some people believe our vocation in life comes at baptism. Saint Cecilia felt a call to consecrated virginity. Are you able to trace your state in life to your baptism? Do you see your choice as an expression of your baptism in Christ?

✸ Cecilia's mother hoped that Valerian, although a nonbeliever, would allow Cecilia to practice her faith. A good marriage cannot be based only on a hope. If you were their friend, what advice about marriage preparation would you give Cecilia and her mother?

Group Discussion

✸ Cecilia's parents believed that marrying her to a good, upright pagan would provide protection for her in a pagan world. "No one would be able to tell that she was Christian," the story says. What do you, as committed Christians, say to this strategy?

𝒮 The moment of Cecilia's death is depicted in the statue by Stefano Maderno (1599) in the Basilica of Saint Cecilia in Trastevere (Rome). She is lying face down with her hands in front of her. One finger is extended on the left hand and three fingers are extended on the right hand, to represent the unity and Trinity of God. This is how she witnessed to her faith and renewed her baptismal promises. How do we renew ours? How do we witness to our baptism?

Read ⟶ *Reflect* ⟶ *Respond*

Matthew 5:14; 28:18–19
1 Corinthians 7:12–16
Catechism of the Catholic Church 3, 1239, 1619–1620

❦

The Sacrament of Confirmation: Christian Maturity

Saint Helena

As mother of Emperor Constantine, Helena was a woman of influence; however, she was also a woman of sorrow, deprived of her marriage. Her faith in Christ, which she embraced late, became the center and strength of her life.

Personal Reflection

☘ The office of emperor demands the "balance of tremendous power with moderation, prudence, and justice." Helena reflected that "the pull of emotions could unbalance the best of judgments." Reflect on your own emotions. Are you able to express them with virtue, or do you feel a constant struggle?

☘ Popular legend believes that Helena discovered the cross of Jesus while in the Holy Land preparing ground for a new church. Whether or not this is true, she did discover the true meaning of the cross during her pilgrimage. During those years of walking in the footsteps of Jesus, she found peace of heart in giving herself freely for the honor of God. What does the cross mean to you?

Group Discussion

☘ Serious problems assailed the imperial family. Helena asked herself what she could do "to heal our family, to bring our focus back to Christ and serving the Church." All of our families experience problems, some more serious than others, but all are hard to deal with. Often they arise from a forgetfulness of religious principles and devotion. Discuss ways to bring the focus back to Christ.

🕮 "By this sign you shall conquer." These words led Constantine to victory in battle and inspired him to grant religious freedom to the Church. Consider how Confirmation is the sacrament of Christian victory in life's struggles.

Read ⤍ Reflect ⤍ Respond

Luke 4:18–19
John 17:21–23; 20:21–22
Acts 1:14
Ephesians 1:13–14
Catechism of the Catholic Church 1290, 1308–1309, 2364, 2400

Saint Lorenzo Ruiz

Everything seemed to go wrong for this young Catholic husband and father. Yet in the midst of an unbelievable situation he called on the grace of his Confirmation and received the ultimate reward.

Personal Reflection

🕮 Lorenzo wrestled with this question: Is it better to pretend to renounce the faith and live, or to die and abandon my family? Have you ever been tempted to pretend you were not Catholic to avoid some ridicule or prejudice?

🕮 Without any knowledge of where he was going, Lorenzo boarded a ship to escape capture. One week after the ship docked he was imprisoned by the Japanese for being a Christian missionary. In fact, Confirmation "confirms" our baptismal vocation to spread the Gospel. Do you feel prepared to witness to your faith in the expected and the unexpected?

Group Discussion

▨ Lorenzo was facing death unwittingly and unwillingly. His story is a perfect witness to the power of the sacrament of Confirmation because, after struggling against his fate, he prayed for strength and found himself filled with holy purpose. He won the greatest victory in martyrdom. Share occasions when you felt the power of your Confirmation.

▨ Back in the Philippines Lorenzo was falsely accused of murder. The occupying Spaniards picked him out because he was half Chinese and half Filipino, and, therefore, considered a second-class citizen. At Pentecost the Holy Spirit came on all believers of every background. How do you rate yourself, your parish, your group on openness and acceptance of those who are different from you?

Read ⟶ Reflect ⟶ Respond

Luke 17:1–10; 24:36–49
Acts 1:8
2 Corinthians 2:14–17
2 Maccabees 6:18–28
Catechism of the Catholic Church 1285, 1296, 1302

⟨❀⟩

The Holy Eucharist: Source and Summit of Christian Life

Saint Thomas Aquinas

One of the Church's greatest theologians, Thomas Aquinas wrote works of theology that still sustain our faith and eloquent hymns that express our prayer. His intellectual astuteness was matched only by his humility of heart.

Personal Reflection

❀ When asked to reply to a difficult theological question, Thomas turned to his formidable knowledge and to adoration of the Blessed Sacrament. Do you feel prepared to respond to questions about faith from family or acquaintances? If you are unsure of what to say, how do you seek an answer?

❀ Thomas was not only a learned man, but also a humble man. Reflect on the interplay of these two attributes. Ask yourself how situations in your own life might be influenced by this kind of balance.

Group Discussion

❀ Because others recognized his fine mind, his goodness, and his devotion, Thomas was given the opportunity to pursue a priestly vocation. Within your parish or family have you approached anyone about a priestly or religious vocation? Have you considered spiritual or financial ways to support vocations?

❀ Thomas wrote some of the most important Eucharistic theology, as well as some of the most sublime Eucharistic hymns. Find ways to deepen devotion to the Eucharist, personally, within the family, and as a parish. One suggestion might be to encourage expression of devotion through special liturgies, holy hours, processions, and private adoration.

Read ·•· Reflect ·•· Respond

Matthew 6:19–21; 18:1–4
1 Timothy 2:7
Hebrews 4:12–14
Leviticus 10:10–11
Catechism of the Catholic Church 1324, 1380–1381, 2625, 2712–2719

Saint Elizabeth Seton

Elizabeth Seton began life as a wealthy New Yorker, enjoying her husband and children amid a busy social circle. Tragedy left her widowed, but God gave her the treasure of faith and called her to be a religious foundress and mother to many.

Personal Reflection

🕉 Because of the tragic illness and death of her husband while in Italy, Elizabeth was welcomed into the Filicchi home. Here she had a chance to witness Catholic life within a family. Would a visitor be attracted to Catholicism by observing how you live?

🕉 Unexpectedly Elizabeth's life of privilege and prominence had been turned upside down. Yet in imitation of Jesus, she gave herself completely to alleviate the sufferings of others by forming the Sisters of Charity. Think of how you respond to the small or large reversals and disappointments of life. Do they make you more Christlike and giving?

Group Discussion

🕊 William Seton became a devout Episcopalian during his long illness. Reflection on death often draws the sick and those around them to deeper faith. Consider how you can improve your care for the ill. What value do you see in ministry to the sick?

🕊 Many non-Catholics are drawn to the Catholic faith because of our belief in the Real Presence of Christ in the Eucharist. How do you personally or as a parish offer opportunities for people to witness Eucharistic devotion?

Read ⟶ Reflect ⟶ Respond

John 6:35, 51
1 Corinthians 10:16–17
1 John 4:11–12
Catechism of the Catholic Church 1329–1330, 1373, 1375

The Sacrament of Reconciliation: Return to My Father

Saint Rita

In Rita's time many animosities took root among the regions and neighborhoods of Italy. Justice was administered by local families, and feuds often proved deadly. Rita made it her mission to bring about reconciliation rather than revenge.

Personal Reflection

- When her husband did not return home, Rita's first instinct was to pray for his safety. Consider your first reactions under stress. Is God your first recourse?

- Paolo's relatives and Rita's sons accused her of weakness. However, Rita was confident that "forgiveness takes more strength than revenge." When you feel cheated, overlooked, or insulted, how do you react?

Group Discussion

- Rita preferred to surrender her sons into God's hands than see them guilty of murderous revenge. In his mercy, God allowed both boys to fall ill and to receive the Sacrament of Reconciliation and Viaticum before they died. Discuss the values at stake here.

- She is now seen as "the saint of the impossible" because in her own life she faced so many impossible situations, and in each she found that with God all things are possible. Share times when reliance on God worked a "miracle" for you or for someone you know. How do you interpret the times when nothing seems to happen despite prayer?

Read ⟶ *Reflect* ⟶ *Respond*

Matthew 5:43–45
Ephesians 4:23–32
2 Corinthians 5:17–21
Galatians 5:22–6:1
Romans 16:17–20
Job 12:10
Catechism of the Catholic Church 1489, 2302–2306,
   2836–2844

Saint Augustine

Augustine went from being a self-confessed sinner to one of the most influential figures in Church history—he is known as the Doctor of Grace. His *Confessions* have been instrumental in reconciling many persons with the Church.

Personal Reflection

❧ Intellectually honest, Augustine found that he was held back from conversion by his long unmarried relationship with the mother of his son. Is there anything that keeps you from embracing wholeheartedly practicing the faith?

❧ Augustine prayed, "Jesus, my God, where was I when I was not thinking of you?" Have you ever realized that the thought of God was not even in your consciousness when you made a poor decision? How can you live in awareness of God's presence?

Group Discussion

❧ As he struggled with the idea of conversion, Augustine cried out, "How long, O Lord?" The answer he received was, "Take up and read." He picked up the Bible and read, "Let us live honorably. . . . put on the Lord Jesus Christ, and make no provision for the flesh" (Rom 13:13–14). Reflect together on this dialogue between Jesus and Augustine. Do you have confidence in the power of God's Word in Scripture?

Both Augustine and his friend, having been reconciled with the truth, prepared for baptism with fasting, prayer, and penance. What preparation is recommended in your parish for those adults preparing for the sacraments of initiation? How would you suggest that an adult who has been away from the faith prepare for the sacrament of Reconciliation?

Read ⇢ Reflect ⇢ Respond

Luke 15:32, 19:10

Acts 17:27

2 Corinthians 3:17

Joel 2:12

Psalms 6, 32, 38, 51, 102, 130, 143 (penitential psalms)

Catechism of the Catholic Church 1422, 1468–1470, 1707, 1730, 1739–1742

⟨❦⟩

The Sacrament of Anointing of the Sick: Sending Home

Saint Alphonsa
of the Immaculate Conception

This daughter of India rejected marriage in order to consecrate herself entirely to Christ as a religious. Constant bouts of illness threatened to put an end to her desire until she received several visions confirming her choice. Suffering continued, but so did her witness of joyful offering.

Personal Reflection

⟨❦⟩ Alphonsa wrote in her journal that "a day without suffering was a day wasted." Reflect on your own relationship with suffering. How can you profit from the inevitable aches and pains of life?

⟨❦⟩ She told God, "I would like to make novitiate . . . but even more, I want to do your will." Are you able to pray as freely to God?

Group Discussion

⟨❦⟩ Because of her many serious illnesses Alphonsa would have received this sacrament of healing many times. She continually recovered after the sacrament was administered and prayers were offered for her cure. What devotion do you have toward the sacrament of the Anointing of the Sick? Do you believe it is well understood and valued in your parish?

❦ Alphonsa often turned to Mary. Does your parish have a ministry of support for the dying? If not, consider how to organize a way in which prayers, companionship, or household support could be offered to the dying and their families.

Read ⟶ Reflect ⟶ Respond

Matthew 25:36
Acts 4:9–10
Colossians 1:24
2 Timothy 2:11–12
Catechism of the Catholic Church 1513–1515, 1520–1523, 1532

Saint Damien de Vuester

Strong and energetic, this young priest generously gave himself for the spiritual and material good of the leper colony in Hawaii. Nothing seemed too much for him. He spent himself completely and joyfully until he was totally identified with his people, declaring himself a leper with them.

Personal Reflection

❦ Damien, with only nine years of experience as a priest, volunteered for the leprosarium knowing that he intended to stay there. Reflect on this obvious heroism and examine your own generosity in difficult situations.

❦ The service Damien rendered to individual lepers, cleaning their wounds, cheering their spirits, bringing them the sacraments, were acts of anointing of the sick. How can you be this blessing for those who suffer?

Group Discussion

⟐ The people banished to the leper colony felt abandoned by everyone, including God. This led them to abandon all virtue and to indulge in violence and vice. Examine together situations in your community that are marked by poverty or crime. If you could alleviate the problem or raise the morale, what would you suggest be done?

⟐ Although he served the lepers willingly, Damien often requested assistance. Finally, near the end of his life, that help came. The arrival of these generous individuals ensured that his work would continue. Consider the numerous ministries and services within your parish community. How can you invite and welcome collaborators?

Read ⟐ Reflect ⟐ Respond

Mark 6:13
Matthew 10:7–10
Luke 5:30–32
James 5:14–15
Catechism of the Catholic Church 1499–1501, 1511–1513, 1517–1525

☙

The Sacrament of Holy Orders: Laying on of Hands

Saint Noël Chabanel

Noël Chabanel was a Jesuit missionary martyred at the age of thirty-six. He was blessed with a fine mind, but he could not master the Huron language, so his priestly ministry was minimal and he had to constantly battle discouragement. After several reprieves, he was ingloriously martyred at the hands of a disgruntled Huron.

Personal Reflection

☙ After five years in New France, Noël was completely demoralized. He considered himself worthless because he could not communicate with the Hurons, and everything about their life repulsed him. How would you have encouraged him and strengthened his priestly self-image?

☙ He not only felt useless but also humiliated when the Hurons made him the butt of jokes. Reflect on your relationships. How do you treat those who cannot measure up to the norm of your group? Is your reaction undue cruelty or extra kindness?

Group Discussion

☙ What is your attitude toward the priests who serve in your parish? Do you compare talents and competence, or do you try to identify the gifts each one brings? Think of the common gift each priest brings to you. Do you try to promote this attitude among your fellow parishioners?

🎗 Even after making a sincere gift of his whole life to the mission, Noël retained the struggles and repugnance he experienced before. What does this say to you about the confidence we should have in grace? How does this realization apply to your particular life situation?

Read ⤳ Reflect ⤳ Respond

Matthew 28:19
Mark 10:45
John 4:34
2 Timothy 2:3–4
1 Peter 2:5
Catechism of the Catholic Church 849, 1548–1550, 1562–1566

Saint Thomas Becket

Always a man of great integrity, Thomas became a true man of God's Church as archbishop of Canterbury. Although he did not seek the office, he gave himself completely to the graces of his ordination. The challenges of this office obliged him to stand against the will of his king and eventually face martyrdom.

Personal Reflection

🎗 When people take advantage of one another, as King Henry II took advantage of Thomas, friendship often turns sour, or "to black hatred," as Thomas predicted. Think about your relationships with both family and friends. Are you generous or self-serving?

🎗 Thomas found in his personal prayer and penance the strength he needed to be a good archbishop and to defend the Church. Are there sacrifices you have to make to be loyal to the Church and to your vocation in life? What prayers sustain you?

Group Discussion

🙖 There is good reason for the Church's stance that a clergyman cannot serve in a public office. When Thomas resigned as chancellor, he thwarted the king's plans to consolidate power and wealth in his own hands. Discuss these two legitimate spheres of power. How can a Catholic be loyal to both Church and state?

🙖 Thomas was hunted down in his own cathedral and murdered within sight of the altar. The men who assassinated him took advantage of a foolish statement of the king to carry out a personal vendetta. Discuss how you can promote and defend the dignity of the Church and her ministers in the face of growing antagonism against religion.

Read ⭢ *Reflect* ⭢ *Respond*

Matthew 16:19
Psalm 25
Sirach 15:14–15
Ezekiel 18:20
Acts 7:59
Catechism of the Catholic Church 888–896, 1463, 1586, 2474

The Sacrament of Matrimony: Sign of the Covenant

Blessed Peter To Rot

As local catechist at the time of the Japanese invasion, Peter found himself leader of his parish. He was the face of the Church to his enemies. With all his strength and ingenuity he nurtured the Church in hiding, and ultimately gave his life as a witness to faith and to the sanctity of marriage.

Personal Reflection

- Peter and his wife, Paula, inspired and comforted each other. However, their arranged marriage had not always been harmonious. With time and effort, it became one of love and devotion. How can unforeseen trials and cultural pressures strengthen a marriage?

- It is said that Peter To Rot was devoted to Sacred Scripture and always carried the Bible with him in his rounds as catechist. How strong is your devotion to God's word in Sacred Scripture?

Group Discussion

- Peter To Rot was an ideal catechist, not just instructing others, but also leading prayer services, baptizing, witnessing marriages, encouraging, and helping those in need. Recognizing that he served in a missionary church and during a time of war, how does Peter To Rot's example raise the bar for parish catechists and other pastoral workers?

⚜ To Rot was described as an "extraordinarily ordinary" man. How does he witness to the fact that holiness is natural to the married state?

Read ⟶ Reflect ⟶ Respond

Matthew 19:5-6
2 Peter 1:5-7
Ephesians 5:21
Deuteronomy 10:12
Catechism of the Catholic Church 897–913, 1604–1606, 1638, 1645, 1804, 1816

Saints Zélie and Louis Martin

Zélie and Louis Martin were uniquely qualified for the honor of being canonized together. Both had desired a life of consecration to God, but his plan called them to live in a consecrated marriage where they created, with their children, a holy family.

Personal Reflection

⚜ The Martins made a point of keeping alive the memory of their four deceased children. They maintained a family devotion to them, asking their intercession in times of particular need. This is a beautiful example of the meaning of the Mystical Body of Christ. Do you have a living relationship with family members or friends who have gone on to God?

⚜ Louis and Zélie made great personal sacrifices for their beloved daughters. First Louis and then Zélie gave up their prized business ventures in order to center on the immediate needs of the family. In your own life determine where your priorities lie. What would you willingly give up for your family?

Group Discussion

❧ Right from the beginning Louis and Zélie agreed that their marriage would be a mutual journey to holiness. For this they prayed daily. Saint Thérèse referred to the family created by her parents as "holy ground." How do you envision such a family in our day?

❧ Zélie's cancer was not cured despite the great faith put in the pilgrimage to the shrine of Our Lady of Lourdes. Yet, to her daughters, Zélie explained Our Lady's words to Saint Bernadette, "I will not make you happy in this world, but in the next." Do you believe your generation is doing a good job of imbuing the next generations with a true belief in heaven?

Read ⤳ Reflect ⤳ Respond

Matthew 7:17–20
John 14:1–3
Ephesians 5:21
Galatians 6:2
1 Timothy 6:6–8, 11–12
Catechism of the Catholic Church 1601, 1639, 1641–1643, 1652–1653, 1656

Alphabetical Listing of Saints

About the Authors

 SISTER MARIE PAUL CURLEY, as a child, found her imagination captured by the stories of the saints. Her early fascination continues today as a Daughter of St. Paul: in addition to co-authoring this book, she has produced children's storybooks for Catholic cable TV, as well as an English adaptation of an animated series on the saints. Sister Marie Paul continues to write for print and screen, including her recent book, *See Yourself Through God's Eyes: 52 Meditations to Grow in Self-Esteem* (Pauline Books & Media). For more resources on the saints in this book, or to contact Sister Marie Paul, visit: www.pauline.org/mariepaulcurley.

 SISTER MARY LEA HILL, a member of the Daughters of St. Paul since 1964, has enjoyed communicating the faith through a variety of apostolic assignments. Her skills as a storyteller were honed as director of audiovisual productions when Pauline Books & Media first produced animated features in the early 1980s. An editor and author for many years, Sister Mary Lea has written several books, including the best-selling *Basic Catechism* (co-authored with Sister Susan Helen Wallace), *Prayer and You* and *Blessed Are the Stressed*. Sister Mary Lea can be found on Twitter as @crabbymystic.

BOOKS & MEDIA

A mission of the Daughters of St. Paul

As apostles of Jesus Christ, evangelizing today's world:

We are CALLED to holiness
by God's living Word and Eucharist.

We COMMUNICATE the Gospel message
through our lives and through all
available forms of media.

We SERVE the Church
by responding to the hopes and needs
of all people with the Word of God,
in the spirit of St. Paul.

For more information visit our website: www.pauline.org.

BOOKS & MEDIA

The Daughters of St. Paul operate book and media centers at the following addresses. Visit, call, or write the one nearest you today, or find us at www.paulinestore.org.

CALIFORNIA

3908 Sepulveda Blvd, Culver City, CA 90230 310-397-8676
3250 Middlefield Road, Menlo Park, CA 94025 650-369-4230

FLORIDA

145 S.W. 107th Avenue, Miami, FL 33174 305-559-6715

HAWAII

1143 Bishop Street, Honolulu, HI 96813 808-521-2731

ILLINOIS

172 North Michigan Avenue, Chicago, IL 60601 312-346-4228

LOUISIANA

4403 Veterans Memorial Blvd, Metairie, LA 70006 504-887-7631

MASSACHUSETTS

885 Providence Hwy, Dedham, MA 02026 781-326-5385

MISSOURI

9804 Watson Road, St. Louis, MO 63126 314-965-3512

NEW YORK

115 E. 29th Street, New York City, NY 10016 212-754-1110

SOUTH CAROLINA

243 King Street, Charleston, SC 29401 843-577-0175

TEXAS

No book center; for parish exhibits or outreach evangelization, contact: 210-569-0500, or SanAntonio@paulinemedia.com, or P.O. Box 761416, San Antonio, TX 78245

VIRGINIA

1025 King Street, Alexandria, VA 22314 703-549-3806

CANADA

3022 Dufferin Street, Toronto, ON M6B 3T5 416-781-9131

¡También somos su fuente para libros,
videos y música en español!